Modernist Soundscapes

UNIVERSITY PRESS OF FLORIDA

Florida A&M University, Tallahassee
Florida Atlantic University, Boca Raton
Florida Gulf Coast University, Ft. Myers
Florida International University, Miami
Florida State University, Tallahassee
New College of Florida, Sarasota
University of Central Florida, Orlando
University of Florida, Gainesville
University of North Florida, Jacksonville
University of South Florida, Tampa
University of West Florida, Pensacola

Modernist Soundscapes

AUDITORY TECHNOLOGY AND THE NOVEL

ANGELA FRATTAROLA

UNIVERSITY PRESS OF FLORIDA

Gainesville · Tallahassee · Tampa · Boca Raton

Pensacola · Orlando · Miami · Jacksonville · Ft. Myers · Sarasota

This book may be available in an electronic edition.

23 22 21 20 19 18   6 5 4 3 2 1

LIBRARY OF CONGRESS CATALOGING-IN-PUBLICATION DATA
Names: Frattarola, Angela, author.
Title: Modernist soundscapes : auditory technology and the novel / Angela
    Frattarola.
Description: Gainesville : University Press of Florida, [2018] | Includes
    bibliographical references and index.
Identifiers: LCCN 2018007668 | ISBN 9780813056074 (cloth : alk. paper)
Subjects: LCSH: Technology in literature. | Sound in literature. | Modernism
    (Literature) | Sound—Recording and reproducing.
Classification: LCC PN56.T37 F73 2018 | DDC 809/.93356—dc23
LC record available at https://lccn.loc.gov/2018007668

The University Press of Florida is the scholarly publishing agency for the State
University System of Florida, comprising Florida A&M University, Florida Atlantic
University, Florida Gulf Coast University, Florida International University, Florida
State University, New College of Florida, University of Central Florida, University
of Florida, University of North Florida, University of South Florida, and University
of West Florida.

UNIVERSITY PRESS OF FLORIDA
15 Northwest 15th Street
Gainesville, FL 32611-2079
http://upress.ufl.edu

Contents

Acknowledgments

As the daughter of an Italian immigrant mother who raised five children on her own, I have never had to look far for a role model. My mother, the most loving and strongest individual I know, is a seamstress who taught herself the English language and made sure each of her children went to college. I was told from a young age that I was born in America so that I could have more opportunities and that it was my responsibility to find them. While my mother did not always understand the practicality of a PhD in literature, I would not have had the gumption, drive, or confidence to pursue my studies without her.

Along the way, I have gathered a huge debt to colleagues. My love of modernism and philosophy began with the undergraduate seminars of Vincent Sherry and Panos Alexakos. My focus on modernism and sound began in graduate school and developed through the patient guidance of Perry Meisel, Martin Harries, and Patrick Deer. As I moved on to teaching modernism at Nanyang Technological University (NTU), I learned a great deal from the wonderful students there, who enthusiastically analyzed passages from modernist novels with me. I also feel fortunate to have found such nurturing and insightful colleagues at NTU; I want to thank them and the visiting scholar Ronald Schleifer, who generously gave feedback on my ideas for this book. My inspiring and smart colleagues in the Expository Writing Program of New York University, especially the reading group who provided invaluable feedback on my book proposal, also deserve a huge helping of thanks. Lastly, I would like to thank Tania Friedel for her thorough copyediting and years of uplifting conversation, and Jackie Portner for her lifelong friendship and support.

Introduction

Published in 1902, Rudyard Kipling's short story "Wireless" depicts a "Marconi experiment," performed by an amateur wireless enthusiast on a cold Saturday night in a pharmacy in Cornwall (130). As he describes wireless technology to the narrator of the story, the enthusiast mixes scientific terminology of the day with mystical language, explaining that while "nobody knows" how "Electricity" works, "It" causes the "magic" of the "Hertzian waves" (132); the "coherer," he clarifies, "will reveal to us the Powers—whatever the Powers may be—at work—through space—a long distance away" (132). The hesitating dashes of this sentence indicate not only the speaker's excitement but possibly gaps in his knowledge, suggesting that even enthusiasts did not fully grasp the science behind the wireless. For most (and many still today), it was an unexplainable "wonder" based on "Powers" beyond their comprehension (Kipling 132).

Despite these intimations of magic, the beginning of the story seems designed to educate turn-of-the-century readers on the basics of the wireless, as the enthusiast, an electrician, defines induction and uses the metaphor of the familiar technology of the steam engine to explain how the coherer, battery, and Hertzian waves work. The enthusiast domesticates the unfamiliar technology by personifying and gendering "the Power—our unknown Power—kicking and fighting to be let loose," explaining, as he sends a message, "There she goes—kick-kick-kick into space" (138). Here, once again, the story oscillates between familiarizing the technology and emphasizing the "strangeness" of sending a message through "space" (138). Throughout the short story, Kipling represents the wireless ambivalently, on the one hand conventionalizing the technology through definitions, metaphors, and personification, while on the other defamiliarizing the technology by calling its "Power" "magic."

The "magic" of the wireless is enhanced by the aura of the "glittering shop," where lights reflecting on glass jars and fixtures create a "kaleidoscope" of "gorgeous patches" of color (Kipling 134). It is amid these colored lights and exotic scents that the consumptive chemist who works in the pharmacy starts to move "machine-like" and inexplicably to recite Keats's "The Eve of St. Agnes" (138).

Fascinated by the chemist's trance, the narrator tries to rationally understand the event and ultimately explains the mystery of the trance with the same vocabulary of Hertzian waves and induction. He notes the similarities between the chemist and Keats, which could have prompted "the power" to "snatch him" (142): "it's the identical bacillus, or Hertzian wave of tuberculosis, *plus* Fanny Brand [the name of the chemist's female visitor, which resembles Keats's fiancée, Fanny Brawne] and the professional status which, in conjunction with the main-stream of subconscious thought common to all mankind, has thrown up temporarily an induced Keats" (140). This easy slippage between the technology of the wireless and what the narrator believes to be a supernatural channeling of Keats is Kipling's way of revealing to the reader how the public perceived new auditory technologies through a mystical lens. Even the electrician in the story acts "as though in the presence of spirits" when Morse code is picked up by the machine (138).

In the end, however, the reader must question whether Kipling is suggesting that either the wireless or the recitation of Keats's poem is supernatural. William B. Dillingham convincingly argues that the narrator should not be assumed to be Kipling and is, in fact, an unreliable narrator. Dillingham notices that after the trance, when the narrator asks the chemist if he has ever read Keats, the chemist replies that he does not have the time to read poetry. This answer, however, indicates that the chemist is perhaps not telling the complete truth about his ignorance of Keats, since he already knew that Keats was a poet (Dillingham 137–38). If the chemist was even vaguely familiar with the poem, the conversation and events of the night, which are reminiscent of many images in the poem (a cold hare, a remark about the coldness of a grave, smoke, a "young breast" in a gold frame, rain), would have been enough to put the poem in his mind. If we consider this, along with the "new and wildish drink" containing chloric ether that the chemist drinks, it is easy to deduce that the poem's recitation is a simple revelry into which the chemist falls, conjured by the images and mood of the evening (Kipling 132). Kipling implies that what may seem supernatural may not be so. Likewise, just as the wireless may seem like a "spiritualistic séance," it can be scientifically understood (142).

Although Kipling's detailed descriptions of the technology display a fascination with the wireless, it is the recited lines of poetry that excite the narrator the most. In fact, while the narrator came to the pharmacy to watch the marvels of the wireless, he ends up engrossed by what "comes through" the chemist, exclaiming of the last lines of Keats's poem: "These are the pure Magic. These are the clear Vision. The rest is only poetry" (Kipling 140, 141). Whereas the overheard wireless transmissions between two ships are "quite pathetic" in their inability to fully communicate, the poetry recitation makes the narrator drip with sweat, as his "every sense hung upon the writing" (143, 142). Oddly enough, in a story titled "Wireless," it is the poetry that creates the dramatic climax; the poetry, not the technology, is the "pure Magic."

Even though Kipling's short story was written earlier than the modernist novels I analyze, which span from 1915 to 1958, it embodies a central idea of this study: European and North American literature at the turn of the century became increasingly concerned with and influenced by the developing auditory technologies of the time. Like the novels I examine, Kipling's short story subtly does the work of educating readers and familiarizing them with a new auditory technology. Yet, just as technology is secondary to the "pure Magic" of literature in Kipling's short story, technology, too, is secondary to aesthetics in the modernist novel. Although modernist writers were influenced by auditory technologies that altered sound perception, allowing people to listen to sounds in novel ways and making sound a reproducible object, the medium of the modernist novel was still written text. While these words could rouse the inner ear, they still required that a reader visually engage with words crafted on a page.

There is an important difference, however, between early literary representations of auditory technologies like Kipling's and the modernist use of such technologies. As these technologies became increasingly common in popular culture and homes, early twentieth-century writers did not treat them with the same mystification and wariness that we see in Kipling's short story and similar early works such as Auguste Villiers de l'Isle-Adam's novel *L'Eve Future* (1886), where a character named Thomas Edison creates a seductive android with golden phonograph records. Whereas the wireless and phonograph play prominent roles in these plots, auditory technologies play only minor roles within the modernist novels of this study. Instead, their influence can be discerned in how these novelists meticulously describe characters listening to one another and the soundscape, as well as the ways in which they experiment with form to make their novels sound out.

Although there have been productive debates about the time period, geography, and characteristics of modernism, and the movement has rightfully been widened to include a range of works that go beyond the canonical, *Modernist Soundscapes* stays within a somewhat conventional and limited scope in order to focus on reevaluating the modernist novel in relation to the early twentieth-century soundscape. Aside from Jean Rhys, who was born in Dominica but moved to England at the age of sixteen, the writers I examine—Dorothy Richardson, Virginia Woolf, James Joyce, and Samuel Beckett—are British and Irish. While Beckett is often understood as straddling modernism and postmodernism, I follow Peter Childs's assessment of his novel *Murphy* (1938): "the elements of religious scepticism, deep introspection, technical and formal experimentation, cerebral game-playing, linguistic innovation, self-referentiality, misanthropic despair overlaid with humour, philosophical speculation, loss of faith and cultural exhaustion all exemplify the preoccupations of modernism" (introduction). Indeed, I argue that some of the above characteristics that we tend to associate with modernism, specifically its formal and linguistic innovation and skepticism toward traditional ways of knowing the world, are in part a result of a growing awareness of and shift toward sound perception made possible through new auditory technologies.

By exploring how modernists represent the act of listening, describe the soundscape, and formally make their narratives auditory, we can come to a deeper understanding of early twentieth-century notions of auditory experience: experiences that were shaped by both innovations in technology and a developing skepticism toward vision. Although not all auditory experiences were unifying and immersive, my analyses will reveal a contrast in modernist representations of sensory experience: vision is often represented as distancing and judgmental, while audition is represented as connecting and inclusive. Recent studies such as Viet Erlmann's *Reason and Resonance* astutely warn against idealizing audition as the polar opposite of vision, which is conventionally associated with rationality and objective analysis. Sound and audition cannot be limited to the irrational: in fact, they allowed for new methods of scientific research by the turn of the century, as doctors used stethoscopes, for instance, to diagnose their patients. While I do not want to affirm what Jonathan Sterne fittingly calls the *audiovisual litany*, which "elevates a set of cultural prenotions about the senses (prejudices, really) to the level of theory" ("Sonic Imaginations" 9), this tension between vision and audition coheres with a larger historical skepticism of vision that the critic Martin Jay, in *Downcast Eyes: The Denigration of Vision in Twentieth-Century French Thought*, locates within French writers, artists, and thinkers. While Jay concentrates on how vision went from being the most valued sense to a "denigrated" sense in the twentieth century, my research suggests that modernists responded to this denigration by creating characters who conscientiously listen to the noisy soundscape, the prosody of voice, and music. I propose that, like the auditory technologies of their time, modernist novelists tend to use auditory perception to bridge the distance between subject and object, shifting the subject from an "objective" observer to a reverberating body, attuned to the moment.

This burgeoning skepticism of a Cartesian, visual-based perspective of the world is a part of the larger breaks with tradition that we have come to associate with North American and European modernism. As the theories of Darwin, Marx, Nietzsche, and Freud seeped into culture, assumptions about one's ability to rationally understand the self and society were put into question. The mass weaponry, death, and destruction of World War I further destabilized the public's faith in civilization and humanity. And all the while, rapid developments in capitalism, urbanization, science, technology, and industrialization continued to change people's interactions with one another and their lived experiences. Surveying these shifts, Richard Sheppard argues that modernists "felt that the 'logocentric' understanding of reality on which classical modernity and the liberal humanist epoch had been based was being called into question or shattered by the experience of modernity in its contemporary configuration" (34). I contend that one of the ways that modernists questioned logocentrism (and, by association, a philosophical tradition from antiquity to the Enlightenment that equated vision with knowledge) was to focus their attention on the auditory perception of their characters as well as of the reader.

While some critics interpret modernist aesthetics as solipsistically turning inward, or simply reflecting the chaos of the time period, I understand modernist writers as reveling in the break with tradition and putting forward possibilities for living that could forge new communal connections.[1] As Sheppard helpfully clarifies, drawing on Fredric Jameson, modernist works "are not just reflexes, transcriptions, or symptoms of a profound cultural upheaval, but, simultaneously, responses through which authors of those works try to pictorialize their understanding and so make sense of that upheaval" (23). As assumed ideas of humanity being rationally motivated and connected through stable social bonds were put into question, modernists, I argue, were inspired by the new forms of intimacy materialized through auditory technologies to connect characters through listening and sound. Instead of surveying the world as distanced observers, they questioned such presumed objectivity and strove to represent their characters and engage their readers more intimately through sound.

My focus on the auditory dimension of modernism builds on Steven Connor's 1997 essay "The Modern Auditory I," in which, citing new auditory technologies and an increase in noise from industrialization and war, Connor asserts that in the modernist period, "stimulating subjective experiences formed round the auditory rather than the visual, or at least formed in a certain contest between the two" (205). Connor holds that modernist novels reflect an aural notion of selfhood that complicates visual modes for understanding the self. Connor's proposition that the "auditory self is an attentive rather than an investigatory self, which takes part in the world rather than taking aim at it," is revisited throughout this study, not in hopes of affirming a dualism between vision and audition, but to demonstrate how modernist writers imply this distinction (219). Modernist characters frequently feel uncomfortable under the judgmental eyes of others and instead strive to create intimacy, connectivity, and community through music, voice, and shared listening experiences. Yet we cannot idealize audition; the sense of hearing is continually proven to be subjective and prejudiced in modernist texts. All the same, narratives that emphasize audition offer modernists an alternative way of ordering the world and presenting subjectivity. We cannot close our ears to the world when sounds literally make our bodies vibrate in sympathy.

Just as important as the modernist representation of listening and the soundscape are the ways in which modernists tried to intimately connect the reader with the text by stimulating the reader's inner ear. These writers did not want the reader just to envision settings and characters; they wanted the reader to hear the narrative. Modernist novels encourage the reader to listen with what Garrett Stewart calls the *reading voice* by defamiliarizing language and therefore heightening one's attention to the sounds of words. The representation of noise (the "tick, tick, tick" that repeatedly interrupts Woolf's *Between the Acts*), interior monologue (the stream of consciousness found in Joyce's *Ulysses* and Rhys's novels), and repetition (Beckett's looped phrases) are the main ways that modernists make their narratives auditory so that the reader cannot read merely for plot and meaning but must slow down and become aware of the sounds represented on the page.

Aside from the modernists' adherence to what Jay calls the "denigration" of vision at the turn of the century, I maintain that modernists wrote novels that prompted one's reading voice because they were living in an age in which the public was increasingly being asked to be active listeners—tuning into radio stations, making and buying phonograph recordings, talking over distances through telephones, and hearing sound become synchronized with film. As the public became more accustomed to auditory technologies, instead of being baffled and amazed at the technology, they started to pay attention to sound fidelity, background noise, and nuances in sound. In turn, companies competed to bring consumers the best sound quality. For example, by 1925, telephone companies started to measure sound in decibels to regulate noise within their communication systems, and film companies tested different methods for synchronizing film and sound. As consumers became discriminating listeners, sound became an aesthetic object. Emily Thompson perceptively sums up the influence of such innovations on twentieth-century listening habits:

> Radios, electrically amplified phonographs, public address systems, and sound motion pictures transformed the soundscape by introducing auditors not only to electrically reproduced sound but also to new ways of listening. As people self-consciously consumed these new products they became increasingly *sound conscious*, and the sound that they sought was of a particular type. Clear and focused, it issued directly toward them with little opportunity to reflect and reverberate off the surfaces of the room in which it was generated. (*Soundscape* 233–34)

New sound technologies undoubtedly changed the ways in which people understood and listened to sound. Instead of being clearly attached to their sources, sounds were now disembodied. No longer shaped by only the acoustics of their origin, sounds now could be isolated and amplified. As modernist writers participated in and experienced this amplified and mediated soundscape, their narratives were shaped by these new listening practices.

To pursue the significance of this technologically driven *sound consciousness*, I contextualize a modernist's work within a particular auditory technology in each chapter. My characterizations of turn-of-the-century auditory technologies are primarily drawn from Jonathan Sterne's *The Audible Past: Cultural Origins of Sound Reproduction* and Emily Thompson's *The Soundscape of Modernity: Architectural Acoustics and the Culture of Listening in America, 1900–1933*, both seminal historical examinations of how auditory technologies grew out of medical, scientific, and architectural contexts and shaped early twentieth-century listening practices. Although these historical accounts tend to focus on America, while I discuss mainly British and Irish writers, I hold that listening experiences in the Western world were fundamentally similar. Because the patents that developed technologies such as the phonograph, headphones, talkie, and tape recorder were the same across the Atlantic, I have to presume that the public's experiences were comparable. While the content and pace of development may have been different, especially between broadcasting in America and the BBC, the gradual changes in auditory perception were the same: sounds, once separated from their sources, became aesthetic objects; listeners encountered voices and noises from afar intimately piped into their home or headspace through headphones; the public became more aware of background noise as sounds were inadvertently recorded or produced by sound-reproducing machines.

The innovations of the turn of the century of course had important nineteenth-century predecessors such as the phonautograph (a machine for writing sound waves), stethoscope, and telegraph, each of which honed the Victorian public's listening skills and made sound quantifiable. John M. Picker's profound study *Victorian Soundscapes* demonstrates that it was "a period of unprecedented amplification . . . alive with the screech and roar of the railway and the clang of industry, with the babble, bustle, and music of city streets, and with the crackle and squawk of acoustic vibrations on wires and wax" (4). While Picker offers convincing evidence of Victorian characters (and writers) being preoccupied with their need for communication or for silence, I would argue that it is not until the modernist period that the novel becomes saturated with sound—both in content and form.[2] While the eye has not lost its importance in the modernist novel, the ear has joined it to present a more complete sensory experience.

The writers taken up in *Modernist Soundscapes* grew up and developed their artistry just as auditory technologies were becoming household items and common experiences. For example, Dorothy Richardson wrote a column for the film magazine *Close Up* and was an avid defender of the silent film. Going beyond film criticism, James Joyce helped to open a cinema in Dublin in 1909, and he once discussed the possibility of making *Ulysses* into a film with Sergei Eisenstein. In *Ulysses*, Leopold Bloom thinks about how interesting it would be to have gramophone recordings of the dead at their graves so that their relatives could still hear them. And today, we can listen to old scratchy gramophone recordings of Joyce reading excerpts from *Ulysses* and the last pages of "Anna Livia Plurabelle" from *Finnegans Wake*. Although she did not record her voice on the gramophone, Virginia Woolf broadcast three talks on the BBC between 1927 and 1937. She often listened to gramophone records, and she has her characters do the same in *The Years* and *Between the Acts*. Similarly influenced by gramophone recordings, Jean Rhys wrote that she was "haunted by popular songs" and has the narrator of *Good Morning, Midnight* liken her inner speech to a gramophone record (Rhys, "Songs"). Rhys also allowed the actress Selma Vaz Dias to adapt *Good Morning, Midnight* into a dramatic monologue for radio (written in 1949 and broadcast on the BBC in 1957) (Pizzichini 273–74). Finally, Samuel Beckett wrote specifically for radio, television, and film. Beckett revealed the great potential of radio drama with plays such as *All That Fall*, *Words and Music*, and *Cascando*, which were broadcast on the BBC. And, most importantly, Beckett hinges the entire plot of *Krapp's Last Tape* on the technology of the tape recorder.

The assumed division between technologies of mass culture and modernist aesthetics has in recent years been adequately challenged. It makes sense to question not only how modernists interacted with the developing technologies of their time but also how such technologies influenced their radical experiments in form. Sara Danius does just this in *The Senses of Modernism: Technology, Perception, and Aesthetics*, which argues that technologies of the senses—from the automobile to the X-ray—are "*constitutive* of high-modernist aesthetics" (3, emphasis in original). As Michael North explains in his analysis of film and photography, new technologies gave "modernism a formal model and not just another type of subject matter" (12). Though modernists were often ambivalent about technology and mass culture, mounting studies have shown that the inventions witnessed by these writers affected their art form. Without falling into the trap of technological determinism by assuming that modernist writers were inevitably compelled to write in a certain way due to technology, we can still explore how auditory technologies at the turn of the century influenced the ways in which the public perceived sound and, consequently, the ways in which writers crafted their art.

While much of the literary criticism of the twentieth century has been complicit with what Jay calls *ocularcentrism*, the intersections between modernism and sound studies have finally begun to be mined in twenty-first-century scholarship.[3] More recently, Sam Halliday's *Sonic Modernity: Representing Sound in Literature, Culture and the Arts* draws on the work of musicians, theorists, artists, and writers to consider how sound is configured among the senses in such texts, and Josh Epstein's *Sublime Noise: Musical Culture and the Modernist Writer* examines the influence of modernist music on writers such as Joyce, T. S. Eliot, Edith Sitwell, E. M. Forster, and Ezra Pound. This research on music and modernism continues important work begun by Brad Bucknell in *Literary Modernism and Musical Aesthetics: Pater, Pound, Joyce, and Stein* and complements Philipp Schweighauser's *The Noises of American Literature, 1890–1985: Toward a History of Literary Acoustics*, which shows how fictional representations of noise reflect larger social concerns and transitions. Melba Cuddy-Keane's "Modernist Soundscapes and the Intelligent Ear: An Approach to Narrative through Auditory Perception" is also an essential essay in this field, as it develops terminology to examine sound and listening in literature. Using Woolf and her representation of the urban soundscape as a case study, Cuddy-Keane asserts that in the modernist period, technology, the modern city, and "a growing interest in cognitive perception gave rise to a new aurality, which in turn made its mark upon narrative, in new inscriptions of sound" (383). My research extends Cuddy-Keane's work by looking specifically at auditory technologies, additional modernist writers, and the philosophical implications of this modernist emphasis on audition. Just as the editors of *Broadcasting Modernism*, Debra Rae Cohen, Michael Coyle, and Jane Lewty, argue that the radio "intermittently ebbed and flowed as direct subject matter, as a platform for artistic expression, or as a subliminal force shaping the dynamics of modernist textualities," the same could be said for the auditory technologies that will be discussed in the coming chapters: the sound film, phonograph, headphones, and magnetic tape recorder (2).[4]

The stimulating scholarship listed above is proof of the exciting readings and cultural insights that can be generated when considering the auditory dimension of modernist writing. This book contributes to the field by exploring how auditory technologies shaped not only the way in which these writers represented listening and the soundscape but the very form of their narrative. My first chapter questions why the early twentieth-century soundscape was called by its contemporaries "the age of noise" and considers how the changing soundscape influenced listening practices. In particular, I examine how auditory technologies altered sound perception by creating new paths for intimacy through listening, by exposing listeners to a cosmopolitan and bohemian world of new sounds, and by aestheticizing noise and sound through mechanical reproduction.

Yet, aside from the technological influences of the time, why else might modernist literature take a turn to the auditory and emphasize sound in ways that literature of the previous generation did not? Scholars such as Connor, Sterne, David Michael Levin, and Don Ihde hold that auditory experience has been neglected in modernity and philosophy, where sight is traditionally privileged. More importantly, some of these writers suggest that while the eye has a tendency to be distancing and analytical, the ear has the potential to connect humans to one another and their environment. Building on Jay's argument that the denigration of vision began with turn-of-the-century thinkers such as Henri Bergson and modernist artists, I postulate that modernists include the auditory as a way of subverting visual-based notions of rationality and subjectivity rooted in antiquity and the Enlightenment. While audition should not be aligned with the irrational, formal innovations and representations of listening and the soundscape allowed modernists to fragment their linear narratives and disrupt the rationalizing syntax of their sentences.

As I move to examining novels, I begin with Dorothy Richardson's *Pilgrim-*

age (1915–67), a multivolume work that follows the life of Miriam Henderson through free indirect discourse and stream of consciousness. Although Richardson, in an essay called "About Punctuation," suggests that her irregular use of punctuation is an attempt to make the reader listen to her prose, her novels do not formally experiment with sound in the same ways that Woolf, Joyce, Rhys, and Beckett do. Instead, I connect Richardson's film column for the magazine *Close Up*, where she criticizes the talkie for its unnatural speech and argues for the importance of the musical accompaniment of silent film, with her fiction, where she pays explicit attention to the bonding qualities of music and voice. For Richardson, the musical accompaniment of silent film is essential for connecting a viewer with the film while allowing for private meditation; conversely, the awkward enunciation of the early talkies ruined the aesthetic experience of film for her. Although she does not represent film in her fiction, Richardson repeatedly uses moments of listening to music to grant her characters a reprieve from their self-conscious inner speech, enabling them to be more receptive to others. Similarly, listening to the musical qualities, or prosody, of speech creates intimacy among Richardson's characters, allowing them to transcend their selfish concerns and connect with one another. Yet, while prosody can express the ineffable depths of characters, Richardson's protagonist Miriam sometimes essentializes groups based on their dialect, revealing that her attention to prosody can lead to stereotyping. Although Miriam seems unaware of her own dialect-based stereotyping, she is critical of male characters with "camera-like" eyes that objectify and linguistically categorize the world from a distance. In contrast, Miriam embraces music, silence, prosody, and an "inward eye" that aids her in becoming a writer by the end of her lifelong pilgrimage.

Next, I consider Woolf's work, which, similar to Richardson's *Pilgrimage*, is filled with descriptions of acts of listening. Yet Woolf also incorporates onomatopoeia to make her prose sound out. While research has been done on Woolf's relationship with auditory technologies, her representation of the soundscape has yet to be closely examined. Woolf's onomatopoeia indicates a desire to represent the sounds of the world without mediation—a drive that was helpfully modeled by the phonograph, which some hoped would allow composers to make music from recorded real-world sounds rather than relying on the mediation of musicians. My evaluation of Woolf's use of onomatopoeia begins with *Jacob's Room* (1922) and reaches a climax with her later works *The Waves* (1931), *The Years* (1937), and *Between the Acts* (1941). These novels are overwhelmingly sound driven, with characters consistently directed and influenced by the soundscape. While characters often feel alienated and scrutinized when they are looked at, the act of listening has the power to unite them, even if only temporarily. Similar to the experience of the phonograph, which allowed mass-produced recordings to be listened to in the privacy of the home, communal listening connects Woolf's characters, while still permitting individual thought. On the level of form, Woolf's onomatopoeia stimulates one's reading voice so that the reader too can be momentarily united with the text. This aestheticizing of noise is similar to the experience of listening to "found sound" recordings such as the one played in *Between the Acts*, where real-world sound fragments are juxtaposed, and the listener relies on the sound itself for meaning. I further contextualize Woolf's desire to manipulate and control real-world sound with her diary entries and essays on World War II, which suggest the importance of listening in wartime England.

Joyce, too, strove to make his novels sound out with onomatopoeia. But in this next chapter, I concentrate on his use of interior monologue, an attempt to make inner speech be heard. I question how the common turn-of-the-century practice of listening to the telephone, phonograph, and radio through headphones may have aided modernists in conceiving of interior monologue as an aestheticized object that could be commodified through the novel form. Using Sterne's argument that headphones created a "private acoustic space," I postulate that listening to voices and music through headphones created a new sense of a personal, objectified space within one's head. As attention was turned to this headspace, modernists could conceive of their inner speech as a product that could be aesthetically rendered. Just as headphones brought unfamiliar sounds and voices into one's private headspace, Joyce represents the stream of consciousness as a collage of voices and sounds from literature, religion, popular culture, and the soundscape. In *Ulysses* (1922), Joyce creates what I call an *auditory cosmopolitanism*, by allowing the languages and sounds of the surrounding world to penetrate and influence the interior monologues of his characters. For Stephen, this means that his interior monologue is a medley of different languages and discourses. For Bloom, such cosmopolitanism is produced by his empathy and receptivity to the plights and concerns of others, which enter and direct his stream of consciousness.

Unlike Joyce, who celebrates auditory cosmopolitanism, Jean Rhys shows how characters can internalize the antagonistic voices of popular culture and a judgmental bourgeoisie. Advertisements, songs, books, and the voices of others impinge on the interior monologues of Rhys's characters, often forming a dialectic between bohemian and bourgeois sensibilities. In particular, the popular songs that are integrated into Rhys's first-person novels enhance the auditory nature of her interior monologues. While the songs referenced in *Voyage in the Dark* (1934) and *Good Morning, Midnight* (1939) sometimes foster automatic responses and clichéd understandings for her narrators, they can also instill a sense of defiance and comfort, making music one of the few channels available for a momentary sense of expression. I contextualize Rhys's interior monologues with her short stories, which often depict popular gramophone recordings and their Bohemian associations. Such representations clarify Rhys's understanding of how the bohemian voice was commodified and purchased by a public with an appetite for lurid tales of the underbelly of society. Rhys's interior monologues let the reader feel as if one is eavesdropping on the private life of a bohemian woman, just as popular gramophone recordings let listeners feel as if they were eavesdropping on the bohemian world—a practice made even more intimate with headphones. Like Richardson, who uses her heroine to push against the male gaze by valuing prosody and music, Rhys focuses on the voiced interior monologue of her characters to subvert the reader's desire to envision her female characters.

While Samuel Beckett, too, crafted interior monologues, it is his use of repetition that I take up in the last chapter of my study. Considering his poetry, radio plays, and drama, not to mention his study of languages and practice of writing in two languages, there is no doubt that Beckett had an ear especially tuned to the acoustic aspects of language. As Beckett started to repeat and loop phrases in his second novel, *Watt* (1953), the French radio technician Pierre Schaeffer started experimenting with splicing and looping magnetic tape recordings in the studios of the Paris radio station Radio Television Français (RTF). Building on the geographical and historical coincidence of these events, this chapter argues that the magnetic tape art of *musique concrète* can serve as an entry point to analyze the effect of Beckett's repetition. Just as *musique concrète* uses the tape recorder to decontextualize real-world sounds through looping techniques, allowing them to be appreciated for their musical qualities rather than their real-world associations, Beckett uses repetition to decontextualize words and phrases, allowing them to be appreciated for their sound rather than their meaning. The recorder's storing and replaying of speech exemplifies Beckett's repeated suggestion in his fiction that the subject is spoken and alienated through language. Paradoxically, while his repetition empties words of meaning, this same repetition, through the course of his fiction, generates its own internal effect and meaning. This, I argue, is done by the familiarity established in the reader's inner ear—a familiarity that is similarly exploited in *musique concrète*. Stripping away a fictional world that his reader can visually picture, Beckett leaves his reader with only a voice, repeating the same basic phrases with minor variations.

One might question why a study like this does not focus on poetry, since modernist poetry most obviously beckons the reader to sound out words. It is true that several modernist poets understood their art to be musical. Langston Hughes, for example, explicitly draws a connection between his book-length poem *Montage of a Dream Deferred* (1951) and "Afro-American popular music," remarking that his poetry contains "passages sometimes in the manner of the jam session, sometimes the popular song, punctuated by the riffs, runs, breaks, and disc-tortions of the music of a community in transition" (387). More generally, T. S. Eliot states that a poem can begin as "a particular rhythm before it reaches expression in words" and compares the qualities of poetic verse to instrumental themes and the movements of a symphony ("Music" 32). Edith Sitwell, Gertrude Stein, and Ezra Pound took Eliot's analogies of music and poetry one step further by putting their words to music. Sitwell's *Façade* poems are, in her own words, "patterns in sound" and were recited with musical accompaniment (Sitwell xii). Even without musical accompaniment, the repetition and minimalism of Stein's prose and poetry make all her work distinctly oriented toward the ear.[5] Collaborating with the American composer Virgil Thomson, Stein wrote two operas, *Four Saints in Three Acts* and *The Mother of Us All*. Pound, too, composed operas such as *Le Testament de Villon* and *Cavalcanti*, in addition to writing the musical study *Antheil and the Treatise on Harmony* and music reviews for magazines.[6] On the link between poetry and music, Pound is clear: "both in Greece and Provence the poetry attained its highest rhythmic and metrical brilliance at times when the arts of verse and music were closely knit together, when each thing done by the poet had some definite musical urge or necessity behind it" (91). But as Pound's exploration of the poetic tradition and music demonstrates, music and poetry blended for many poets throughout time, so that poetry has always been understood to become more potent through its proximity to music.

This study focuses on the modernist novel because its immersion in sound is exceptional for the novel genre. The realism of the novel, moreover, is able to reflect the subtle changes that auditory technologies brought about in sound perception. Richardson and Woolf exemplify the intimacy made possible through headphones, the radio, the phonograph, and the telephone in their representation of shared listening experiences, which intimately connect characters through voice, music, and the soundscape. Joyce and Rhys also create intimacy by letting the reader eavesdrop on the interior monologues of their characters.

Yet, they simultaneously reveal how these same technologies brought foreign and marginalized voices, music, and sounds into the home by creating interior monologues that include the cosmopolitan and bohemian. Beyond bringing nonlocal sounds into the home, the phonograph and tape recorder also aestheticized noise through mechanical reproduction. Such aestheticizing is found in Woolf and Beckett as they experiment with defamiliarizing words, allowing them to be heard before they are understood.

This survey of auditory narrative attempts to add a new perspective on why modernists developed some of the general characteristics that we associate with the period: "the recurrent act of fragmenting unities (unities of character or plot or pictorial space or lyric form), . . . the refusal of norms of beauty, the willingness to make radical linguistic experiment, all often inspired by the resolve (in Eliot's phrase) to startle and disturb the public" (Levenson 3). Woolf's and Richardson's attention to and incorporation of noise, voice, and music fragments the unity of pictorial space and plot, while Rhys's and Joyce's use of stream of consciousness disrupts the unity of character. Woolf's noisy onomatopoeia and Beckett's repetition test the reader's desire for beauty and flout the reader's conventional expectations on the sentence and plot level. Such radical formal experimentation, which most consider a defining trait of modernist literature, is, I argue, in part due to the ways in which auditory technologies, along with a growing skepticism of vision, changed how modernist writers conceived of and experienced sound.

1

The Modernist Soundscape

Ocularcentrism and Auditory Technologies

Let us try to imagine for a moment the modernist soundscape.[1] While the Western world may not have gotten noisier in the early twentieth century, there is evidence that people perceived the world as noisier. Emily Thompson helpfully shows that in the Victorian period the "sounds that so bothered Carlyle and Goethe were almost identical to those that had been identified by the Buddha centuries earlier: organic sounds created by humans and animals at work and at play" (*Soundscape* 116). Victorians tolerated the "clanking din of the factory, the squeal of the streetcar, and other new sounds" as part of the soundscape, but still predominantly complained of the noises created by humans (street musicians especially) and animals (Thompson, *Soundscape* 117). It was not until the early twentieth century, according to Thompson, that machine-generated noises started to impinge on the everyday lives of people. As a 1925 article from the *Saturday Review of Literature* reveals, the soundscape and people's lives were now dominated by "the steady burr of the motor," "the clank clank of the elevated," "the chitter of the steel drill," "clattering ties of the subway," "the drone of the airplane," and the "recurrent explosions of the internal combustion engine" (qtd. in Thompson, *Soundscape* 117). Hillel Schwartz confirms the significance of coalescing noises from auditory technologies (the microphone, radio, telephone, and phonograph), public transportation (the elevated train and subway), World War I, construction, factories, steam locomotives, industrial whistles and bells, machine shops, cash registers, washing machines, sewing machines, vacuum cleaners, typewriters, printing machines, automobiles, trucks, and motorcycles: "In this 'Age of Noise,' as people began to call it, hearing was crucial in order to make one's way in the world and to keep from being run over when crossing the street or the train tracks" ("Indefensible Ear" 491–92). Thus, between 1860 and 1930, noise changed from being understood as a sporadic disturbance or clash of particular noises to a continual background noise that was, potentially, psychologically disruptive (Schwartz, "Noise" 6).

As a consequence of such noise, anti-noise societies such as Julia Barnett Rice's Society for the Suppression of Unnecessary Noise, which was started in 1906, flourished during this period. Such societies continued, even into the 1950s, when Edith Sitwell became the vice president of the Noise Abatement Society of London's Mayfair district (Greene 431).[2] Some members of the upper class believed that "the refined mind and cultivated self-control" were "threatened by the mechanical and non-mechanical sounds of the lower classes, the lowest emotions and brutal self-diffusion" (Bijsterveld, "Diabolical" 168). For others, noise indicated that machines were not running efficiently, making them a threat to public health (Bijsterveld, "Diabolical" 173). Yet these same noises of a typical Western city at the turn of the century could just as easily be positively interpreted as the by-product of production, labor, and commerce. Rather than categorizing the noise of the early twentieth century as an overall negative experience for people, it is helpful to keep in mind that the soundscape in general is a complex intermingling of sounds that create a sense of community among those within the range of hearing. For acoustic "signals are always reminders of the dominant institutions of the community and reflective of its social and economic base" (Truax 61). Just as R. Murray Schafer explains that "acoustic communities" were once "defined by the range of church bells" or the "area over which the muezzin's voice can be heard as he announces the call to prayer from the minaret," the early twentieth-century urban community was defined by industrial, electrical, and human sounds (*Our Sonic Environment* 215). The daily experience of such sounds allowed people to identify themselves as modern city dwellers.

Equally important within the modernist soundscape were the sounds of World War I, which were made by the telephone, wireless, loudspeaker, tanks, aircraft, and artillery. In the trench warfare that dominated the Great War, projectiles were aimed without relying on a direct line of sight with the enemy, altering the dominance of sight that one would assume to be typical in war. A soldier who was trying to hide from the enemy was reliant on his auditory perception to hear approaching bullets and bombs. Robert Graves, in his autobiography, *Good-Bye to All That*, attests to the significance of sound in World War I through his generous use of onomatopoeia: shells that go "whoo-oo-oooooooOOO-bump-CRASH!" (94); "the roar of artillery" and "shells bursting" until "the whole air rocked and shook" (107). In one scene, as Graves hears "a curious singing noise in the air, and then flop! flop! little pieces of shell-casing . . . buzzing down all around," a sergeant remarks, "They calls [*sic*] them the musical instruments" (94–95). This same sergeant then advises the soldiers to avoid wasting their energy hitting the ground every time that they hear incoming artillery. Instead, he recommends, "Listen by the noise they make where they're going to burst" (95). Eventually, the soldiers learn to "pick out at once the faint plop! of the mortar that sends off a sausage, or the muffled riffle noise when a grenade is fired" (Graves 112). Erich Maria Remarque's *All Quiet on the Western Front* (1929) likewise affirms that in addition to having an eye and feel for the land, a good soldier must have an "ear for the sound and character of the shells" (97). Italian futurist Luigi Russolo, in a chapter called "The Noises of War," written in 1916 during a break from the front, also attributes a soldier's survival to his ability to listen: "From noise, the different calibers of grenades and shrapnels can be known even before they explode. Noise enables us to discern a marching patrol in deepest darkness, even to judging the number of men that compose it. From the intensity of rifle fire, the number of defenders of a given position can be determined. There is no move-ment or activity that is not revealed by noise" (50). Of course, visual cues were still of great importance, and the Great War was not the only one to be noisy. But one gets the sense that World War I was the first mass war with weapons so loud as to make a soldier's "ears [sing] as though there were gnats in them" or cause a "vibration" that "made [one's] chest sing" (Graves 112).

This modernist soundscape, consisting of the noise of war and urban life, galvanized the sound poetry and avant-garde music of the period. Just as lis-teners interpreted the noise of industry differently, artists too ranged in their responses to noise. For example, the futurist F. T. Marinetti's sound poem *Zang Tumb Tumb*, which first appeared in journals between 1912 and 1914, revels in the noise of the Battle of Adrianople in the First Balkan War, which he witnessed as a reporter. The poem exemplifies Marinetti's idea of *parole in libertà* (words in freedom) and makes use of unconventional typography along with onomatopoeic words that represent the sounds of gunfire and ex-plosions.[3] The Dadaists likewise created sound poetry, but their intent was to combat the mechanization of modern life, consumerism, and nationalism, and to allow the individual body to be heard. When the German poet Hugo Ball opened the Cabaret Voltaire in Zurich in 1916, he explained in his Dadaist manifesto that his sound poems were meant not only to disrupt the accus-tomed reception of language but "to get rid of all the filth that clings to this accursed language, as if put there by stockbrokers' hands, hands worn smooth by coins" (221). The *simultaneous poem*, in which poets would recite words and make noise at the same time, and *chants nègres*, "whimsical abstractions designed to evoke the rhythms and 'semantics' of African songs," were also performed at the Cabaret Voltaire to fulfil the Dadaist objective of subverting the Western ideology inherent in European language through one's sense of hearing (McCaffery 119). Although they took different positions, Dadaists and futurists explicitly incorporated the modernist soundscape into their poetry to jolt the reader with a sense of reality and to subvert the conventional logic of language.

Both incorporating and contributing to the turn-of-the-century soundscape, modernist music broke with the musical tradition in much the same way that writers broke with the literary tradition. Two of the more notorious examples of music that appropriated the soundscape are Erik Satie's ballet *Parade* (1917), which used a typewriter, lottery wheels, pistol shots, foghorn, and Morse code apparatus, and George Antheil's *Ballet Mécanique* (1926), which included airplane propellers, sirens, and player pianos. Both of the premieres of these works resulted in violent reactions from audiences, and both were closely linked with modernist visual art: Pablo Picasso designed the costumes and sets for *Parade*, and in a letter, Antheil describes his score as "us[ing] time as Picasso might have used the blank spaces of his canvas" (71).[4] Similarly, Jean Cocteau, who wrote the one-act scenario of *Parade*, explains that the score "was meant to supply a musical background to suggestive noises, e.g. of sirens, typewriters, aeroplanes and dynamos, placed there like what Georges Braque so aptly calls 'facts'" (326). In both these descriptions, sound is used like scraps in a collage, as a way of incorporating the materials of modern life into a score.

In his 1913 "The Art of Noises: Futurist Manifesto," Russolo reasons that because the public's ears have grown accustomed to "variegated noises," they have come to "demand more and more violent acoustic emotions" (179). In his manifesto, Russolo catalogues the noises that the modernist artist must not only contend with but encounter as an aesthetic experience:

Let us wander through a great modern city with our ears more attentive than our eyes, and distinguish the sounds of water, air, or gas in metal pipes, the purring of motors (which breathe and pulsate with an indubitable animalism), the throbbing of valves, the pounding of pistons, the screeching of gears, the clatter of streetcars on their rails, the cracking of whips, the flapping of awnings and flags. We shall amuse ourselves by orchestrating in our minds the noise of the metal shutters of store windows, the slamming of doors, the bustle and shuffle of crowds, the multitudinous uproar of railway stations, forges, mills, printing presses, power stations, and underground railways. (180)

As Russolo summons his reader to experience the city with her ears above all else, he is participating in the larger cultural shift of artists and modern technologies drawing the public's attention to the value and significance of audition. While the sounds Russolo lists are not all specific to modern technology, it becomes clear from the above sampling of sounds that mechanical and urban noise intensified the soundscape of everyday life for an early twentieth-century Western public. As we will see and hear throughout this study, avant-garde poets and composers were not alone in this desire to aestheticize and incorporate such real-world sounds. Although grounded in a different ethos, modernist fiction writers too attempted to cut and paste the soundscape into their art—sometimes to jolt the reader into listening more closely, sometimes to disrupt the linearity of their prose, and often to represent the effect of these shared auditory experiences.

Keeping in mind this more general sense of the modernist soundscape and the ways that such noise inspired European poets and composers to break with the artistic traditions that shaped them, in the next two sections of this chapter I will consider what I believe to be the two most important contexts for my reading of auditory narrative in the modernist novel: first, a growing skepticism of and break with a philosophical tradition that valued vision above the other senses; and second, a climax in the popularization of auditory technologies that altered sound perception—creating new pathways for intimate connections, bringing sounds from different cultures and walks of life into the home, and aestheticizing noise through mechanical reproduction. As the public became disillusioned with vision and inundated with auditory technologies, modernists realized that if they wanted to be heard, they had to appeal to the reader's ear.

Ocularcentrism

Thus, from the outset in formal philosophy, thinking has been thought of in terms of *seeing*. . . . If one considers how easy it is for sight unlike the other senses to shut out the outside world and if one examines the early notion of the blind bard, whose stories are being listened to, one may wonder why hearing did not develop into the guiding metaphor for thinking.

Hannah Arendt, The Life of the Mind

In Greek philosophy, sight was considered the noblest sense, metaphorically associated with the work of the mind and search for truth. For instance, Plato referred to the "eye of the soul," and in the first paragraph of *Metaphysics*, Aristotle holds that humans prefer vision above all other senses because it "makes us know and brings to light many differences between things." In *Downcast Eyes*, Martin Jay argues that from Plato to Descartes, sight has generally been the privileged sense: "From the curious, observant scientist to the exhibitionist, self-displaying courtier, from the private reader of printed books to the painter of perspectival landscapes, from the map-making colonizer of foreign lands to the quantifying businessman guided by instrumental rationality, modern men and women opened their eyes and beheld a world unveiled to their eager gaze" (69). Although the primacy of vision was not without its complications and exceptions, thinkers such as Locke and Descartes "maintained a faith in the linkage between lucidity and rationality, which gave the Enlightenment its name. And both distrusted the evidence of the competing major sense organ, the ear, which absorbed only unreliable 'hearsay'" (Jay, *Downcast* 85). Despite the eye's ability, as Hannah Arendt explains above, "to shut out the outside world," from antiquity to the Enlightenment, seeing has been equated with knowing and, as the word *seeing* suggests, insight.

Such privileging continued through the Victorian period and was bolstered by innovations that made printing less expensive, as well as by the growth of museums, galleries, exhibitions, advertisements, and window displays. For example, the British National Gallery of Art opened in 1838, while in 1851, Victorians were presented with displays of commodities at the Great Exhibition in the Crystal Palace, in which "goods became spectacle, arranged by place of origin but divorced from the processes of production featured in earlier expositions" (Spear 196). Photography allowed the public to see the world in new ways, beginning with the daguerreotype in 1839 and culminating with the first salon for photography in 1893. As Kate Flint persuasively argues, "Victorians were continually being invited to look, to engage in [the] active interpretation of what they saw" ("Seeing" 27). Indeed, the popularity of optic devices such as the kaleidoscope, stereoscope, diorama, and zoetrope, in tandem with inventions such as the graphic telescope, the binocular microscope, the stereopticon ("magic lantern"), and the photographic camera, established the eye as the dominant sense for exploring and categorizing the world in the Victorian period.

This is evident, too, in the Victorian novel, where illustrations often encouraged readers to gain insights from images as they followed a narrative.[5] As nineteenth-century "novelists wrote dramatic scenes intended for illustration," literary critics cultivated visual metaphors to describe their work, appreciating literature that made use of "portrait, landscape, sketch, touch, graphic delineation, color, light, and shadow" (Spear 191). In addition to novels that focused on realist visual details, nineteenth-century poetry, painting, and aesthetic theory often made "the eye the preeminent means by which we perceive truth" ("Painterly" par. 1). While all the senses were represented and engaged in Victorian art, the eye was often relied on as the most dependable mode for revealing a person's character as well as personal insights.

Jay registers a shift, however, in this privileging of sight at the end of the nineteenth century. Photography, which nurtured the proliferation of images and the desire to gaze, also taught viewers to be skeptical of images, which could be manipulated by artists through techniques such as double exposure. Similarly, the impressionist and postimpressionist art movements, "broadly construed, can be understood as a laboratory of postperspectivalist optical experimentation, with a subcurrent of outright antiretinalism culminating in Duchamp" (Jay, *Downcast* 170). Jay also includes among the forces that weakened the eye's dominance at the turn of the century the philosopher Henri Bergson, the symbolists, and Marcel Proust's *In Search of Lost Time*, where the "voyeuristic gaze . . . might be understood to have a sinister implication" (*Downcast* 183). Visual technologies, philosophy, and art movements thus aided in "the dethroning of the dominant scopic regime," opening the way, one could infer, for the exploration of other senses (Jay, *Downcast* 150). Though, for Jay, the pinnacle of visual skepticism manifests in the late twentieth century, with French thinkers who harbor a "deep-seated distrust of the privileging of sight" such as Georges Bataille, Michel Foucault, and Jacques Lacan—to name only a few—he locates the beginning of this skepticism at the turn of the century, with modernism ("Rise" 309). According to Jay, though early modernist visual art and literature exhibited a flurry of innovation around "new visual experiences," "this initially euphoric exploration of new visual practices ultimately led to a certain disillusionment" (*Downcast* 150).

The idea that modernism heralded a disillusionment with vision has been taken up by a small group of literary critics, who have begun to investigate how early twentieth-century writers were influenced by the mechanical reproduction of images. For instance, Michael North, Karen Jacobs, and Sara Danius propose that visual technologies made the public more aware of the subjective and limited nature of the naked eye.[6] Photography and film could zoom in on a subject to expose what is normally overlooked or pull out to include a wealth of details that the human eye could never record. Film in particular could slow down motion, allowing viewers to scrutinize movement in radically new ways, or fast-forward a picture, making a familiar object suddenly unfamiliar.

Jacobs postulates that this new, seemingly objective mediation caused a "crisis of belief in the continuity between seeing and knowing, and a commensurate cognizance of the subjective mediations of embodied visuality" (19). This in turn caused modernists to develop what Jacobs calls an "internal gaze," a gaze that brought value to their work by affirming that the modernist writer could see a hidden inner truth, which was not debased through the limitations of the human eye (19). Though using different terminology, Danius similarly holds that a "sensory crisis" was instigated by technologies of perception, which caused modernists to shift their focus to subjectivity and aesthetics (3). These assessments of modernism are insightful and revelatory; they help us understand from a historical perspective why modernists might have turned their efforts to stream of consciousness and psychological realism. If seeing could not equal knowing any longer, then perhaps knowledge was not the ideal goal for the writer; the writer instead should concentrate on exploring the internal world. I, however, contest that this turn should be understood as a crisis. *Crisis* implies that perception in the past was somehow authentic or unproblematic and that modernist formal experimentation came from a negative experience of disorientation. While there undoubtedly was turmoil in this period—indeed, it is one of the period's defining characteristics—we can just as easily tell a story of modernism in which writers revel in the destabilization of vision. Perhaps modernist writers even aided in compromising the dominance of the eye, intentionally subverting the power of vision and resorting instead to *auditory* experience.

Though visual technologies made twentieth-century thinkers and writers question the objectivity and reliability of the human eye, modernity as a whole still remains dominated by visual paradigms. In fact, one could argue that the proliferation of images from the mid-nineteenth century onward, dubbed by Jean-Louis Comolli the "frenzy of the visible," has obscured the importance of sound in modernity (122). Presenting an alternative narrative, Sterne attests that though "the philosophical literature of the Enlightenment . . . is littered with light and sight metaphors for truth and understanding," audition, while not necessarily a superior mode of sensory perception, is an essential part of modernity (*Audible* 3). By examining how modernist writers represent sound and audition, this study further fills in what Sterne calls "the audible past." Auditory perception was a valuable way for these writers to push back against the dominance of vision. Modernists, thus, did not necessarily feel themselves to be in a state of crisis as their faith in vision was shaken. Rather, their attention to the soundscape, voice, music, inner speech, and the acoustics of words indicates a sense of liberation from an ocularcentrist orientation of the self and the world. This shift is reflected in their negative representations of vision and their tendency to represent sound and the act of listening as a means to achieving intimacy and connectivity.

Within philosophical discourse, Don Ihde, Jean-Luc Nancy, and David Michael Levin have persuasively argued that once we destabilize the privileging of vision, we can begin to discover the thoughts and experiences that are facilitated through our sense of hearing. Tracing the equation of knowledge with vision through Greek philosophy, Levin works against "philosophical texts subservient to the visual paradigm" and "ocularcentrism—a paradigm based on the dual nature of the Gaze, the one practical and aggressively active, the other theoretical and contemplative, panoramic, stationary, unmoved, dispassionate, disembodied, outside time and space" (30). To conceive of a self that is not limited to the subject-object dualism engendered by an "aggressive" and "dispassionate" gaze, Levin believes that we must cultivate our listening skills (182). Similarly, Nancy suggests that a developed sense of listening can allow for a different sense of self: "To listen is to enter that spatiality by which, at the same time, I am penetrated, for it opens up in me as well as around me, as well as outside, and it is through such a double, quadruple, or sextuple opening that a 'self' can take place" (14). While Ihde does not make such claims for auditory perception, he too notes how "sound permeates and penetrates my bodily being" (45). He asserts that "phenomenologically I do not merely hear with my ears, I hear with my whole body" (44). To varying degrees, each of these writers sets out to explore how, while observed objects and people are kept at a distance, sound waves envelope a body, immersing the listener in the sounds of her environment.[7]

According to Levin, Martin Heidegger's concept of *Gelassenheit*, translated as a sort of "releasement" or "letting go," can be achieved through responsive and open listening (225–26). In fact, Heidegger has "made us most aware of the deeper roots of the vision of the Greeks," and in his later work he advocates listening as a way to come to experience Being (Ihde 6). Heidegger writes: "Listening to . . . is *Dasein's* [for Heidegger, "being-in-the-world"] existential way of Being-open as Being-with for Others. Indeed, hearing constitutes the primary and authentic way in which *Dasein* is open for its ownmost potentiality-for-Being—as in hearing the voice of a friend whom every *Dasein* carries with it" (206). Though Heidegger is still immersed in visual metaphors, he often makes an appeal to the ear as a way to realize Being.[8]

While I want to be cautious about affirming an artificial dualism of vision and audition, labelling vision as distancing and negative and audition as connecting and positive, my close readings of modernist novels indicate that because audition entails a physical permeation, modernists turned to representations of auditory experience to connect their characters to their surroundings and one another. Listening is often used to immerse modernist characters in the moment (what Joyce called an *epiphany*, Richardson called *being*, and Woolf simply called the *moment*), to cause them to feel a heightened sensory delight in existence. Because sound is ephemeral and fleeting, as Kate Lacey explains in her study of broadcasting and listening practices, "listening is always also caught up *in the moment*," facilitating "a sense of presence" (55, emphasis in original). Modernists thus intuited this potential for auditory experience to awaken an individual to an attuned sense of being and of openness to the other. As modernists attempted to create realistic portrayals of human psychology, representations of listening, inner speech, and sound became integral to creating characters with vivid interior lives who were still connected to the outside world.

I argue that modernists used sound to counteract traditional, Cartesian concepts of subjectivity, and, by extension, linear narrative conventions. Such a revelatory understanding of sound perception seems to be what T. S. Eliot implies when he describes the poet's *auditory imagination* as

> the feeling for syllable and rhythm, penetrating far below the conscious levels of thought and feeling, invigorating every word; sinking to the most primitive and forgotten, returning to the origin and bringing something back, seeking the beginning and the end. It works through meanings, certainly, or not without meanings in the ordinary sense, and fuses the old and obliterated and the trite, the current, and the new and surprising, the most ancient and the most civilized mentality. (*Use of Poetry* 118)

Eliot's suggestion that the sounds of the words that the poet listens to within his auditory imagination have the power to reconnect with the "primitive" and "ancient," bringing echoes of nonverbal associations into language, resonates with Theodor Adorno and Hanns Eisler's claim (quoted at length below) that because audition has been less manipulated by technology, it remains an "archaic" sense. While I disagree with the claim that audition has not been affected by technology, I do believe that modernists tried to connect with the reader's auditory imagination by disrupting their narratives with onomatopoeia, stream of consciousness, and repetition, so that the reader could listen to "syllable and rhythm, penetrating far below the conscious levels of thought and feeling" (Eliot, *Use of Poetry* 118). While taking into account Viet Erlmann's argument "for the ear's intimacy with reason," we can connect the heightened attention to sound and auditory perception in the modernist novel with a desire to tap into the "primitive and forgotten" resonances of language and sound—a desire to break with the conventions of the realist novel by making the written text sound out (Erlmann 307; Eliot, *Use of Poetry* 118). But was it only this new understanding of the limitations of the naked eye sparked by visual technologies and a growing philosophical skepticism of vision that prompted modernists to amplify their novels? What role did auditory technologies play?

In their 1947 work *Composing for the Films*, Adorno and Eisler claim that audition has the potential for connectivity because, unlike vision, it has not been corrupted by capitalism and technology:

> The human ear has not adapted itself to the bourgeois rational and, ultimately, highly industrialized order as readily as the eye, which has become accustomed to conceiving reality as made up of separate things, commodities, objects that can be modified by practical activity. Ordinary listening, as compared to seeing, is "archaic"; it has not kept pace with technological progress. One might say that to react with the ear, which is fundamentally a passive organ in contrast to the swift, actively selective eye, is in a sense not in keeping with the present advanced industrial age and its cultural anthropology.
>
> For this reason acoustical perception preserves comparably more traits of long bygone, pre-individualistic collectivities than optical perception. (74)

Studies by historians such as Sterne and Thompson have taught us that radio broadcasting, the mass production of phonograph records, telephones, and sound in film inevitably made the ear a part of modernity. With the popularization of a slew of auditory technologies at the turn of the century, audition was as technologically enhanced and changed as vision; no longer was the ear the "passive" organ once assumed. Yet, just as Eisler and Adorno believed that the ear can bypass the eye's tendency to perceive the world as "separate things, commodities," modernist writers too suggest that auditory perception may allow for a different way of being in the world as well as a novel conception of the self. Unlike Eisler and Adorno, however, I propose that it is *because* of the developing auditory technologies of the time that modernists were able to conceive of audition as allowing greater receptivity to the other. It is not because audition remained untainted by technology but quite the opposite: because technologies such as the phonograph, headphones, radio, telephone, sound film, and tape recorder created new modes for connectivity and new forms of intimacy through the ear, modernists were inspired to experiment with ways to make their narratives auditory. This next section will explore how auditory technologies clarified the power of sound and listening for both artists and the general public by isolating the sense of hearing for intimate connections, facilitating interactions with distant and unfamiliar sounds, and aestheticizing noise through mechanical reproduction and manipulation.

Auditory Technologies

New Channels for Intimate Connections

The first telephone conversation was held between Alexander Graham Bell and Thomas Watson in 1876. Thomas Edison first heard himself singing "Mary Had a Little Lamb," reproduced through indentations made from vibrations on a tinfoil cylinder, in 1878. Guglielmo Marconi's wireless telegraph crossed the English Channel in 1899. And in 1906, a voice was unexpectedly broadcast to navy personnel, launching the development of the modern radio.[9] What these technological breakthroughs all have in common is that they forged a new means of connecting one human to another. These technologies opened networks for communication that were not based on the "observer-observed duality" inherent in face-to-face communication (Connor, "Modern" 207). In addition to creating new channels for (potentially) intimate communication, sound-reproducing technologies brought new sounds, voices, and music into the private home, making them available for the average person to study, manipulate, and enjoy in an intimate setting.

While each of the above auditory technologies created new paths for intimacy, the telephone exemplified this quality. Although the "theatreophone" was initially used to transmit live musical performances, the technology soon became a popular method for conversation. The telephone isolated listeners from the sounds of their immediate environment and required that they direct all their attention to a voice that, as advertisements repeatedly insisted, was as present as someone speaking right in front of them. A Bell Telephone advertisement, for instance, chastises, "Discourtesy on the part of telephone users is only possible when they fail to realize the efficiency of the service. It will cease when they talk over the telephone as they would talk face-to-face" (qtd. in Sterne, *Audible* 266). The public had to be taught that a disembodied voice constituted the same human presence as a living face. Gradually, the voice was granted the weight of individual presence.

Advertisements from the 1910s and 1920s emphasized that whereas one's grandfather "could not be heard nearly so far as he could be seen, . . . the telephone has vastly extended the horizon of speech" (qtd. in Sterne, *Audible* 168). This advertisement implies that with the telephone, one could now connect beyond the scope of vision; indeed, one could now communicate with someone who could not even be seen with the aid of a telescope: "Talking two thousand miles is an everyday occurrence, while in order to see this distance, you would need to mount your telescope to a platform approximately 560 miles away" (qtd. in Sterne, *Audible* 168). Whether advertisements suggested business or erotic communication, importance was dominantly placed on the immediacy and intimacy of presence that the telephone guaranteed.[10]

By isolating the voice from other environmental sounds, the telephone brought a heightened attention to the voice alone and granted listeners a new type of exciting aesthetic experience based on the sound of a vocal exchange. As Emily Thompson writes, "It was as if the telephonic conversants were speaking directly and intimately into each others' [*sic*] ears, oblivious to not only the distance between them, but also the space around them" (*Soundscape* 235). The telephone's ability to create intimacy where there was physical distance exposed people to exchanges between genders and classes that would have been less acceptable in face-to-face social situations. Even within the Victorian home, Michèle Martin clarifies, "the barriers that their society had built in order to preserve privacy did not work with the telephone, and there was no time to construct new ones" (146). These compromised boundaries and the aestheticization of voice aided modernist writers and the general public in bringing new significance to the act of listening and to the prosody of voice. Without visual clues, a listener had to decode an individual's mood and unstated intentions by voice alone. This attention to voice is represented throughout Dorothy Richardson's *Pilgrimage*, where, although Miriam does not use the telephone much, she relies on the prosody of voice to deduce a person's qualities.

The intimacy of the telephone was heightened by the use of headsets, which piped sound into the most private of spaces, the mindscape. Headsets, which were typically used with the telephone, phonograph, and radio, assisted in separating the senses, so that one's sense of hearing became isolated and thus more self-consciously used and theorized. In groups or alone, people trained their ears to hear the often garbled and soft early recordings and broadcasts. As the users of technology became more familiar with the strengths and weaknesses of the microphone and loudspeaker, they were able to create "new forms of public intimacy"—for example singers developed "crooning" styles, and politicians had "fire-side chats" (Lacey 62). With radio in particular, there was "a range of techniques to try to persuade" listeners that they were "in an intimate dialogue with the broadcast voice, a privatized exchange that willfully ignored the reality of the public dynamic" (Lacey 115). While the effect of having sound brought into the privacy of the headspace and home was an intimate one, the experience of simultaneously listening to phonograph recordings, broadcasts, and sound films created cultural connections among the public. Whereas one's acoustic environment was once determined by direct experiences within one's range of hearing, the modernist soundscape was dramatically altered by technologies that brought voices, noise, and music from distant places into the private space of the home and head.

As auditory technologies created new possibilities for intimate connections and the private reception of sounds among their users, these technologies gave modernist writers a way to imagine sound as linking strangers, friends, and family through shared communal listening experiences. We see this repeatedly in Dorothy Richardson's *Pilgrimage* and Virginia Woolf's novels, where music and the soundscape unite characters through their shared auditory perception. Whereas vision generally creates distance among their characters, listening can create intimate connections. The reader experiences this too, as Woolf's onomatopoeia allows the reader to participate in the shared listening experiences of the characters. As readers are forced to slow down their reading and pronounce the sounds on the page within their own mindscapes, they are brought into a more intimate connection with the text.

Although this aspect of intimacy will be most discussed in my chapters on Richardson and Woolf, it is worth noting that the modernist use of stream of consciousness also brings readers into an intimate connection with characters. This will become apparent as my chapters on Joyce and Rhys examine how we eavesdrop on the cosmopolitan and bohemian interior monologues of their characters. While there may seem to be a tension between, on the one hand, the intimacy created through auditory technologies and, on the other, the ability of such technologies to enable a cosmopolitanism by bringing nonlocal voices, music, and ideas into the home, I hold that the very reason why this cosmopolitanism was so potent was because it brought those sounds intimately close to the listener. Auditory technologies, thus, could intimately connect the listener to both the familiar and unfamiliar, the local and the cosmopolitan. Lacey attests that "privileging an acoustic subjectivity throws into disarray conventional distinctions between interior and exterior worlds, public and private, active and passive, even subject and object" (6). I would extend this to the act of listening to auditory technologies, which blurred and disrupted these traditional binaries so that the act of listening to a public address in the privacy of the home could simultaneously be a deeply personal, interior experience and an outward-oriented, connective public experience. This is reflected in the modernist interior monologue, where, as my chapters on Joyce and Rhys will show, personal interior speech is constituted by a mixture of internal, cosmopolitan, and local forces.

Cosmopolitanism and Bohemianism

By bringing new sounds into the intimate space of the home, auditory technologies also became a means for expanding the provincial worlds of listeners. Amateur radio, in particular, according to Sterne, "was from the start based on a kind of cosmopolitanism" (*Audible* 208). In his study of American radio in the 1930s, David Goodman cites a document from the Ohio Municipal Light Department that paints an ideal picture of a rural "farm wife" who, thanks to electricity, can turn on a radio that "brings the world and its entertainments into the home" (qtd. on 229). Referring to this document, Goodman writes that while some appreciated "the prospect of a more cosmopolitan world entering American homes," others preferred the radio "to project a familiar world, to speak truths rather than provide a stream of unsettling new perspectives" (228). The BBC, which unlike American radio was nationally funded, purposely cultivated programs such as its "Group Listening Scheme," which encouraged the public to listen actively together to differing voices and ideas on world issues (Lacey 140–41). Revealing how John Reith, the first general manager of the BBC, pushed against the term *listener-in*, Lacey explains the implication: "the idea was about listening *out* to different ideas and different voices" (141). Indeed, by opening the BBC up to members of the Bloomsbury Group such as the Woolfs, John Maynard Keynes, and E. M. Forster, Reith showed his willingness to compromise his own "cultural and moral imperatives" (Avery 35). As Todd Avery persuasively argues through his analysis of these BBC talks, "Bloomsbury writers saw radio as a potential partner in the advancement of a utopian internationalism grounded in the tenets of their ethical aestheticism" (36). Although the radio could bring a nation together both by fostering the act of simultaneous listening and by focusing the public's attention on common concerns and ideas, it also exposed listeners to "a wide range of literary and ideological opinion" (Avery 139). While broadcasts could often confirm stereotypes and nationalist rhetoric, they also gave a voice to different cultures and classes.

Likewise, the phonograph, which was first marketed for businesses and families to record speech, eventually became a machine that could enable music to travel far distances.[11] Citing composers such as Colin McPhee and Steve Reich, who were exposed to Balinese gamelan and African music through phonograph recordings, Mark Katz attests that "recordings and with them musical influence, traveled not only from north to south and west to east, but from east to west as well" (15–16). Recordings were particularly important in expanding the audience for jazz. Although listeners might "be far removed geographically and culturally from the urban centers in which the music flourished," consumers and curious, budding musicians could easily buy phonograph recordings of this new genre or come across recordings in phonograph parlors (Katz 73). In addition to expanding one's generic palette, the phonograph also "placed the full spectrum of musical timbre in the public domain, thereby increasing the listeners' sensitivity to timbre" (James 257).

Auditory technologies did not just bring unfamiliar sounds and music into the home, they also aided musicians in expanding the conventions of music and composition. As early as 1925, the Austrian composer Hanns Eisler warned audiences against attending concerts "only as guardians of cherished traditions," advising them not to "cling to a standard of beauty" or "look up reference books to see 'whether it is right' or whether this chord was 'allowed' a hundred years ago" (341). This line of thinking was targeted to audiences such as the ones listening to Ernst Krenek's *Jonny spielt auf* (1927), which incorporated a shocking mix of railroad trains, loudspeakers, jazz, and a telephone. Composer Edgard Varèse further bent the conventions of music in 1936 by advocating for science labs that could create "an entirely new magic of sound" through electronic instruments (186).[12] Varèse, who along with Satie was part of French and American bohemian circles, composed *Poème électronique* from a collage of bells, sirens, electronic sounds, machine noise, and animal noise (first heard at the 1958 Brussels World's Fair and later performed at the Greenwich Village club the Village Gate).[13] These (often bohemian) composers encouraged listeners to be receptive to the idea that the everyday noises of modern life and nonmainstream genres could be incorporated into classical music.[14]

As the public was pushed to question its standards of music by bohemian composers and was exposed to new types of music and voices from different cultures and classes through auditory technologies, a sense of cosmopolitanism was fostered. Through these technologies, the physical realities of others, different from oneself, were affirmed by an auditory presence. This is clarified in my chapter on Dorothy Richardson, where the central character of her *Pilgrimage*, Miriam, listens carefully to the dialects and accents of different characters and thereby begins to open herself to different nationalities. However, the concepts of cosmopolitanism and bohemianism are developed most thoroughly in my chapters on James Joyce and Jean Rhys. In their novels, a character's stream of consciousness is shaped by external voices, texts, and the soundscape. For Joyce, in *Ulysses*, interior monologues take on an auditory cosmopolitanism that ranges from Stephen's incorporation of foreign languages and texts to Bloom's consideration of the plights and stories of the different people he encounters throughout the day. In contrast, the interior monologues of Rhys's characters incorporate the popular songs and advertisements of the time and a bohemian voice that defines itself against the bourgeoisie. Although people had been exposed to the ideas and voices of others long before the advent of auditory technologies, and although technological mediation does not guarantee exposure to cosmopolitan or bohemian sounds, these popular auditory technologies made members of the public more aware of their role as listeners and multiplied the possibilities for potential encounters with new and foreign sounds. If listening, as Lacey suggests, "becomes an active way of engaging analytically and politically with the plurality of the world," then auditory technologies expanded the world with which listeners could engage, as they brought sounds from afar into the home (176).

Aestheticizing Noise through Mechanical Reproduction

Auditory technologies separated sounds from their sources, allowing sounds to be, as Schafer writes, "torn from their natural sockets and given an amplified and independent existence" (*Our Sonic Environment* 90). While Sterne rightly contests definitions of sound reproduction that insinuate disorientation and "the primacy of face-to-face communication," such as Schafer's *schizophonia*, we do get the sense that early listeners were shocked to hear sounds separated from their sources (*Audible* 21).[15] When phonograph recordings of Robert Browning were played after his death in 1890, for instance, the *Times* described them as an "extraordinary séance" (qtd. in Picker 123). In the early 1900s, an Edison phonograph advertisement titled "The Acme of Realism" depicts an incredulous child applying a hammer to a phonograph as he searches for the musicians responsible for the songs he hears; a caption informs consumers that the child is "looking for the band" (qtd. in Sterne, *Audible* 264). About the same time, the London Gramophone Company asked Francis Barraud to paint over the phonograph in his Victorian dog portrait, *Dog Looking at and Listening to a Phonograph*, with *its* gramophone, implying that the fidelity of its recordings could confuse even the keen senses of one's canine companion. The mere name of the Victor Talking Machine Company (started in 1901) already implies the confusion of a sentient "talking machine" rather than a machine that records and replays sound. Though these advertisements make use of dogs and children, instead of suggesting that potential customers could be so bewildered by a talking machine, they reveal how strange it must have been for turn-of-the-century consumers to grasp the mechanical reproduction of sound.

The phonograph stands out among other sound-reproducing technologies for its ability to record, store, and replay a sound repeatedly. In fact, one of the uses that Edison suggested for the phonograph was as a connection for the telephone "so as to make that instrument an auxiliary in the transmission of permanent and invaluable records, instead of being the recipient of momentary and fleeting communications" ("Perfected" 646). By making a sound permanently storable and reproducible—a literal object—the phonograph radically changed the relationship between a sound and its source, subverting the essential primacy of the source. Picker astutely demonstrates how the Victorian period first saw sound transformed "into a quantifiable and marketable *object* or *thing*, a sonic commodity" (10). Sterne echoes this, asserting that "between around 1750 and 1925, sound itself became an object and a domain of thought and practice, where it had previously been conceptualized in terms of particular idealized instances like voice or music" (*Audible* 2). The magnetic tape recorder took this subversion a step further, as it allowed people to splice, loop, and layer recorded sounds with much more ease and flexibility.

Walter Benjamin, in his famous discussion of the loss of the aura through mechanical reproduction, holds that a reproduction lacks the original's "presence in time and space, its unique existence at the place where it happens to be" yet satisfies the desire of the masses "to bring things 'closer' spatially and humanly" (200, 223). Similarly, these auditory technologies could reproduce sounds independent of their sources, disturbing the aura of the original sound event; but, at the same time, they allowed listeners to enjoy and manipulate sounds in new and possibly more intimate ways. Discussing sound theory in relation to film, James Lastra argues that because *all* sounds are transformed by their acoustic contexts, distinctions cannot be made between an original and copy: "reproduction is simply a special case of representation, with no essential theoretical priority" (137). In compromising the hierarchy between presence and mediation, the phonograph, film sound, and tape recorder reconfigured the very notion of original and copy. Sounds were disassociated from the authority of their sources and could be manipulated, just as any other material, for artistic creation.

As the phonograph, in Edison's words, allowed the "indefinite multiplication of . . . sounds, without regard to the existence or non-existence of the original source," composers realized that they were no longer confined by the temporal and spatial limitations of the orchestra ("Phonograph" 32). As early as 1890, the Italian tenor Giovanni Sbriglia described the use of several phonographs in a Strauss concert in Madison Square Garden:

> During the performance of a polka entitled "The Phonograph" and dedi-
> cated to Edison, the Viennese maestro, to the applause of the public which
> demanded an encore, raised his baton . . . but the orchestra did not move,
> and the polka was repeated by twelve machines that the Phonographic
> Society had placed around the platform of the orchestra. (qtd. with elision
> in Szendy 84)

Taking such experimentation even further, the 1930s German movement Grammophonmusik used the gramophone as a musical instrument by speeding up and slowing down recordings, as well as dubbing recordings over one another (Katz 100). Artists in other mediums were likewise eager to experiment with sound made tangible: Guillaume Apollinaire, for example, suggested that the phonograph be used in a poem, and Dziga Vertov tried to use recorded "found sounds" in his art but became frustrated with the quality of recordings (Kahn 9, 10).

The manipulation of sound and the art of splicing and looping sound reached new heights with the magnetic tape recorder. Patented by Fritz Pfleumer as "sounding paper" in 1928, the magnetic tape recorder became affordable to consumers (home-recording hobbyists, composers and musicians, teachers, historians, and the business world) between 1945 and 1955 (Brøvig-Hanssen 135).[16] The mechanical reproduction of the tape recorder was best exploited in *musique concrète*, which treated sounds as a malleable material not beholden to their sources. With a donation from the architect Paul Williams, John Cage established the Project of Music for Magnetic Tape (1951–54), a group of composers and electronic music pioneers who scored five compositions designed for magnetic tape, one of which, *Williams Mix*, is "a juxtaposition of hundreds of spliced tapes" (Brøvig-Hanssen 146). By decontextualizing and manipulating mechanically reproduced sounds through looping and splicing them in unexpected places, not to mention juxtaposing and layering them in unexpected ways, composers were able to create an entirely new understanding of what constitutes music. Moreover, such music encouraged listeners to perceive the noise around them with a new appreciation.

The mechanical reproduction of sound contributed to the aestheticizing of noise, as sampled noises detached from their originating sources and arranged in a certain pattern could begin to sound like music. Yet auditory technologies also created occasions where the public had to listen to the mechanical noise of a reproducing technology, drawing the listeners' attention to the quality and nuances of such sounds. Because auditory technologies picked up ambient background noise, there developed a practice of closely listening to and appreciating the noises that we customarily ignore. As Lacey points out, "minute details, fleeting sounds, could be amplified both figuratively and literally, attracting a level of attention never possible before" (56). Similarly, in Sterne's description of the "audile technique" engendered through sound-reproducing technologies, he mentions "the construction of sound as a carrier of meaning in itself" (*Audible* 176–77). Beginning with telegraphy, which was completely reliant on listening to Morse code for meaning, and continuing with technologies such as the phonograph, radio, and telephone, listeners had to discern between the sounds of the medium and the intended mediated sound.

This focused attention to mechanical noise, which auditory technologies required and proliferated, is an important historical context for the rise of onomatopoeia in early twentieth-century sound poetry. Rubén Gallo explains that sound poets were influenced by the radio not just because they could now broadcast to faraway countries and continents but because "the wireless introduced a series of new sounds: the buzzing and crackling of receivers, the high-pitched screeches of interference, as well as the short-and-long beeps of Morse code" (205–6). Yet, these newly aestheticized sounds can also be heard in the modernist novel. This aestheticizing objectification of sound as independent from the authority of its source helped modernist writers conceive of sounds as meaningful in and of themselves.[17] As the background noises of the soundscape were inadvertently picked up by reproducing technologies, listeners became more aware of how their ears filter out such noise and its significance in everyday life. A consideration of how novelists, much like the composers above, felt a new freedom to capture and manipulate real-world sounds, will be taken up in in chapter three, which contextualizes Woolf's incorporation of onomatopoeia in the phonograph's ability to capture noise. The repetition of Beckett's fiction too is best appreciated when read as a form of *musique concrète*—a music made from recorded and manipulated sound. Just as the mechanical reproduction of sounds with a tape recorder encourages a listener to focus on the texture and quality of the sound itself rather than its source, Beckett repeats and loops words to encourage his reader to focus on the sounds of words rather than their meaning.

Far from concurring with Adorno and Eisler's claim that "to react with the ear . . . is in a sense not in keeping with the present advanced industrial age and its cultural anthropology," this study holds that auditory perception was brought to the forefront of modernism through technological advancements in the phonograph, headphones, radio, sound film, and tape recorder (74). These technologies opened modernists up to new experiences of intimacy, cosmopolitanism, and the aestheticizing of noise, turning their attention to the ear and the possibilities it held for their narratives and characters. This, along with a growing skepticism of vision and an increasingly noisy urban soundscape, are the reasons why modernists became more aware of listening and sound, and why they began to represent the prosody of voice, noise, music, inner speech, and the sound of language itself with the utmost care and detail.

2

Music and the Prosody of Voice

Dorothy Richardson and the Transformation from Silent Film to the Talkie

In her September 1929 "Continuous Performance" column for the film magazine *Close Up,* Dorothy Richardson re-creates the experience of seeing and hearing her first talkie, *Hearts in Dixie.* Richardson describes the big-studio production musical (the first to employ a largely African American cast) as portraying "the pathos and humour of Negro life in the southern States" ("Dialogue" 195). Having already expressed in a previous column her belief that speech would ruin the silent film's "perfection of direct communication," Richardson enters the theater full of "fear" and "curiosity" ("Almost" 190; "Dialogue" 193). At first, she finds herself "holding back [her] laughter," but then she admonishes herself, remembering that with "the crude, the newly-born" medium, the audience must be taught "how to hear Talkies" ("Dialogue" 193). The film presumably begins with just that: actors introducing the audience to the new form of the talkie. But Richardson can only comment on the awkward and unclear quality of the speech: "adenoids, large and powerful, at once mufflers and sounding-boards, were the most immediate obstacle to communication between ourselves and the semi-circle of young persons on the screen, stars, seated ostensibly in council over speech-films" ("Dialogue" 193). Richardson hesitates to call what she is hearing a human voice, capable of expression. Instead, she only refers to the spoken voice by one of its anatomical parts, implying a sense of cold detachment from what she hears. Speech, here, is ironically an "obstacle to communication."

After a poetic recitation that, for Richardson, is "slow and laboriously precise in enunciation," she is relieved to find the film "restored to its senses by music" ("Dialogue" 193, 194). She explains that the music of "cotton-gatherers" in the fields is able to "unify seer and seen": "Song, partly no doubt by reason of the difference between spoken word and sustained sound, got through the adenoidal obstruction and because the sound was distributed rather than localised upon a single form, kept the medium intact" ("Dialogue" 194). To Richardson, the unnaturalness of filmic speech obstructs a viewer's ability to connect with the film, while music is able to bridge the distance between the audience and what it sees. The music allows Richardson to lose herself in the film, to forget that she is a spectator in a theater. But as soon as the music stops, and silence ensues, Richardson is "flung back into such a seat of such a cinema on such date," with only the "hissing of the projector" to be heard ("Dialogue" 194). Instead of a cohesive aesthetic film experience, the audience, theater, screen, and projector "[fall] apart into competitive singleness" ("Dialogue" 194). Without sustained music, the audience is held apart in oppositional self-consciousness.

Richardson was not alone in her dislike of the talkie. Bryher (Winifred Ellerman), who financed *Close Up*, and fellow contributor H.D. were similarly wary of how the talkie would derail the art form of silent film. Anne Friedberg explains that the founders of the international magazine tended to look at silent film as a form of Esperanto, a universal language in images (21). Yet, beyond artistic differences, there were significant technological setbacks in the first attempts to synchronize sound and film. In her survey of the various experiments to put sound to film in the first two decades of the twentieth century, Emily Thompson explains that the film industry "basically gave up," reasoning that "the public clamored for silent films; why change an already successful product?" (*Soundscape* 244). Although she does not discuss speech in particular, Thompson documents the "difficulty in maintaining synchronization between sound and image," as well as "the problem of providing sound loud enough for everyone in the theater to hear" (*Soundscape* 243).[1] It was not until the 1927 Vitaphone feature *The Jazz Singer* that producers began to recognize the viability of synchronizing film with speech and music. Most importantly, the race to produce the most efficient sound system for film "led listeners to listen more closely than ever before" (Thompson, *Soundscape* 247). One can just imagine Richardson in the theater straining to determine whether the amplified voices seemed acceptable to her ears, which, as this chapter will show, were finely tuned to the cadences, tones, and rhythms of speech.

Indeed, throughout her film criticism, it is the speech of the talkies that Richardson most abhors. Although she argues that speech impedes an audience's ability to concentrate on and participate with a film (even with technological improvements), in the review above, she is most annoyed by the technology's inability to capture the nuances of the human voice. She jokes that the actors' "respective mouths opened upon their words widely, like those of fish, like those of ventriloquists' dummies, those of people giving lessons in lip-reading. And the normal pace of speech was slowed to match the effort" ("Dialogue" 193).

About another bit of dialogue, she complains that it "inevitably had to be announcement, clear announcement in the first place to us, the audience" ("Dialogue" 195). In other words, the line of dialogue was not presented in a tone that was natural to the narrative but instead was announced to the audience in a formal, clearly enunciated, and artificial way. In such speech, all prosody and human warmth is lost, and the aesthetic experience is ruined as the audience is reminded that they are watching and listening to a film. Except for when the film breaks into song, Richardson holds that voices are "perfectly unintelligible . . . slow, enunciatory, monstrous" ("Dialogue" 194). Hence, it is the prosody of speech that the early talkies cannot capture. For Richardson, without tonal and rhythmic texture, vocal sound in film is merely a medium for linguistic information, a "barrier to intimacy" ("Thousand" 167).

Perhaps Richardson's disgust with the talkie's initial lack of prosody can help explain why it is that in her fiction, she pays the utmost attention to the musicality of voice in everyday life.[2] In line with the film review above, in the thirteen novel-chapters that make up her life's work, *Pilgrimage* (1915–67), Richardson goes to great lengths to describe the prosody of voice and the power of music, both of which connect and expose the ineffable depths of her characters. We see characters "unify" through their experience of prosody and music, which have a power to forge intimacy and express emotions that cannot be conveyed linguistically. Language, on the other hand, which Richardson generally associates with ideology and the male gaze, is often perceived to be an "obstruction to communication." Instead, silence, music, and the prosody of voice (rather than the content of what is being said) are valued by Richardson in her fiction. These sonic experiences create a continuity for Richardson's characters not unlike the continuity that musical accompaniment creates in silent film. Although musical accompaniment in film varied widely—from improvised piano playing to scores performed or prerecorded by an orchestra—Richardson perceives such music as an antidote to the "adenoidal obstruction" of communication created by speech in film ("Dialogue" 194).

This is not to say that Richardson is not interested in vision and imagery. Indeed, she values the silent film so much because it works through the seemingly universal language of images. And critics have rightly noticed the influence of the visual aspects of cinema on her writing. In her introduction to a reprint of Richardson's film column, Laura Marcus concludes that her "representations of reading and writing are . . . distinctly visual and cinematographic" (155). Carol Watts likewise remarks, "If *Pilgrimage* is a narrative in search of an aesthetic form, then the moving image of silent cinema finally provided it" (18). Richardson herself suggests this kinship when she contrasts a conventional narrative that takes "the form of a conducted tour, the author leading, visible and audible" and a filmic narrative, in which "the material to be contemplated may be thrown on the screen, the author out of sight and hearing" ("Autobiographical" 562). Referencing Richardson's preference for the latter method of narrative, Paul Tiessen writes, "Richardson saw in cinema the model for the potential of novels to bring a reader to perfect contemplation without the interfering commentary of a conductor" (86).

More generally, critics have recognized the cinema as a model for modernists such as John Dos Passos, William Faulkner, Virginia Woolf, and James Joyce, noticing parallel structures (for example, montage) and tracking the influence of film on modernist techniques.[3] Yet, similar to the insightful cinematic readings of Richardson's *Pilgrimage*, these studies often focus predominantly on the visual aspects of film.[4] Richardson, however, is always conscious of both "sight and hearing" (Richardson "Autobiographical" 562). This chapter will try to remedy the above critical imbalance by first examining Richardson's representation of music as a unifying force and then revealing her fascination with the prosody of voice over the ideological implications of language. I argue that by keeping in mind Richardson's dislike for the unnaturalness of the stilted speech of the talkies and her appreciation for the musical accompaniment in silent film, we can better understand her representation of music and the prosody of speech in her fiction.

Music: Creating Openness, Intimacy, and Transcendence

In Richardson's most passionate *Close Up* column defending silent film, she is careful to mention that it is "silent film, with musical accompaniment" that has the power to "translate" "each man's individual intensity of being" ("Tear" 200). According to Richardson, music is just as important as the visuals in a silent film because it fosters "the concentration that is essential to collaboration between the onlooker and what he sees" ("Musical" 163). Apparently, Richardson did not require total silence in the cinema. In fact, silent films were never completely silent: music was played regularly, patrons talked during the film, and the projector made noise. Weighing the different effects of an orchestra versus a lone piano player with a film, Richardson concludes that "any kind of musical noise is better than none," noting that one time when the orchestra did not show up, "the pictures moved silently by, lifeless and colourless, to the sound of intermittent talking and the continuous faint hiss and creak of the apparatus" ("Musical" 163).

Amidst the mechanical "hiss and creak" of the film projector, musical accompaniment, which was initially improvised but eventually followed "cue sheets" and later scores, brought a human dimension into the theater.[5] As Kurt London, an early theorist of film music, explains, "it was the task of musical accompaniment to give [film] accentuation and profundity" (35). We can explore the effect of musical accompaniment further by considering what Roland Barthes calls the "grain of voice," a term he also applies to instrumental music. Borrowing Julia Kristeva's theory of the *pheno-text* and *geno-text*, Barthes distinguishes between music that follows the "constraints of style" (the pheno-song), and music in which the musician's body is present and felt (the geno-song) ("Grain" 188). In the pheno-song, the "verbal and cultural content" dominates; in the geno-song, "the purely sonorous, bodily element of the vocal utterance" dominates (Dunn and Jones 1–2). Explaining his preference for the geno-song, in which the musician's bodily interaction with the instrument is valued over technical perfection, Barthes proclaims, "I am determined to listen to my relation with the body of the man or woman singing or playing and that relation is erotic" ("Grain" 188). Viscerally feeling the grain in the musical accompaniment of a film could allow the viewer to physically connect with the musician and bring that erotic bodily presence into the film experience. This perhaps can help explain the "collaborative" qualities that Richardson celebrates in the musical accompaniment of film.

Of course, this notion that music can connect people is not a new idea brought about by the musical accompaniment of silent film. Music has always been an integral part of communal bonding. Building on Anthony Storr's *Music and the Mind* (1993), Oliver Sacks writes,

> People sing together, dance together, in every culture, and one can imagine them doing so, around the first fires, a hundred thousand years ago. This primal role of music is to some extent lost today, when we have a special class of composers and performers, and the rest of us are often reduced to passive listening. One has to go to a concert, or a church or a musical festival, to recapture the collective excitement and bonding of music. In such a situation, there seems to be an actual binding of nervous systems, the unification of an audience by a veritable "neurogamy" (to use a word favoured by early Mesmerists). (2528)

This waning "primal role of music" was perhaps revived through the modern experience of listening to musical accompaniment with a silent film. Although the audience did not sing together, Richardson implies that music allowed the film to make more demands of the audience, keeping them from falling into passivity and thus recapturing the "collective excitement" that Sacks mentions (Richardson "Musical" 163).

According to Richardson, the musical accompaniment of silent film enabled her to "collaborate" not just with the visual images of the film but with other viewers in the theater ("Musical" 163). Richardson's column suggests that she was very aware of her fellow audience members. In one of her first articles, for example, she calls the cinema a "sanctuary" and "escape" for housewives in the afternoon ("Continuous Performance" 160). In another, she defends the children who sit in the front rows ("front-rowers") and argues that they are not straining their eyes in a stifling theater, as some chastise, but are becoming informed critics of the stock characters and plots of the cinema ("Front" 173). She even suggests that the cinema has a civilizing effect on those who are not exposed to art; people who have no prospects except work "are living new lives. Growing" ("Cinema" 181). Taking in the significant communal role of the cinema, Richardson likens its "all-embracing hospitality" to that of a church and concludes that "film is a social art, . . . a small ceremonial prepared for a group" ("Increasing" 171; "Almost" 191). Although the collective experience of the cinema was predominantly a visual one, Richardson stresses that musical accompaniment is essential in preventing the audience from becoming detached and passive viewers, bonding them as an audience as they creatively collaborate with the visual images. In Richardson's fiction, although music does not connect a viewer to an image, it serves as an important means for her characters to connect with one another, while also, like the theater, offering a hospitable escape from judgment and self-restraint.

As we come to know the protagonist of *Pilgrimage*, Miriam Henderson, through free indirect discourse and stream of consciousness, we see that she too thinks of the "primal role of music" that links her with humanity and allows her to transcend her temporal preoccupations (Sacks 2528). For instance, while visiting the Broome family for Christmas, she is awakened by music in the middle of the night, and "the perfect velvety darkness" (reminiscent of a dark cinema theater) heightens her experience of the sound:

There was nothing between her and the sound that had called her so gently up from her deep sleep. . . . It came from far back amongst the generations where everything was different; telling you that they were all the same. . . . In the way those people were playing, in the way they made the time sound in the air, neither instrument louder than the others, there was something that *knew*. Something that everybody knows. (*Interim* 300–301, emphasis in original)

The music brings back "a tide of remembered and forgotten incidents" and "[sends] her forward to to-morrow," collapsing linear time by merging her past and future with the present (*Interim* 301). Because the sounds enter directly into her ears and vibrate through her body, she feels no distance between the music and herself. This is because Miriam senses the grain of the music—"the way those people were playing." She cannot discriminate one instrument from another because the "'instrument' that sounds is the entire orchestra united in sound. The surrounding, penetrating quality of sound maximizes larger unities than individuals as such" (Ihde 79). The music conveys a paradoxical knowledge ("something that *knew*") by echoing back to past generations that may seem different but are the same as Miriam.

Even though Miriam does not participate in creating the music of the above scene, she still feels connected to the musicians as well as past generations of music makers. This type of experience and form of knowledge that is based on listening is Richardson's response to the distancing and analytical tendencies of vision, the sense that is most often associated with rational knowledge. While the scientific and technological thrust of modernity encouraged surveying the world as a "separated object of knowledge," Richardson shows that music and sound can convey an intuitive knowledge that is not reliant on analytical and "objective" methods of observation (Connor "Modern" 203). As Steven Connor maintains, whereas "visualism signifies distance, differentiation and domination," "the auditory self provides a way of positing and beginning to experience a subjectivity organized around the principles of openness, responsiveness and acknowledgement of the world" (203–4, 219). While we want to avoid essentializing and polarizing vision and audition, Richardson's representation of Miriam tends to bear out Connor's claims. For Miriam, vision is often associated with separation and judgment, while music connects her with others and instills a sense of liberation.

Richardson's first novel-chapter, *Pointed Roofs*, begins with Miriam about to leave her family and English home for a teaching job in Germany. The night before she leaves, Miriam dreams of the German staff "crowded round her, looking at her" with "dreadful eyes"; they "saw her as she was, without courage, without funds or good clothes or beauty. . . . They looked at her with loathing" (*Pointed* 21). Once in Germany, Miriam for the most part avoids "risking . . . any meeting of the eyes"; instead, she covertly judges and "scrutinizes" others as they do the same to her (38). Although not all looking is negative, positive experiences of vision are often disturbed by prying eyes. For example, Miriam "stare[s] easily and comfortably up into" the "great mild eyes" of Pastor Lahmann, with whom she has a connection, until Fräulein Pfaff's "eyes had spoiled it" (127, 130). Visual perception highlights her differences and separation from her German surroundings, reminiscent of the "competitive singleness" Richardson experienced when viewing *Hearts in Dixie* without music accompaniment. When Miriam listens to the German girls sing and play the piano, however, an activity that offers her relief from "hard-eyed observation"—the "cunning and malicious" eyes that "cut like sharp steel"—she escapes into a "featureless freedom," opening a liberating outlet for exchange (*Pointed* 36, 38, 39, 43).

Listening to one of the girls play piano, Miriam feels that the music "came nearer and nearer. It did not come from the candle-lit corner where the piano was. . . . It came from everywhere. It carried her out of the house, out of the world" (*Pointed* 43, suspension points in original). In his phenomenological study of auditory experience and voice, Don Ihde informs us that while the field of vision is generally in front of us, our hearing is *omnidirectional*, accounting for why Miriam feels surrounded by the music (75). Ihde continues: "In the overwhelming presence of music that fills space and penetrates my awareness, . . . I [am] momentarily taken out of myself in what is often described as a loss of self-awareness that is akin to ecstatic states" (78). Because of this, inner speech can be silenced when one is "'in' the music" (Ihde 135). Music envelopes Miriam and allows her momentarily to pause in her self-conscious inner speech, signified by the ellipses of the narrative. Paradoxically, the music is "near" and intimate, yet it also carries her "outside" of herself, transcending the particulars of her environment. As Miriam learns to "let herself go" and play the piano as the Germans do, she sits "grave and happy . . . with unseeing eyes, listening, for the first time" (*Pointed* 56, 57). The practice of listening and "unseeing" opens Miriam to new experiences and contributes significantly to her maturation.

Just as with the above scene, engendering a receptive openness through music is exactly what Richardson deems to be the role of musical accompaniment in film. She writes that music is "essential. Without it the film is a moving photograph and the audience mere onlookers" ("Continuous Performance" 161). If a film is good, music enhances the viewer's ability to connect with it; yet if a film is "bad," musical accompaniment "help[s] the onlooker to escape into incidentals and thence into his private world of meditation" ("Musical" 162). We see this as well in Richardson's fiction, where Miriam slips into a meditative state with the aid of music. For example, listening to the piano in a darkened room where "no eyes could meet and pilfer her own," Miriam "seem[s] to grow larger and stronger and easier as the thoughtful chords came musing out into the night . . . She found herself drawing easy breaths and relaxing completely . . . everything was dissolved, past and future and present and she was nothing but an ear, intent on the meditative harmony which stole out into the garden" (*Backwater* 204, 205). The narrator personifies the music as "thoughtful," "musing," and "meditative," which allows Miriam to unselfconsciously be in the moment, "finding herself" in a state of relaxation. Reduced to only "an ear," Miriam experiences a loss of self-awareness and temporality, escaping her social and familial obligations.

Yet music does not automatically transport a listener to a heightened meditative state. In *Pointed Roofs*, this is often because Miriam has to undergo a "transformation" of her "English ideas of 'music'" (36). Just as the two English girls in the school "were learning in Germany not to be ashamed of 'playing with expression,'" so too must Miriam learn to play the piano "as she had always dimly known it ought to be played and hardly ever dared" (45). In Germany, Miriam learns how to play with abandon and to appreciate music that is not marked by "English self-consciousness" and technical perfection yet is bodily and expressive (44). These contrasting styles resonate with Barthes's distinction between the constrained style of the pheno-song and bodily sonority of the geno-song, which beckons one to discern an "erotic," physical relation between the listener and musician ("Grain" 188). This clarifies not only why Miriam attaches a sense of shame to this type of expressive playing, but also why Miriam describes the bodies of the musicians that affect her so much. For example, with the first young German girl who "amaze[s]" Miriam with her piano playing, she "notice[s] the firmly-poised head, the thick creamy neck that seemed bare with its absence of collar-band" (*Pointed* 35). After listening to her play, Miriam receives a hug from the young girl that seems "more motherly than her mother's" (36). Experiencing the "grain" of the girl's piano playing brings Miriam into a newfound intimacy with the young girl.

This attention to the body is echoed when Miriam herself first plays with such "grain." With just the first chord, she feels she "had confessed herself" so that "anyone hearing it would know more than she could ever tell them" (*Pointed* 57). As she plays, she feels "her whole being beat out the rhythm," and "[finds] herself sitting back, slackening the muscles of her arms and of her whole body" (57). This type of playing develops in Miriam, as, back in England, she plays a Beethoven sonata, "using her body as the instrument of its gay wild shapeliness, spreading her arms inelegantly, swaying her, lifting her from the stool with the crash and vibration of its chords" (*Tunnel* 28). This bodily surrender to the music is not just liberating for Miriam: it allows her to expose herself to those around her more than she can in words. As Miriam describes bodies playing the piano in Germany—one that "threw back her head" with music "flow[ing]" from her hands, another who played with "a slightly swaying body and little hands that rose and fell one against the other"—she places her own body into an erotic relationship with the other girls, opening herself up to a sensual connection with those around her (*Pointed* 44, 46). Despite the cultural and linguistic differences among the girls, playing and listening to music creates for them an intimate kinship.

Similarly, when an Australian girl sings "with an expressive power which was beyond anything in Miriam's experience," Miriam is initially aghast at the lack of technical perfection: "Not a note was quite true. . . . The unerring falseness of pitch was as startling as the quality of the voice. The great wavering shouts, slurring now above, now below the mark, amazed Miriam out of all shyness. She sat up, frankly gazing—'How dare she? She hasn't an atom of ear—how ghastly'" (*Pointed* 46–47, suspension points in original). Yet, although the performance reminds Miriam of "the cry, hand to mouth, of a London coal-man," she still gives "the fullest applause of the evening" to the singer (47). Just within the time of listening to the song, Miriam goes from feeling disgust at her impropriety and imperfection to appreciating "the certainty of the body, of thrill" (Barthes, "Grain" 189). This development in the appreciation of the "grain" of music is integral to Miriam's maturation and development as an artist.

And yet, when a musician plays in what Barthes would call the constrained style of the pheno-song, Miriam remains distant and detached, as such music fails to create a physical connection. Ironically, this is implied when she listens to her eventual lover and intellectual mentor, Hypo Wilson, play Beethoven's Seventh Symphony. Miriam questions whether Hypo is "revealing himself" and compares his boisterous playing to "an impatient schoolboy" (*Revolving* 365). In the end, she decides that "something disappears in listening with the form put first" (*Revolving* 365). In his excellent analysis of vision, music, and silence in *Pilgrimage*, David Stamm notes that Miriam "listens to [Hypo's] music as a detached observer who, standing both physically and emotionally outside, analytically follows the forms and technical details rather than its emotional message" (131). In this instance, Miriam's analytical tendencies, which Stamm links to a visual mode of "detached observation," override her connection to the music. Similarly, when Miriam goes to the orchestra with her first romantic partner, Michael Shatov, the lengthy scene depicts her as initially unable to appreciate the music beyond "a shape of tones," but then "a single flute-phrase, emerging unaccompanied, drop[s] into her heart" (*Clear* 297, 298). Miriam confirms to herself that it was not the music that changed but her state of mind: "she had gone part of the way towards the changeless central zone of her being" (*Clear* 299).

Instigated by the orchestral music, Miriam envisions a garden scene through "an opening inward eye" and begins to conceive of herself leaving London for "green solitude" (*Clear* 299). This scene is linked indirectly to a foundational "bee memory" of a garden, first rendered in the short story "The Garden" (published in the *Transatlantic Review*) and repeated throughout *Pilgrimage*. Carol Watts's detailed reading of the relationship between the short story and *Pilgrimage* postulates that this is an "ur-memory," where "the child's consciousness discovers itself in a rapturous and animistic compact with the natural world" (20, 21). The beginning of Miriam's consciousness is associated with this garden scene, and the memory of it kindles within her a sense of her presence—her being. Equally important, the music sparks a new idea for Miriam's sense of her future; she suddenly can see herself as a writer living in a less urban environment. The music to which Miriam listens facilitates her inward eye, a mode of internal visualization to which I will return later in this chapter. This also resonates with the general significance of the *moment* in modernism, akin to Joyce's epiphany. Music, in its ability to kindle a physical sense of presence and internal vision, brings a heightened sense of Miriam's "being" in the moment.

When Miriam is in this open state of mind, music helps her tune into "the changeless central zone of her being" (*Clear* 299). While Miriam perceives Hypo to be preoccupied with "becoming," she sees her own ideal as one of "being," "the overwhelming, smiling hint, proof against all possible tests, provided by the mere existence of anything, anywhere" (*Clear* 362). Though she connects this state to silence, it also is found in moments of listening. Indeed, the above description of "being" is echoed in one of the last musical scenes of *Pilgrimage*, where Miriam plays the piano and sings with the young women at St. John's Wood. In a passage made more immediate through the first-person narrative, Miriam thinks, "Playing accompaniments, I felt all about me an awareness, conscious in the few, shared, like an infection, to some extent by all, of the strangeness of the adventure of *being*, of the fact of the existence, anywhere, of anything at all" (*March* 638). Music here makes Miriam attuned not only to her own existence but to the existence of everything around her, creating intimacy—"infections"—with others. It is no wonder, then, that Richardson saw music as fundamental to an audience's ability to connect with a film.

Although this scene is from *March Moonlight*, Richardson's last novel-chapter, coming nineteen years after her enthusiastic praise of musical accompaniment in the cinema, it still resonates with her adamant claim that the right type of music can facilitate "the concentration that is essential to collaboration between the onlooker and what he sees" ("Musical" 163). The dark and intimate setting of silent film unified the audience through a shared experience of music and visual imagery. As this experience was threatened by the talkie, Richardson's fiction reflects a heightened appreciation of the power of music to connect her characters. Conversely, the unnatural enunciation of the talkie also sharpened her appreciation for the prosody of voice, which, for Richardson, holds the power to forge intimacy. Richardson shows how the accent, intonation, and timbre of voice can expose emotional depth more than semantic meaning, which Miriam often associates with the patriarchal system of language. Yet, just as Miriam has moments when she cannot get beyond a detached, formal analysis of music, her relationship to voice likewise is not always one of connectivity.

Representations of Voice and Prosody in *Pilgrimage*

Richardson, who perceived filmic speech to be "slow and laboriously precise in enunciation," preferred to imagine film voices through subtitles ("Dialogue" 193). Richardson describes such imagining when she reports that the "tall letters" of a film's title "fill the hall with a stentorian voice," while subtitles are "more intimately audible than the spoken word. It is the swift voice within the mind" ("Captions" 164; "Dialogue" 196). This comment reveals that Richardson was tuned into her reading voice, as she enjoyed imagining and mimicking the particular qualities of different voices. The unrealistic speech of the talkie cannot compete with this intimate inner voice. It is this nuanced attention to voice, which was perhaps sharpened by reading subtitles and jarred by the imperfect speech of the first talkies, that we find throughout *Pilgrimage*, where the conventions of dialogue are defamiliarized through attention to prosody over content.

Barthes clarifies that "sometimes an interlocutor's voice strikes us more than the content of his discourse, and we catch ourselves listening to the modulations and harmonics of that voice without hearing what it is saying to us" ("Listening" 255). The reasoning behind this, he postulates, is that "listening to the voice inaugurates the relation to the Other: the voice by which we recognize others . . . indicates to us their way of being, their joy or their pain, their condition; it bears an image of their body and, beyond, a whole psychology" ("Listening" 254–55). We see this in Miriam's attention to what she calls the "singing shape" of the voice, which has "a meaning without the meaning of the words" (*Interim* 440). As Miriam tries to decipher the psychology of those she encounters through their prosody, Richardson likewise encourages the reader to listen to the voices of her characters and come to understand them through their voice.

Richardson consistently describes the prosody of voice, emphasizing Miriam's ear for such sounds. For instance, in the speech of her Irish friend, Densley, Miriam discerns "the Celtic shape of its tone, the first two words on one middle note, then one two notes higher with a curve in its course that brought it two notes lower than the opening words, then ding dong up and down, the last drop curving up at its end" (*Dawn's* 148). She notices the "subdued buzzing, barking and fluting of English voices . . . springing delicately, consciously beautiful, from note to note upwards and downwards in the scale" (*Dawn's* 159–60). Richardson often foregoes visual renderings of characters and instead presents meticulous descriptions of voice, reminding the reader to hear characters through one's reading voice.

For Miriam, voices are not just a means to receive a linguistic message; they are a song to be listened to.[6] Talking with her sisters, Miriam feels that "each tone was a confession and a song of truth"; she wonders, "Was there any one who fully realized how amazing it was . . . a human tone. . . . Perhaps that was what kept life going" (*Honeycomb* 464, first suspension points in original). In this particular example, it is the "low, secure, untroubled tone of a woman's voice" that Miriam praises: "There was nothing like it on earth. . . . If you had once heard it . . . in your own voice, and the voice of another woman responding . . . everything was there" (*Honeycomb* 464, suspension points in original). This scene exemplifies the complex representation of voice found throughout *Pilgrimage*: the prosody of the voice is emphasized over the content of what is said, and it has the power to convey a deep meaning that would only be vulgarized through words, represented through the ellipses. Yet, there is also a risk of essentialism in Miriam's assumption that there is an innate link between women and this quality of voice. While this risk will be taken up in more detail later in this chapter, here Miriam's statement implies that there is a right and wrong tone for a woman's voice and that to be a woman, one should ideally be able to perform this "low, secure, untroubled tone."

Although Miriam is constantly taking in sights, she repeatedly listens to voices as a way to go beyond the surface image one presents to the public, a skill that takes on importance as she moves out of her parents' house and must judge people on her own. For instance, the "metallic quality" of one character's voice "expressed, for Miriam, in sound, that curious sense of circumspect frugality," while the "soft horrible slurring flatness" of another's "suggested evil" (*Pointed* 52; *Honeycomb* 402). Referring to one of the young German girls she teaches, "Miriam note[s] the easy range of the child's voice, how smoothly it slid from birdlike queries and chirpings, to the consoling tones of the lower register"

(*Pointed* 18). When an old man in the park makes a comment to Miriam, what exactly we are not told, she notes a "strange . . . conviction in the trembling old voice" (*Tunnel* 97, suspension points in original). She associates this tone with an elderly masculine way of presuming "things that might look true about everybody at some time or other, and were not really true about anybody—when you knew them" (*Tunnel* 97). And the "gentle, unaggressive movement" of her close friend Jean's "peculiar cadences" convey "her whole self," so that "after she had spoken there lingered within the air, rather than the meaning of what she said, its sound" (*March* 566). By listening to the prosody of speech, Miriam abstracts qualities such as "frugality," "evil," consoling tenderness, presumptuousness, and selfhood. Richardson successfully defamiliarizes the convention of dialogue, causing the reader to linger over these imagined voices. Instead of just trying to picture characters, the reader tries to *hear* her characters.

Miriam takes this attention to voice even further when she registers the sound of a voice while neglecting the content of dialogue. In one of her first visits to the Wilson family, she notices that Hypo, who has a "high, huskily hooting voice . . . a common voice, with a cockney twang," "made little short statements . . . and little subdued snortings at the back of his nose in the pauses" (*Tunnel* 112, 113). Later in the evening, Miriam hears his wife, Alma, make "little faint encouraging maternal sounds" at their children, while another guest presents a "monologue" of "high-voiced clever sayings," which are "punctuated by soft appreciative sounds from Alma and little sounds from Mr. Wilson" (*Tunnel* 114, 115). Although we do get some dialogue and physical descriptions of these characters, the narrative is generally devoted to Miriam's apprehensions and interpretations of their prosody: their "snickerings," "a soft squeal," "a rotund crackle," a voice "large and tenor and florid," another "bass and crisp and contemptuous" (*Tunnel* 113). A few novel-chapters later, while talking with Grace Broome, Miriam marvels at how it is the act of exchanging vocal sounds, rather than what is said, that connects people: "Leaping into her mind came the realization that she was sitting there talking to someone . . . *marvellous* to speak and hear a voice answer. Astounding; more marvellous and astounding than anything they could discuss" (*Interim* 319, suspension points and emphasis in original). Richardson, through Miriam, attempts to draw attention to how the sound of a voice is laden with meanings that we barely consciously register. Even with herself, Miriam notices "within the inflections of her voice, statements clearer than any spoken words" (*Dawn's* 138). In doing this, Richardson stands out among modernist writers in her desire to capture the prosodic subtext of social interactions. Because the voice "comes from internal passageways: the mouth, the throat, the network of the lungs," it is "the equivalent of what the unique person has that is most hidden and most genuine" (Cavarero 522). Such meditations on prosody not only allow Miriam to become more intimate with other characters but also allow the reader access to another form of character development. From these descriptions of prosody, one can also begin to grasp why Richardson was so appalled by the stilted speech of the first talkies.

In *Pilgrimage*, Miriam's attention to prosody justifies her disregard for "the clever superficially true things men said" (*Tunnel* 113). Miriam belittles the ideological substance of language, which she associates with masculinity, and instead listens to speech for the ineffable qualities of intimacy that can be found in relationships. Miriam's close readings of speech reveal that "voices are the very texture of the social, as well as the intimate kernel of subjectivity" (Dolar 540). For instance, when Miriam nurses Mrs. Bailey, the woman who runs a boarding house where she rents a room, she listens to and partakes in the small exchanges of talk between the sick woman and her visitors. While in her bedroom, she hears,

> the accumulated intercourse [break] through the silence in a low-toned remark. It seemed to come from every one and to bear within it all the gentle speech that had sounded since the world began. . . . Taking her share in the remarks that followed, Miriam marveled. . . . she was aware, within the controlled tone of her slight words, of something that moved her, as she listened, to a strange joy. It was within her, but not herself; an unknown vibrating moulding force. . . . (*Deadlock* 34–35, final suspension points in original)

This thought ends with an ellipsis, denoting that the tone conveys an ineffable feeling. The narrator does not bother to render the group's remarks. Instead, Miriam lingers over the vocal tones that register a closeness among the group, which, like the music cited above that "came from far back amongst the generations," echoes back to the first bonds of humanity. In sharing such human tones, Miriam feels herself (literally, through vibrations) take part in something that transcends herself.

Because Miriam places such value on the prosody of speech, she also notices how dialects, accents, and foreign languages contain different sounds. In Mrs. Bailey's boardinghouse, Miriam encounters people from different countries and develops her understanding of these strangers by overhearing their voices through the house. As she comes to know Shatov, for example, his Russian accent becomes "the sound of Russia"; "in the rich, deep various sound and colour of its inflections, in the strange abruptly controlled shapeliness of the phrases of tone carrying the whole along, the voice *was* the very quality he had described, here, alive: about her in the room" (*Deadlock* 43, emphasis in original). Although listening to voices lets Miriam connect with others while avoiding the risk of being caught gawking, these aural indicators are also sometimes essentialized by Miriam, as they become linked to one's body and disposition. In fact, throughout *Pilgrimage*, there is a tension within Miriam as she, on the one hand, listens to music and prosody to foster intimacy and connectivity and, on the other, is compelled to analyze sound to formulate judgments based on her own prejudice and social relations.

With her eye and ear for detail, Miriam scrutinizes how facial features are a result of certain accents, at times using such features to categorize others. In an episode where Miriam is asked by her Russian friends to explain an overheard fragment of English, she explains that it is a "London Essex" dialect, "the worst there is" (*Revolving* 318). The man who is overheard "appear[s] horribly before [Miriam], his world summarized in his speech that must, *did* bring everything within it to the level of its baseness" (*Revolving* 318). Realizing that the Russians do not empathize with her disgust, Miriam retorts: "There is a relationship between sound and things. . . . It ["deformed speech"] shapes these people's mouths and contracts their throats and makes them hard-eyed" (*Revolving* 319). Ironically, while Miriam criticizes Shatov in this same outing for being "clear as crystal about ordered knowledge, but never questioning its value," she is unable to acknowledge her own rigidity and bias when it comes to "these people," who she assumes to be "hard-eyed" and "base" because of their dialect (*Revolving* 319). Richardson highlights Miriam's inability to extend her criticism of Shatov to herself, just as she highlights many of Miriam's faults. Similar to when Miriam is unable to appreciate Hypo's rendition of Beethoven's Seventh Symphony beyond an analytical response, Richardson suggests that despite the momentary intimacy that can be created through music and prosody, one cannot consistently bypass politics and social prejudice—even through the ear. Here, Richardson conveys the limitations of Barthes's idea that "the voice by which we recognize others . . . indicates to us their way of being" ("Listening" 254).

There is, however, another repercussion to Miriam's attention to accent and dialect: she assumes that if she can mimic the facial features and speech of a particular class, she can come to a better understanding of that class's worldview. This idea is summarized at a dinner in which Miriam talks at length about the various pronunciations of the sentence, "How many irons are in the fire" (*Dawn's* 161–66). Noting that this scene spans six pages, Jean Radford questions its excessiveness and concludes that these seeming "digressions on phonetics, chirography, or sociolinguistics" are part of "the characterization of Miriam as a writer" (132). More specifically, similar to Leopold Bloom's auditory cosmopolitanism discussed in my later chapter on James Joyce, Miriam deliberates on and imitates the speech of others to empathize with people from other classes and walks of life by listening to them. Within her humorous diatribe on how different classes pronounce vowels, depending on who most "desire[s] to keep the mouth closed" or who is most self-conscious about "face-convulsion[s]," Miriam asserts that "if you speak in a certain way you will feel correspondingly" (*Dawn's* 164, 165). Fromm remarks that growing up, Richardson had a "talent for mimicry. There did not exist a speech sound . . . that she was unable to imitate" (589). Similarly, Miriam claims, "I can imitate any sound" (*Trap* 435). By performing another's speech, Miriam tries to inhabit momentarily the life of another—a skill that she must develop on her journey to becoming a mature writer.

While Miriam uses her discerning ear and talent for mimicry to identify with people through their speech, it is this same skill that pushes her to categorize and judge people. For instance, when stereotyping "upper middle-class folks" through their speech, Miriam attempts to mimic the voice to grasp the mindset: "She had already discovered the exact amount of constriction of the throat necessary to its production, and felt it draw the muscles of her nose and mouth into an expression of faintly humorous contempt. . . . It gave a clue to the mode of being that would automatically produce it; disdain of life's external processes, of everything but high ends" (*Trap* 404). Typical of her fastidious ear for prosody, Miriam studies how an upper-middle-class accent would require certain facial and throat constrictions. Yet when she equates this accent with a "mode of being" and "disdain," she goes beyond listening to speech for emotional states and musical connectivity and instead uses speech to justify her prejudice against an entire group. Similarly, she generalizes that the "circular jaw movement" produced from a Canadian woman's accent "must affect her thoughts . . . making them *circular*, sympathetically balanced, easier to go on from than the more narrowly mouthed English speech" (*Interim* 438–39, emphasis in original). Voice no longer indicates a unique individual's bodily grain but instead defines one through class or national stereotypes. Though audition mostly frees Miriam from the distancing analytical mode of vision, Richardson attests that hearing is still determined by the subjective perspective of the listener. Miriam's oscillation between auditory connectivity and judgment signals that Richardson does not idealize speech and music. Such ambivalence is reflected too in the auditory technologies of the time, which on the one hand modelled new ways to connect intimately with others and engendered cosmopolitanism but on the other hand could reinforce stereotypes and nationalist rhetoric.

Skepticism of Masculinity, Language, Vision, and the Talkie

Paradoxically, Miriam reduces people to their speech, while resenting how language determines a person. She dislikes the fact that thought "depends upon the source of one's metaphors"—in other words, language (*March* 607). This is precisely why she is so insistent on representing the prosody of voice, which relays more to Miriam than does the content of words. Adriana Cavarero, drawing on the tradition of oral poetry and psychoanalysis, explores this differentiation between the nonverbal and linguistic aspects of voice, arguing that the voice acts "as the register of an economy of drives that is bound to the rhythms of the body in a way that destabilizes the rational register on which the system of speech is built" (527). By valuing prosody, Miriam destabilizes the rational and limiting structures of language, which she repeatedly disparages as myopic and systematic. While prosody and music often forge moments of intimacy and transcendence for Miriam, language and vision make her feel judged, objectified, and distanced from others. We see this connection between language and vision when Miriam explains that the "clever phrases" of men are "like a photograph":

> There was truth in it, but not anything of the whole truth. . . . Clever Phrases that make you see things by a deliberate arrangement, leave an impression that is false to life. But men do see life in this way, disposing of things and rushing on with their talk; they think like that, all their thoughts false to life; everything neatly described in single phrases that are not true. (*Deadlock* 14)

Miriam here likens language and photography, and she equates phrases, talk, and thought with seeing, impressions, and describing. Employing the metaphor of "seeing" for knowing, Miriam echoes Martin Jay's observation that "unlike the other senses . . . there seems to be a close, if complicated, relationship between sight and language, both of which come into their own at approximately the same moment of maturation" (*Downcast* 8). Through Miriam's critical awareness of the shallowness of visual impressions, Richardson participates in the larger modernist skepticism of vision.

Miriam further complicates the connection between language and vision by indicating that both traditionally construct patriarchal worldviews. Miriam pities the male sex as "hemmed in by women, fearing their silence, unable to enter its freedom—being himself made of words" (*Revolving* 278). For her, men and "'clever' women" who spout "quotations from men" are limited by their preferred discourses (scientific, religious, philosophical, or socialist) (*Tunnel* 251). Though Miriam of course must use language to communicate and pursue her career as a writer, she attempts to subvert the "fals[ity]" of language in her daily life through music, the prosody of voice, and silence, which she experiences with Quakers and within a few of her close female relationships (*Deadlock* 14).

This connection between language and masculinity is clarified in Richardson's film column, where she calls the talkie "a masculine destiny," linking the speech of the talkie with masculinity ("Film" 206). Richardson argues that film is "essentially pantomime": "Vocal sound, always a barrier to intimacy, is destructive of the balance between what is seen and the silently perceiving, co-operating onlooker" ("Thousand" 167).[7] Listening to speech destroys the collaboration between the viewer and moving images because, according to Richardson, the dialogue of the talkie reduces film to a "battle-ground of rival patterns, plans, ideologies" ("Film" 206). Men, and women who speak like men, use language to regulate and theorize the world around them: "Those women who never question the primacy of 'clear speech,' who are docile disciples of the orderly thought of man, and acceptors of theorems, have either been educationally maltreated or are by nature more with the man's than within the woman's camp" ("Film" 206). Though Richardson can seem to be essentializing masculinity and femininity, "her definitions," as Marcus astutely claims, "are radically unstable, veering between the historical and the mythic in the construction of 'woman'" ("Introduction" 157). The "clever phrases" and judgmental vision of men are just as often associated with women, including Miriam herself. What concerns Miriam is how vision and language, as related practices, mediate relationships and reduce life to a set of assumed generalizations.

Yet Richardson excessively idealizes the silent film for the sake of her argument, which drives her to make uncharacteristically absolute statements, such as "life's 'great moments' are silent," while trying to prove that "it is impossible both to see and to hear" ("Tear" 200, 197). Richardson self-consciously jokes about these extreme claims, commenting that in her column on *Hearts in Dixie*, she "foreswore [her] sex by asserting, in bold, masculine, side-taking, either-or fashion, that no matter what degree of perfection might presently be attained by the recording apparatus we were certain that the talkie . . . will never be able to hold a candle to the silent film" ("Tear" 196). Despite her awareness that she is making absolute claims that *all* talkies will *always* be terrible, Richardson concludes by echoing her character Miriam's dualism between her own valuing of being and Hypo's valuing of becoming, maintaining that the talkie is limited to a "destiny of planful becoming rather than of purposeful being" ("Film" 206). Within Richardson's dualisms, the talkie is aligned with masculinity and language, while the silent film is aligned with femininity and musical collaboration. It follows that because the silent film is associated with the feminine, Richardson is equally concerned with the male gaze: how women in particular are looked at by men. Richardson's fiction clearly shows that language, the "clever phrases" of men, are "like a photograph," intricately connecting the male gaze with linguistic ideology (*Deadlock* 14).

Although there are moments in *Pilgrimage* in which Miriam celebrates sight, when she is put into raptures by a beautiful home, landscape, or London street, with the light illuminating it in just the right way, she also at times generalizes vision as masculine, corrupted, and limited. When Miriam is first introduced to the technology of photography, her thoughts are preoccupied with the way in which men look at women and the way in which women respond to this gaze. Attending a lecture on the daguerreotype with her boss, Mr. Hancock, she is offended when he mentions that a passing woman is "pretty" (*Tunnel* 105). Richardson presents Miriam's contradictory thoughts, which unknowingly reflect both her disgust for how men are taken in by such "a deliberate 'charming' feminine effect" and her anguish at feeling that her boss is "bored by her own heavy silence" and unimpressive out-of-date dress (*Tunnel* 105, 108). Miriam supposes that women present themselves to men in this "advertising manner" because men "treat them as works of art" and only notice a woman when she looks beautiful and parrots their own statements; yet Miriam is still subject to these conditions, wishing she had a new dress to attract her boss's eye (*Tunnel* 105, 106). Though Miriam does not connect these thoughts to the lecture on photography, Richardson's irony is apparent. Miriam's argument can easily be extended to the new technology, which further sealed the fate of women as objects for ogling.

Miriam complains that men cannot both criticize women for "talk[ing] shamelessly at a concert or opera" and "stare at them . . . as works of art" (*Tunnel* 106). Such "admiration," she concludes, creates a sense of competition, where women "assert themselves in the presence of other works of art" (*Tunnel* 106). Richardson, however, makes this same contradictory complaint in a film column published nine years after the above fictional scene. She praises women as works of art in silent film, admiring the starlet "in silent, stellar radiance, for the speech that betrayeth is not demanded of her" ("Continuous Performance

VIII" 174). Yet she disparages a woman in the audience who "shamelessly" talks during the film, patronizingly claiming that she "cherish[es]" her, while offering a manual for film viewing that asserts, *"Don't be audible in any way . . . Cease, in fact, to exist except as a contributing part of the film, critical or otherwise, and if critical, silently so"* ("Continuous Performance VIII" 175, emphasis in original).[8] One suspects that Richardson, as represented through Miriam and her film column, would rather that women were silent.

While this silencing may seem sexist, it is usually the systemization and limitations of language that Richardson wants to repress—not women. As discussed earlier, Richardson associates language with masculine ideology, whereas in both her fiction and film column she repeatedly reveres silence as "where truth blossoms" (*Deadlock* 188). All the same, this silence can easily take on a negative aspect when it is part of the silencing of the "male gaze," a type of looking in which Miriam herself partakes. Just as Richardson prefers the "silent, stellar radiance" of the female on the screen, Miriam too enjoys the beautiful female face, which, she laments, can be destroyed with speech ("Continuous Performance VIII" 174). Although Laura Mulvey examines classical rather than early film, her discussion of how film constructs spectators as masculine can help to explain Miriam's pleasure in the silent female image. To borrow Mulvey's terminology, Miriam exhibits a *fetishistic scopophilia* as she takes pleasure in viewing the beauty of the female face, "transforming it into something satisfying in itself" (844).[9] In such cases, Miriam occupies the position Mulvey reserves for the masculine viewer, a position in which, as a daughter who was supposed to be a son, she frequently finds herself.[10]

Miriam's assumption of a traditionally masculine position is exemplified in her reaction to Ulrica, one of the girls at the German boarding school. Gaining satisfaction through the act of looking, Miriam "[feeds] upon the outlines of [Ulrica's] head"; "She wish[es] she could place her hands on either side of its slenderness and feel the delicate skull and gaze undisturbed into the eyes" (*Pointed* 97). With the neuter pronoun *its* and the article *the*, Miriam detaches Ulrica's skull and eyes from her particular personhood, objectifying her beauty. When Ulrica reads aloud, Miriam admires her "rich and full and liquid" voice, though she does not listen to what she says; "hearing no words," Miriam once again longs to "put her hands about the beautiful head, scarcely touching it and say 'It is all right. I will stay with you always'" (*Pointed* 99). Miriam frames Ulrica like a film close-up. As long as Ulrica does not speak, Miriam can maintain this masculine position of guardianship and adoration. Once Ulrica speaks, however, Miriam is left in total disappointment: "Miriam felt as if she were being robbed. . . . This was Ulrica" (*Pointed* 148, suspension points in original). "Robbed" of the beauty of her object, Miriam is appalled by Ulrica's conventional sentiments, which recall how she wept at her confirmation because of the beauty of her dress, her flower bouquet, and the sacrament. Miriam's initial registering of the prosody of Ulrica's reading voice ultimately does not connect her to the character as vision and language distance her and spur analysis and judgment.

Though Miriam is only seventeen in the scene above, as she matures, she oscillates between gazing on the beauty of women and being judgmental of how women perform their roles as objects of beauty. During her time as a governess with the Corrie family, for example, Miriam looks "with hatred in her eyes" at a staged photograph of a woman labeled "Inspiration" (*Honeycomb* 400). She is repulsed by how the woman, who she calls a "*thing*," intentionally tries to attract the male gaze, and she thinks, "She was not a woman, she was a *woman* . . . oh, curse it all. But men liked actresses. They liked being fooled" (*Honeycomb* 400, suspension points and emphasis in original). Miriam likens the woman to an "actress" who performs a stereotype of "femininity" that inspires heroes to take action. For Miriam, it is only in person that women have the power to instill the awe of the fetishized woman. Much later in her life, while Miriam is sitting with Hypo and Alma at dinner, Alma's "eyes rest on Miriam's," and through their passive "dreamy mildness," Miriam is reminded of a photograph she had once seen of Alma (*Dawn's* 162). Miriam "felt she could kneel, with the world's manhood, in homage to the spirit of the womanly woman, yet shared, as the radiance passed, their cramped uneasiness" (*Dawn's* 162). Once again, Miriam occupies a masculine position, seeing women as ultimately "insufficien[t]" beyond their beauty (*Dawn's* 162).

Miriam also finds herself the object of the male gaze. Carol Watts posits that though Miriam has the freedom of a modern woman to walk the streets of London alone, "this world of exchanged glances elsewhere positions Miriam in a more commodified economy of the streets—the object of the male gaze" (64). This is indeed the case when Miriam wanders through a London park, preoccupied with sorting out her romantic relationship with Shatov, and is disturbed by two men looking at her. Miriam senses the "leer of their talk"; as they "[scan] her in the spirit of the images of life they had evoked in their sequestered confidential interchange, they identified her with their vision" (*Deadlock* 208). It is unclear whether Miriam imposes her own thoughts on these men, but regardless, she can find no "refuge" from their stare, which she intuits holds the "unconscious male mind of Europe surprised unmasked"

(*Deadlock* 208). She ruminates on how they perceive women: "One image; perceived only with the body, separated and apart from everything else in life. Men were *mind* and *body*, separated mind and body, looking out at women, below their unconscious men's brows, variously moulded and sanctified by thought, with one unvarying eye. There was no escape from its horrible blindness, no other life in the world to live . . ." (*Deadlock* 208, suspension points in original). To Miriam, their idea of "womanhood" is determined through a distancing and analytical mode of seeing women as only "images" and "bodies." Rooted in philosophy and affirmed through the Enlightenment, rational and "objective" thinking has always been equated with vision—a "blind" and "unvarying eye"—and within this tradition women have always been associated with the body. Miriam astutely brings these two historical strains together to explain how women have been "thought out and systemized" by men through vision and language (*Deadlock* 208).

Hypo comes to embody this masculine way of seeing, especially as his relationship with Miriam becomes romantic and as she feels herself segmented into body parts where "each detail was 'pretty' and the whole an object of desire" (*Dawn's* 231).[11] When Hypo recognizes her beauty, Miriam repeats his words within herself: "You were a lovely person in your blue gown" (*Trap* 465). Internalizing the male gaze by repeating this sentence (about six times), she thinks, "I felt him looking, and felt myself not there but looking on, with his eyes—I was a lovely person in a blue gown" (*Trap* 465). Richardson reveals Miriam's conflicted emotions as she feels "there is something wrong in his way of wanting effects, illusions," and yet she simultaneously absorbs his view of her, illustrated in the mechanical repetition of his compliment and her own sense of absence (*Trap* 466).

After finding herself in this objectified position, Miriam becomes more explicitly critical of Hypo's vision when she takes her friend Amabel to meet him and imagines how he sees her. Assuaging Amabel's anxieties about meeting him, she tells her, "It will just be *us*. And the intelligent eye, blinkered in advance with unsound generalizations about 'these intense, over-personal feminine friendships,' and the clumsy masculine machinery of observation, working in this case like a hidden camera with a very visible and very gleaming lens, will both find themselves at fault" (*Clear* 315, emphasis in original). Miriam reduces Hypo to only an eye, and a blind one at that. His way of looking is circumscribed by the "generalizations" that he makes about women, once again linking vision and patriarchal language. Interestingly, Watts claims that the name *Hypo* is "derived from the 'Acid Hypo' used to fix film" (18). Keeping this origin in mind, we can draw a connection between the way that the camera objectifies women and the way that Hypo sees women with his "hidden camera."

The chapter that immediately follows the above quotation details Amabel and Hypo's meeting and is filled with references to his "investigating" vision and constricted thinking (*Clear* 319). It begins ironically, with Hypo stating, "I SEE," as Miriam immediately notes his inability to see: "his lowered eyelids," "closed shutters," "his picture," "his vision" (*Clear* 316). Later in the same conversation, Miriam "encounter[s] [Hypo's] eyes . . . and [sees] their searching beams . . . a direct gaze" (*Clear* 318). Miriam even hypothesizes that Hypo's seat at the end of the table allows him an advantage, since he has "the longer vista for the impersonal gaze," as she repeatedly notices his "eyes gazing ahead," "a would-be authoritative glance," a "pointed, personal gaze" (*Clear* 319–20). Once Miriam is left alone with Hypo, she humorously concludes (just after Hypo says "I see your point") that "his sightless, entertainment-seeking" eyes, "moving from point to point, searchlights, operated from a centre whose range, however far it might extend, was constricted by the sacred, unquestioned dogmas ruling his intelligence" (*Clear* 327). Since Hypo's "dogmas" determine what he is able to see, Miriam repeatedly argues that his literal sight is hampered: "his eyes fixed on a distant point," a "sightless, contemplative gaze" (*Clear* 334, 396). Richardson's negative rendering of Hypo's gaze exemplifies what Levin philosophically associates with "ocularcentrism—a paradigm based on the dual nature of the Gaze, the one practical and aggressively active, the other theoretical and contemplative, panoramic, stationary, unmoved, dispassionate, disembodied, outside time and space" (30). Though Hypo is the most obvious and extreme case, Miriam extends this argument to anyone, male or female, who maintains an aggressively analytical or distantly theoretical perspective.

The Subversion of Vision

Miriam subverts the hegemony of masculine vision most obviously by her valuing of music and the prosody of voice, already discussed. Yet this subversion happens more subtly through her constant listening for the "happy symphony of recognizable noises" that makes up London and her surroundings (*Interim* 373). She even at one point notes the "sound of dust" that suggests the "empty space" of Mrs. Bailey's dining room and proclaims to a roommate that "she loved rattling windows; loved, loved them" (*Interim* 444; *Trap* 430). Barthes points out the "often underestimated" importance of "a space of familiar, *recognized* noises whose ensemble forms a kind of household symphony: differentiated slamming of doors, raised voices, kitchen noises, gurgle of pipes, murmurs from outdoors" ("Listening" 246). These are precisely the sounds to which Miriam pays attention, from the "tap-tap" and "high squeak" of a door, to the "clear plonk plonk and rumble of swift vehicles," to "cheeping birds," to "the sound of an unaccompanied violin, clearly attacking and dropping and attacking a passage of half a dozen bars" (*Tunnel* 12, 15). Among examples too numerous to mention, Miriam listens to the representation of such sounds to differentiate each new apartment she inhabits. What stands out for the reader is the detail that Richardson employs to describe these sounds and the importance that she attaches to them, even depicting Miriam "finding renewal in the familiar creaking of her floor"—a "happy creaking" that she purposefully retreads (*Interim* 409). In bringing to the forefront the typically ignored background sounds of life, Richardson subverts traditional hierarchies of signification: visual characterizations and settings, along with the content of dialogue, are put on equal footing with the soundscape.

Barthes holds that such noises are one of the ways in which a human "recognizes its territory, its habitat," a recognition that can be disrupted with too much noise "pollution" ("Listening" 247). This is certainly true of church bells, which generally suggest that those within listening range are within that particular community. Indeed, Miriam feels herself a part of the London community once she returns from Germany and hears the church bells of Saint Pancras, which are onomatopoeically described as actively entering her room: "clamouring in the room; rapid scales, beginning at the top, coming with a loud full thump on to the fourth note and finishing with a rush to the lowest which was hardly touched before the top note hung again in the air, sounding outdoors clean and clear while all the other notes still jangled together in her room" (*Tunnel* 21). As Miriam moves around, she is always aware of the bells making her part of an auditory community, and she appreciates the notes of the bells, suggesting that "all one's being, in order not to miss its perfection . . . had to become an attentive ear" (*Dawn's* 204).[12] Miriam even distinguishes between weekday and Sunday sounds, when "the recurrent church bells and the sound of the traffic unburdened by the ceaseless heavy rumble of commerce . . . held a depth no other day could provide" (*Dimple* 491). From the sounds of London to "the never-to-be-forgotten voices of doors from the past," Miriam incessantly orients herself by listening (*March* 628). With "every single, blessed sound indoors and out," she feels herself part of a community and revels in the continuity that sounds create in her life (*Dawn's* 204).

These sounds give Miriam a wider sense of her community, including classes other than her own. In *The Trap*, Miriam shares an apartment with a friend in London and nightly listens to "noisy homecomings," "drunken monologues," the "cobbler, noisily taking down his shutters," "hoarse-voiced lovers," and "thick, distorted voices in strife. Shut in, maddened" (500). Mulling over each sound, Miriam decides that "even at their worst they were life, fierce and coarse, driving off sleep; but real, exciting" (*Trap* 500). She contrasts these sounds with the "innocent sounds" of her roommate's morning rituals of tea, sighs, and cleansing, sounds that inspire "hatred" and make Miriam think of "death" (*Trap* 500–501). For Miriam, it is not just hearing in general that indicates the life around her but listening specifically for the sounds of the downtrodden and different, noises that suggest the diverse life of London. Even listening to Wagner in a theater, her mind wanders, and she concludes, "Every sound in the world, every protest and cry of agony, every relieving shriek of hysteria, is tribute to the sure knowledge of life's perfection" (*Dawn's* 172). Similar to Woolf's notion of sound (discussed in the next chapter), the act of listening has the power to integrate one into life itself.

Although silence is revered in *Pilgrimage*, Miriam's continual attention to voice, music, and the sounds of London demonstrates Richardson's belief that audition is vital to everyday experience. Richardson says as much when she argues that film should be the "reverse" of "daily life," where "the faculty of hearing takes precedence of the faculty of sight and is in no way to be compensated" ("Tear" 197). If we can assume that for Richardson the purpose of the novel is to capture "daily life," then it too should be predominantly concerned with "the faculty of hearing." For Richardson, film was the medium that complemented one's visual capacities, and it could only inadequately convey everyday speech and realistic noise. It makes sense then that in her fiction, the ability to listen to the prosody of voice, music, and soundscape is an essential mode of discerning the world and one's place within it.

In the last novel-chapters, Miriam makes a final push in her subversion of vision by rejecting Hypo's way of seeing and focusing on her "mind's eye." Looking at writers such as Woolf, Vladimir Nabokov, and Ralph Ellison, Karen Jacobs contends that "skeptical philosophical discourses of vision," visual technologies such as photography and film, and anthropological and sociological methods of observation heightened modernists' awareness of the imperfect and subjective condition of the naked eye, which could not record the world as accurately as their mechanical counterparts (2). This in turn fostered a valorization of an "interior gaze," "which relocates visual truths to an 'interior'—literal or conceptual—where they can be recovered only by a properly expert vision" (19).

Similarly, Richardson presents Hypo's "objective" camera-like gaze as imperfect and limited, while Miriam's internal artistic mind's eye sees deeper truths within her subjective mind.

But Miriam's internal eye is not necessarily a "properly expert vision," as one of its most important characteristics is that it is a construct of her stream of consciousness, entirely reliant on her subjectivity. For instance, in the passage quoted above, Hypo's "machinery of observation" is contrasted with Miriam's inward eye, which "consider[s] her many aspects" (*Clear* 315). In a passage quoted earlier of Miriam listening to music with Shatov, it is "an opening in her inward eye" that allows her to see a garden setting and come to her realization of leaving London (*Clear* 299). In the final novel-chapter of *Pilgrimage*, such references become more frequent, as she "sees" memories "within her mind" and recalls people with her "truant inward eye" (*March* 595, 598). Once Miriam begins to write, she makes an effort to withdraw "from everything within sight" and look to "her mind's eye": "she gazed incredulously at the spectacle arisen within her mind and projected thence so clearly that the surrounding room vanished" (*March* 617, 628). Though critics have cited this passage as evidence of Richardson's filmic notions of writing, it is just as much a renunciation of literal sight in favor of an individualistic and multivalent form of knowledge based on memory.

This subversion of vision is found not only in the ways in which Miriam perceives but also in the form of the novel's auditory narrative. Early critics voiced difficulty with Richardson's lack of a distanced perspective, claiming that she did not show Miriam processing her reality and sorting out the significant details from the insignificant. In her study of Richardson, Watts quotes from a contemporary review in which the critic Lawrence Hyde complains that "Miriam receives impressions far faster than she can deal with them. She serves principally as a delicate and efficient receiving instrument, a medium through whom we can look at life so surely and clearly that we forget she is there between us" (qtd. in Watts 4). Watts clarifies, "Richardson's failure, the article suggested, is that the reader is not given a vantage-point. . . . The problem was one of lack of distance" (5). For Watts, these comments are evidence of both the newness of Richardson's stream-of-conscious style and the annoyance of some readers with the work's singular focus on Miriam. To me, this also implies that early twentieth-century readers typically expected novels to be more visually oriented. The reader who looks for a discerning perspective in *Pilgrimage* is instead confronted with the immediacy of an auditory narrative. Though impressionism and subjective viewpoints are integral to modernism, Richardson's form illustrates that stream of consciousness often had to forsake a visual point of view and instead present the self as "a delicate and efficient receiving instrument," with sounds flowing through the mind that are not perceived and explained as a rendered picture. Woolf, in her review of *The Tunnel*, suggests as much when she writes that Richardson's reader "is invited to embed himself in Miriam Henderson's consciousness, to register one after another, and one on top of another, words, cries, shouts, notes of a violin, fragments of lectures, to follow these impressions as they flicker through Miriam's mind, waking incongruously other thoughts, and plaiting incessantly the many-coloured and innumerable threads of life" (71). This stream of prosodic moments must be experienced by readers without the benefit of an ordering distanced perspective.

Richardson's orchestration of prosody, music, and sound demonstrates that she understood audition to be essential to experience and subjectivity. She represents her artistic struggle to create an auditory narrative in scenes where the act of reading is defamiliarized for Miriam, and she is able to hear the words she is reading. Comparing the "music" of Shakespeare to Beethoven, Miriam asserts, "It was the *sound* of Shakespeare that made the scenes real" (*Tunnel* 180, emphasis in original). Reading a philosophical work, Miriam "imagine[s] the words spoken" so that she can critically read the text (*Interim* 407). Struggling to decipher Amabel's strange penmanship in her letters, Miriam deduces that "when meanings were discovered, they sounded; as if spoken" (*Dawn's* 215). Whether Miriam likes or dislikes what she is reading, her ideal is when "it comes so near as to seem spoken rather than written" (*Dimple* 454). Richardson, too, strove for this ideal of having her written text speak out to the reader. While she believed that the purpose of film was to be a "mirror for the customary," "restoring its essential quality" by being "arranged and focused at the distance exactly fitting the contemplative state," Richardson's fiction does not allow us any distance from Miriam's life ("Narcissus" 202). We are immersed in Miriam's subjectivity by listening to her "being," rather than observing a singular, analytical point of view. Consequently, like sounds that bypass the distancing position of the eye and are felt on the body directly, Miriam interacts with the reader on a level of intimacy that few characters achieve.

Although Richardson's representations of music, listening, and prosody do not onomatopoeically sound out, as described in my next chapter on Woolf's fiction, we can still deduce that Richardson wanted her reader to listen to her fiction. In her essay "About Punctuation," Richardson argues that commas and conventional punctuation have "devitalized the act of reading," making it "less organic, more mechanical" (415). Conversely, prose with less punctuation is ideal because "in the slow, attentive reading demanded by unpunctuated texts, the faculty of hearing has its chance, is enhanced until the text *speaks* itself" (415, emphasis in original). Richardson thus was aware of the importance of auditory narrative, and her own sparing use of punctuation helps to tune the reader into the auditory aspects of her narrative for which this chapter has listened. By extension, this chapter suggests a new path for exploring the influence of the cinema on modernist literature—one that considers the role of sound in the cinema, which transitioned from musical accompaniment to speech within the modernist era.

3

Recording the Soundscape

Virginia Woolf's Onomatopoeia and the Phonograph

There is music in the air for which we are always straining our ears.

Virginia Woolf, "Street Music"

When the phonograph was first promoted in the late 1870s, the public, after getting over suspicions of deception, praised its ability to perfectly reproduce speech and music. According to the *New York Graphic* (1878), for example, the French Academy of Science thought that the phonograph demonstrator "was a ventriloquist, and was using that trickery to obtain the results which so amazed them" ("Edison's"). Nine years later, in 1887, the editors of *Scientific American* sheepishly admitted, "Fully familiar as we are and have been with the machine since its inception, it is still impossible for us to listen to it without a feeling of astonishment and a well-defined doubt that our senses are not deceiving us" ("Phonograph" 161). They assured their readers that while the first models may have been difficult to understand, the present model "repeats the voice with perfect articulation and with every inflection" (161). In an 1893 article in *Century Magazine*, a writer who describes himself as "a person professionally interested in music" certified, "It is really music, and not a mere suggestion of music" (Hubert 40). Phonograph recordings were advertised to be "lifelike," "a true mirror of sound," "natural," and "the real thing" (qtd. in Katz 2). The success of Edison's Tone Tests, in which he would challenge audiences to decipher when a live performer stopped and a phonograph took over, reveals how ready the public was to believe that recorded sound was indistinguishable from live sound. Listeners were continually awed by the phonograph's radically new ability to record, store, and replay a sound without regard for its source.[1]

Yet, as Lisa Gitelman astutely observes, while "the first scratchy phonograph records . . . reportedly sounded 'just like' the sounds they recorded, . . . the perceptual condition of sounding 'just like' has continued to change over time and according to expectation and technology" (18). Jonathan Sterne points out that the first demonstrations of the phonograph typically used well-known phrases and songs such as Edison's test recording of "Mary Had a Little Lamb." This allowed listeners, driven by their "desire for the machine to work," to "*help the machine*" (*Audible* 251, emphasis in original). Sterne notes that listeners had to practice an "audile technique" so they could discern between the noise of the machine, which was to be ignored, and the intended reproduced sound (*Audible* 259). Aside from such mechanical noise, listeners heard "the inadvertent sounds of the environment, which rode along unnoticed during the recording process" (DeMarinis 74). Although studios and equipment that reduced such unwanted noises were eventually designed, early phonograph recording brought attention to background sounds that "had been little noticed before" (DeMarinis 74). Since the phonograph did not filter out irrelevant background noise as the human ear does, it fostered a "counter-intellectual, counter-hierarchical sensitivity to the fugitive, the ephemeral, 'the background'" (Lastra 48). This new technology thus influenced sound perception in two dominant ways: it cultivated a selective and nuanced sense of hearing that required listeners to discern mechanical and background noise from an intended recording; and yet it ironically raised awareness of the background noises we tend to filter out when listening.

Despite the limitations of the first phonographs, music composers were excited by the idea of incorporating "real life" sounds into their art. For instance, in 1924, Ottorino Respighi used recordings of nightingales in his piece *Pines of Rome*, and six years later, Walter Ruttmann composed his sound collage, *Weekend*, entirely from recordings of speech, urban noise, and instrumental music. Seeing the phonograph as eradicating the interference of interpretive musicians, the French composer Carol Berard questions, "Why . . . are phonograph records not taken of noises such as those of a city at work, at play, even asleep? . . . If noises were registered, they could be grouped, associated and carefully combined as are the timbres of various instruments in the routine orchestra" (28). In the early 1920s, László Moholy-Nagy too advocated that artists eradicate "the interpretive artist [the musician]" and inscribe grooves into records in order to transform the phonograph "from an instrument of reproduction into one of production" (332). Though early phonographs were scratchy at best and could only record for about four minutes, artists were eager to bypass the mediation of musicians and open the field of musical sound beyond notation.

Paralleling the phonograph's celebrated ability to capture and present real-life sound, modernist writers similarly believed that in breaking with the conventions of the novel, they might record the world around them more directly. A cursory look at their own words affirms their determination to reproduce rather than imitate psychological and sensual experience. Virginia Woolf suggests, "Let us record the atoms as they fall upon the mind in the order in which they fall, let us trace the pattern, however disconnected and incoherent in appearance, which each sight or incident scores upon the consciousness" ("Modern" 150). Using the auditory and visual metaphors of recording, scoring, and tracing, Woolf voices a typical modernist desire to present the inner workings of the mind with directness and immediacy. This aspiration is further articulated by Joseph Conrad, as he maintains that a writer must "snatch . . . a passing phase of life" and "hold up . . . the rescued fragment before all eyes" (1888). Through the "perfect blending of form and substance," modernist writers attempted to make language experiential, to make it a reality unto itself (Conrad 1888). The futurist poet F. T. Marinetti argues that onomatopoeia "vivifies lyricism with crude and brutal elements of reality" (519). Similarly, Luigi Russolo argues that when artists include noise in their work, it has "the power of immediately recalling life itself" (181). While Woolf does not share many affinities with futurism, this chapter will show that she holds a similar enthusiasm for the aesthetic importance of noise, as both Russolo and Woolf value how art can capture "life itself" (Russolo 181; Woolf, "Modern" 151).

While modernist writers were of course limited to the medium of language, they nevertheless tried to mold language so that it could contain the ramblings of the mind, overheard dialogue, and the modern soundscape. The phonograph, in its ability to record, store, and replay real sound, offered a suggestive model for these writers. As it mechanically reproduced sounds for amazed audiences who willingly saw no difference between recorded sound (with all of its crackles and glitches) and the live performer, modernist writers devoted "an unremitting never-discouraged care for the shape and ring of sentences," trying to free the novel from such trappings as plot and quotation marks (James Joyce's particular crusade) in an effort to record "life itself" (Woolf "Modern" 151). Though her focus is on Edison's Tone Tests rather than on modernist literature, Emily Thompson, building on the ideas of Miles Orvell, also draws this connection between "modern artists" who "strove not for realism but for 'reality itself'" and the promotion and reception of the phonograph as not mimicking sound but being a "musical instrument" in and of itself ("Machines" 133, 142). Just as audile techniques had to be developed so that listeners might appreciate phonograph recordings, readers had to approach the auditory narrative of modernist texts with a different set of expectations, not to mention a refined ear.

Virginia Woolf, with her inclusion of a noisy "chuffing" and "ticking" gramophone in her last novel, *Between the Acts*, and her abundant use of onomatopoeia, is a perfect case study for the modernist tendency to aestheticize real-world sound—just as phonographs did. Although Woolf never wrote specifically about the effect of the gramophone on sound perception, we do know that when the Woolfs acquired an Algraphone in 1925, listening to recorded music became an important and consistent part of Woolf's life (*Diary* 3: 42). Leonard Woolf wrote record reviews for the *Nation and Athenaeum* between 1926 and 1929, even keeping a diary of the music that the family played (Clements 161; Cuddy-Keane, "Virginia" 74). In Emma Sutton's estimation, the "excitement of this new acoustic technology, the social as well as domestic uses of the machine, and the potential to listen to music in a variety of settings, are evoked by many of [Woolf's] friends" (10). Although the Woolfs mainly listened to an Austro-German classical and romantic repertoire, they subscribed to the National Gramophonic Society from 1925 until 1926, which exposed them to contemporary orchestral works (Sutton 10–11). The gramophone also gave Woolf the opportunity to listen to jazz recordings that T. S. Eliot brought from America, as well as some folk, early Italian baroque, and non-Western music (Sutton 11).[2] Presumably, this daily experience of listening to phonograph recordings affected Woolf's creative life. Elicia Clements convincingly argues that listening to gramophone records of Beethoven while composing *The Waves* provided Woolf "with a model for a new novelistic 'form'" (161).[3] Although Woolf was immersed in the visual arts through Bloomsbury artists and critics such as Vanessa Bell, Duncan Grant, and Roger Fry, not to mention her great-aunt, the Victorian photographer Julia Margaret Cameron, Woolf claimed, in a letter to Mrs. R. C. Trevelyan, "I always think of my books as music before I write them" (*Letters* 426). This analogy of her books and music suggests not only that Woolf purposefully wove phonic, poetic elements into her fiction but also that she thought of her novels as an art to be listened to above all else—an auditory narrative.

The musical undercurrents and aural quality of Woolf's later fiction have been noted by many scholars.[4] For instance, Garrett Stewart claims that through her "poetic resonance" and "stray reverberations," Woolf performs the "vocal writing" that Roland Barthes valorizes in *The Pleasure of the Text* (261, 279). While Stewart analyzes the phonic elements of *The Waves*, this chapter will concentrate on a more overt example of Woolf's "vocal writing": her use of onomatopoeia, which ranges from birds (nature) to airplanes (the mechanical) to street hawkers (the human). Onomatopoeia becomes a dominant force in Woolf's novels beginning with *Mrs. Dalloway*, published in 1925, the same year that the Woolfs brought a gramophone into their home. The first section of this chapter will survey Woolf's use of onomatopoeia to create fictional soundscapes—"aural landscape[s]" that are "simultaneously a physical environment and a way of perceiving that environment" (Thompson, *Soundscape* 1). As we shall see, Woolf is concerned with both aspects of *soundscape*: she draws the reader's attention to how her characters perceive and are influenced by the sounds they hear, but she also attempts to render the sounds themselves through onomatopoeia, forcing the reader to sound out noisy words that beg to be heard with what Stewart calls the *reading voice*. My second section will explore how these background sounds, for Woolf, create intimate connections among listeners who often feel judged and distanced through vision. Woolf's auditory narratives, however, imply that a shared soundscape has the power to connect people in a chorus, while preserving their individuality. This seeming paradox of communal connections and private individuality is exemplified through the phonograph, which allowed listeners to enjoy mass-produced recordings in the privacy of the home. The potential for sound to allow for individual revelries becomes even more significant in my last section, where I explore how Woolf incorporates the noises of World War II into her diaries and essays. In a similar vein, Woolf's last novel, composed during the war, is full of interrupting onomatopoeia. Yet, Woolf uses the novel form to aestheticize noise, giving her a sense of artistic control over the soundscape of her novel. Just as the phonograph could capture and control sound, Woolf uses her novel to claim agency over the noise of war impinging on her soundscape. Moreover, Woolf's onomatopoeic fragmentation and attention to the qualities of a sound as such are comparable to how phonographs made listeners more aware of mechanical, background, and recorded noises, facilitating "the construction of sound as a carrier of meaning in itself" (Sterne, *Audible* 176–77).

The phonograph is a perfect context for this exploration of onomatopoeia in Woolf's work because it was an invention that made the public more aware of the background sounds that constituted the soundscape.[5] The effects of Woolf's onomatopoeia in her fiction—its presentation of the often-ignored background noises of the soundscape, its ability to connect characters in a chorus while safeguarding individuality, its ultimate role of fragmenting narrative and drawing the reader's attention to the sounds of words as such—are all clarified through a historical awareness of the effects of the phonograph on listeners in the modernist period. For it was the phonograph that prompted listeners to perk up their ears at the background noises of the soundscape that were inadvertently recorded, to experience listening as both communal and public, and to listen to sounds as potentially meaningful in and of themselves. This chapter proposes that in drawing the public's attention to background sounds that typically go unnoticed and in aestheticizing noise, the phonograph inspired modernists to capture and record real-world sounds in their art.

Presenting the Soundscape of "Life Itself"

Just as the phonograph was advertised as producing lifelike sounds and brought the public's attention to the typically ignored background noises of the soundscape, Woolf brought "life itself" into her art by including this newly amplified soundscape in her fiction. The Canadian composer and theorist R. Murray Schafer coined the term *soundscape* and was an advocate for a more thoughtful curation of the "vast musical composition which is unfolding around us unceasingly" ("Music" 29). Schafer divides the soundscape into keynotes, signals, and soundmarks, terms that will be helpful when thinking about the rich array of sounds that Woolf includes in her novels. For Schafer, keynote sounds are background sounds that we do not consciously register but that give us a sense of our daily life: traffic roaring, birds chirping, clocks ticking, and windows squeaking. Signals are sounds that are foregrounded in the soundscape, sounds that we typically pay attention to: the patter of rain, the dressing-bell, an ambulance, the boom of guns. And soundmarks are sounds that are idiosyncratic to a location, such as the call of a familiar street hawker or the bells of Big Ben. Each of the examples listed above is a sound that we hear throughout Woolf's novels, and her onomatopoeic inclusion of these sounds assures that her reader shares in hearing the vital soundscape of her characters.

In her first experimental novel, *Jacob's Room* (1922), Woolf only sporadically incorporates onomatopoeia. The reader listens to cows that "munch, munch . . . then again munch, munch, munch" (37), men that "stamp, stamp, stamp" (102), and trams in Greece that "clanked, chimed, rang, rang, rang" (138). But more often, sounds are conceptually described rather than represented through onomatopoeia. For example, the sound of a clock is described rather than directly represented: "The worn voices of clocks repeated the fact of the hour all night long"; "The frail waves of sound broke among the stiff gorse and the hawthorn twigs as the church clock divided time into quarters" (99, 133). We do once get the clichéd sound of the clock ticking, which is meant to enhance the lonely life of Mrs. Pascoe: "Washing in her little scullery, she may hear the cheap clock on the mantelpiece tick, tick, tick . . . tick, tick, tick. She is alone in the house" (52, suspension points in original). As the reader is presented with the onomatopoeic "tick," instead of a conceptual description of the sound, Woolf's complicated notion of the soundscape becomes clear: it enhances her character's loneliness and separation, as sounds in an empty room only make the emptiness that much more apparent, but it also signifies sameness by referencing a common aural experience with which most readers can identify. Still, the ticking clock does not fragment the narrative or interrupt the character's thoughts; rather, it fills in what Mrs. Pascoe might hear, heightening the realism of the novel.

Published the same year that the Woolfs purchased a gramophone, *Mrs. Dalloway* (1925) reveals an outburst of onomatopoeia, which Woolf seamlessly stitches into her narrative. In the first scene of Clarissa opening her windows and descending onto the street to buy flowers, we hear a barrage of keynote sounds: "squeak," "burst," "flap," "swing, tramp, and trudge," "shuffling and swinging," "jingle," "tapping," "sprung," and "whirling" (1–3). This immersion in sound gives Clarissa the keen sense of "life, London, this moment in June" (4); as the vibrations of the soundscape pass through her, she feels connected to the city and experiences a heightened sense of presence.

Woolf also uses subtle onomatopoeia in her repeated descriptions of Big Ben's bell: "There! Out it boomed. First a warning, musical; then the hour, irrecoverable. The leaden circles dissolved in the air" (2). This last sentence is narrated four times in the novel, making the sentence itself a repeating sound within the novel (2, 51, 102, 203); however, while the verb "boom" suggests the soundmark of the bell, and the repeated sentence enacts the repetition of the bell, sound here is primarily described conceptually. It is markedly different from the church bells of Woolf's later *Between the Acts*, which intrude on characters and readers with a resounding "ding, dong" (199, 200, 201). While Woolf's earlier works consistently sound out with onomatopoeia, such moments are almost always integrated into longer scene descriptions. The reader senses that Woolf is not satisfied with only visually describing a scene but rather wants the reader to hear the "uproar" of London in order to sense the mundane keynote sounds that can have "a deep and pervasive influence on our behaviour and moods" (*Mrs. Dalloway* 209; Schafer, *Our Sonic Environment* 9).

This desire to make her novels sound out with onomatopoeia is explicitly taken up when Woolf begins her most experimental novel, *The Waves* (1931), and questions in her diary, "Could one not get the waves to be heard throughout? Or farmyard noises? Some odd irrelevant noises?" (*Writer's Diary* 141). The auditory narrative of *The Waves* is dominantly conveyed through the rhymes, alliteration, cadences, and rhythms, as well as the voices of the characters, which are set in quotations, drawing attention to their spoken form.[6] Such sonic qualities prompted Woolf to consider adapting the work for the wireless, a gesture that "suggests how much the novel was to her an aural work" (Cuddy-Keane,

"Virginia" 88). Though *The Waves* is intensely visual, as Woolf painstakingly details the course of the sun and its light and shadows in the italicized sections, there is also a continual attention to sound through onomatopoeia: birds "*bubbling*," "*chuckling*" (279), "*chirp[ing]*," and "*twittering*" (179, 251); flowers "*rocking, and pealing a faint carillon as they beat their frail clappers*" (194); the "*thud*" (194, 250, 278), "*drum[ming]*" (227), and "*spattering*" (291) of waves; overripe fruit and steam that "*oozed*" (226, 251); leaves that "*crisped*" and "*rustled*" (290); light that passes with a "*flaunt and flash*" (302); and leaves that a "*blast blew*" (302). In these examples, even objects that we usually assume to be silent such as flowers and light are given an auditory dimension through onomatopoeia. On finishing *The Waves*, Woolf wrote in her diary, "Thus I hope to have kept the sound of the sea and the birds, dawn and garden subconsciously present, doing their work underground" (*Writer's Diary* 165). In these italicized sections, Woolf does not represent the listener of her "underground" soundscape, indicating that it is the reader who is the intended receiver of this sensory experience of background sound. The vivid imagery of these sections is thus matched by rich onomatopoeia and rhythmic syntax, which attune the reader to the background sounds of nature, just as phonograph recordings attuned listeners to the background noise of the soundscape.

While *The Waves* presents the reader with the beautiful sounds of nature, Woolf was equally interested in the cacophonous sounds of the city street. Although writers such as Dickens, Carlyle, and Tennyson as early as 1864 supported a bill to outlaw London street music, and noise abatement societies flourished throughout the early twentieth century, Woolf consistently affirms the importance of such noise. In 1932, the same year that Woolf struck on the idea for her "Essay-Novel" *The Years*, which was "to take in everything, sex, education, life etc." (*Writer's Diary* 183), she published an essay in *Good Housekeeping* in which she observed, "A thousand such voices are always crying aloud in Oxford Street. All are tense, all are real, all are urged out of their speakers by the pressure of making a living, finding a bed, somehow keeping afloat on the bounding, careless, remorseless tide of the street" ("Oxford" 26–27). These sounds often signify economic circumstances: those who cannot procure any other job must sell their services on the crowded streets; those who cannot afford large private houses must listen to others in adjacent apartments and in the streets below. Woolf brings the voices of the street hawker to the forefront of her soundscapes because, as she writes in "Oxford Street Tide," if a "moralist" walks along Oxford Street, he "must tune his strain so that it receives into it some queer, incongruous voices" (25).

Street hawker cries are an essential soundmark in the urban soundscape of

The Years (1937), as they often trespass into the private space of the home. In the section devoted to 1910, for instance, Rose Pargiter visits her cousins Sara and Maggie, sisters who share an inexpensive apartment in a "shabby street on the south side of the river [which] was very noisy" (162). The reader is introduced to their apartment not with a traditional visual setting but through a soundscape setting that takes the reader from the street to the apartment: "The swarm of sound, the rush of the traffic, the shouts of the hawkers, the single cries, and general cries, came into the upper room of the house in Hyman Place where Sara Pargiter sat at the piano" (162–63). The bustle and marketplace of the street are made vivid when they hear a disembodied, anonymous voice come through the window: a man "crying," "'Any old iron? Any old iron?'"; "'Any old iron to sell? Any old iron?'" (171, 172). Shortly after, Woolf represents another street hawker that they hear and draws the reader's attention to the class difference indicated by dialect: "'Nice vilets, fresh vilets,' he repeated automatically as the people passed. Most of them went by without looking. But he went on repeating his formula automatically. 'Nice vilets, fresh vilets,' as if he scarcely expected any one to buy. Then two ladies came; and he held out his violets, and he said once more 'Nice vilets, fresh vilets.' . . . Then he began muttering again, 'Nice vilets, fresh vilets.'" (173–74). Although such phrases are not typical examples of onomatopoeia, their repetition and the phonetic spelling of "violets" allows Woolf to emphasize the aural quality of the street cries. Like the mechanical reproduction of the phonograph, these soundmarks "automatically" play around the sisters, and yet they give a sense of the "real" that Woolf values in the essay quoted above. While the young Pargiter women are still able to maintain a sense of safety and differentiation, particularly through the upper-middle-class token of genteel sound that is the piano, they (like Dorothy Richardson's central character, Miriam) are connected with the modern city, as they encounter the "swarm," "rush," "shout," and "cries" of the urban soundscape.

Woolf, however, does not idealize the sounds of the street, which do in fact denote class struggle and interrupt the thoughts and conversations of her characters. In the "Present Day" section of *The Years*, for example, North Pargiter, just back from a much less hectic Africa, has "his voice . . . drowned by the voice" of a "man crying" on the street, "Old chairs and baskets to mend," a call heard twice in the scene (304). He proceeds to drive through the "hooting" traffic to visit his cousin Sara, and their conversation is interrupted by sounds such as a trombone and a woman practicing her scales: "The voice of the singer interrupted. 'Ah-h-h, oh-h-h, ah-h-h, oh-h-h'" (311). Likewise, in *The Waves*, sounds call characters out of their separate thoughts: "But now listen, tick, tick; hoot,

hoot; the world has hailed us back to it" (332). These street sounds embody the paradox of modern living, in which the proximity of city life unites people at the same time that it isolates them; characters feel differentiated yet are simultaneously a part of the soundscape. These sounds make it difficult for Woolf's characters to live solely within their own thoughts and conventions as they are forced to acknowledge the world outside.

In *The Years*, Woolf shows not only that a city has "its own background noise signature" but that this signature changes over time (Horowitz 41). As Woolf closely follows the lives of the members of the Pargiter family from the 1880s to the mid-1930s, she meticulously weaves together repeated references to sounds to establish the setting and mood of each time period. The 1880 section, for example, is filled with the signal of "the dressing-bell" and the chimes of Saint Paul's and Oxford's bells, which are repeatedly described as "the walloping Oxford bells, turning over and over like slow porpoises in a sea of oil"; "they went walloping one over another," "walloping like a slow porpoise" (37, 44, 50, 63, 65). Likewise, rain is portrayed repeatedly as "making a little chuckling burbling noise in the gutters"; "the gutters chuckling and burbling as they sucked up the water"; "chuckling and burbling in the gutters" (50, 53, 65). Eventually, the sounds of cabs, birds, wind, waltzes, the war, the "hoot[ing]" of cars, and "roar" of London are added into each section.[7] In the World War I section, when London has blacked out its streetlights for protection, Eleanor visits her niece Maggie and feels the "silence [weigh] on her" in the darkness (277). As their dinner is interrupted by the "boom" of the guns, a signal that grows louder (and closer), the narrative is dominated by their anxious listening (287–88). This detailed mixture of keynotes, signals, and soundmarks that changes and suffuses each time period allows Woolf to present historically specific settings without having the narrator describe and explain historical events. In particular, the keynotes of the city soundscape "have imprinted themselves so deeply . . . that life without them would be sensed as a distinct impoverishment" (Schafer, *Our Sonic Environment* 10). Likewise, a narrative without these sounds would seem impoverished.

While, as Don Ihde explains, the "music of daily sound" creates "an auditory texture and background that provides an auditory stability to the world," interrupting sounds (like the guns heard in *The Years*) can be destabilizing (87). Whereas certain sounds are associated with progress and stability, such as the "light high bell of the ambulance" that Peter hears in *Mrs. Dalloway* and calls "one of the triumphs of civilisation," others are associated with class differences, violence, or vulgarity (166). The irony of this scene in *Mrs. Dalloway* of course is that the ambulance is responding to Septimus's suicide—a result of his trauma from World War I and, thus, a mark against civilization. Citing the noise complaints from the seventeenth century to the early twentieth century, Karin Bijsterveld observes that "the noises that were restricted, for instance through licensing, were those made by the poorest classes: the popular entertainers and low-profit traders whose sounds did not fit into the lifestyle of a growing professional urban class longing for peaceful reading and studying" (*Mechanical* 97). The noise that Woolf incorporates into her fiction reflects this cultural ambivalence toward the urban soundscape, which could give a sense of both stabilization and intrusiveness.

Lecturing on Woolf's fiction after her death, E. M. Forster praised her novels for being "not about something" but for being that "something" itself (*Virginia* 7). Woolf is able to accomplish this by being tuned into what Forster elsewhere calls "rhythm," which can hold a novel together (*Aspects* 165). Forster explains that the "function of rhythm" is "not to be there all the time like a pattern, but by its lovely waxing and waning to fill us with surprise and freshness and hope" (*Aspects* 167). Woolf makes her novels *be* something, rather than just *describe* something, by weaving surprising onomatopoeic rhythms throughout her narrative. She presents soundscapes and shows how her characters perceive and are influenced by those sounds, consequently adding a new dimension to the realism of conventional visual settings of the novel. As this chapter suggests, it is no coincidence that in this same period, the phonograph's ability to capture and amplify sounds heightened the public's awareness of the background and foregrounded sounds of their acoustic environment. Just as the phonograph could produce "life-like" sounds, the novel too now had to keep up and present a more complete rendering of the soundscape.

Soundscape Listening: The Chorus and the Judgmental Eye

In his examination of vision and visual technologies in the early twentieth century, Michael North suggests that photography and film presented the public with pictures that did not necessarily match its own perspectives, revealing the eye to be an imperfect and subjective medium. One's ability to perceive "objectively" was put into question when faced with a machine that could zoom in or out on a visual to present a detailed account that the human eye could never produce. North clarifies that the camera, first "celebrated . . . as objectivity incarnate, also came to serve as one of modernity's most powerful emblems of the subjectivity of perception and knowledge" (11). Similarly, one could claim that while the phonograph was praised for supposedly reproducing sound perfectly, it brought the public's attention to the subjective nature of hearing, which regularly filters out background sound. The many background noises that were either produced or picked up by the phonograph revealed to listeners that the audile technique of filtering out background noise was always already a part of auditory perception. Extending North's argument, it becomes apparent that by producing recordings that did not match exactly with perceived reality, the phonograph challenged the assumption that our sense of hearing is objective. Furthermore, phonograph recordings of real-world sounds from different cultures or speeches of famous figures exposed people to novel sounds, destabilizing the notion that the world one person hears is the same for all.

As the phonograph initiated a recognition of background noise and an acute understanding of the subjective nature of hearing, novelists reacted by depicting sound and peripheral noise as integral to the subjectivity of their characters. Since it is one of the ways that her characters retain a sense of individuality within shared aural experiences, the subjectivity of hearing is a primary concern for Woolf. We see such subjective listening demonstrated with the onomatopoeia in *Mrs. Dalloway*. For instance, as Big Ben's and Saint Margaret's bells strike half past eleven, the sound momentarily unites Clarissa and Peter through their shared aural experience but then sparks personal associations in Peter. The following lengthy passage traces Peter's thoughts, which fluctuate from remembering a happy time with Clarissa to thinking of a death knell and Clarissa's ill health:

It is half-past eleven, she says, and the sound of St. Margaret's glides into the recesses of the heart and buries itself in ring after ring of sound, like something alive which wants to confide itself, to disperse itself, to be, with a tremor of delight, at rest—like Clarissa herself, thought Peter Walsh, coming down the stairs on the stroke of the hour in white. It is Clarissa herself, he thought, with a deep emotion, and extraordinary clear, yet puzzling, recollection of her, as if this bell had come into the room years ago, where they sat at some moment of great intimacy, and had gone from one to the other and had left, like a bee with honey, laden with the moment. But what room? What moment? And why had he been so profoundly happy when the clock was striking? Then, as the sound of St. Margaret's languished, he thought, She has been ill, and the sound expressed languor and suffering. It was her heart, he remembered; and the sudden loudness of the final stroke tolled for death that surprised in the midst of life, Clarissa falling where she stood, in her drawing room. (53)

Woolf here is instructing readers on how to react to the onomatopoeia of her narrative: let the sound "glide into the recesses of the heart and bury itself"; let it spark a chain of individual and common associations, from "profound happiness" to "languor and suffering." The sound is "alive" because it is not static and is interpreted in different ways almost simultaneously, as Peter remembers an intimate moment with Clarissa but quickly switches to the more common aural association of a death knell. Peter's inability to place the exact memory that the bell conjures, its "extraordinary clear, yet puzzling" quality, bears out Russolo's suggestion that noise "is never revealed . . . entirely" and "holds innumerable surprises" (181). Yet, despite this intensely personal resonance, the bell also unites Peter with other characters, as they too hear the bells throughout the day.

As always, Woolf has it both ways: the subjectivity of listening secures the individuality of her characters while at the same time sound can potentially unite them through simultaneous listening and common cultural associations. Several critics have noticed this paradoxical implication of sound in Woolf as well. For example, Pamela Caughie helpfully contextualizes Woolf's representation of Big Ben's bell, which connects both friends and strangers alike, to new modes of listening engendered by the radio and gramophone that provided "intimacy-in-isolation" ("Virginia" 336). Kate Flint makes a similar claim in her illuminating essay on urban noise in Woolf's fiction, where she argues that "Woolf's awareness of the potentially unifying effects of sound goes hand in hand with her registering the reverse of this process" ("Sounds" 190). Although, for Woolf, "individual subjectivity inevitably conditions how we register noise," such noises can also "reveal the connections that exist between people in the urban environment" (Flint, "Sounds" 194). Beyond just connecting characters through their shared listening experiences, however, Woolf implies that her characters become part of a chorus as they listen to the soundscape. This concept resonates with how early phonographs changed the public's perception of who could be considered musical—from only musicians and composers to anyone with an ear for music appreciation (Katz 61). As phonographs enabled the general public to listen closely and repeatedly to internationally recognized artists, the public's horizon of what constituted "good music" was expanded. This newfound sense of appreciation made the role of the listener more distinguished so that, as one contributor to the *National Music Monthly* (1917) wrote, "If one loves to listen to good music, one *is* musical" (Faulkner 131, emphasis in original). Similarly, even if Woolf's characters are not explicitly contributing to the chorus of the soundscape, they participate in it and feel intimate with one another simply by listening.

Woolf's idea of the chorus is most clearly articulated in what was intended to be the opening essay of her "Common History book," "Anon" (*Writer's Diary* 335). Here, Woolf posits a theory about the first experiences of the English with song. She imagines a prehistoric England with a lush forest housing "innumerable birds" singing, which are heard by only "a few skin clad hunters" ("Anon" 382). Connecting the inspirational soundscape of bird songs with the first human endeavors at song, Woolf wonders, "Did the desire to sing come to one of those huntsmen because he heard the birds sing, and so rested his axe against the tree for a moment?" ("Anon" 382). Though Woolf deduces that the hunters did not have the leisure to create songs and poetry, she proposes that the "voice that broke the silence of the forest was the voice of Anon," the first poet who "is the common voice singing out of doors . . . lifting a song or a story from other people's lips, and letting the audience join in the chorus" ("Anon" 382). The voice of this anonymous poet, like the birds chirping, inspires participation and communes with the common audience, drawing them together in a chorus as they collectively listen to and identify with the voice of Anon. Similar to Richardson's idealization of the musical accompaniment of silent film and her fictional representation of music as facilitating collaborative and intimate connections, Woolf holds that Anon's audience "shared in the emotion . . . and supplied the story" ("Anon" 382). For both novelists, "hearing is a way of touching at a distance and the intimacy of the first sense is fused with sociability whenever people gather together to hear something special" (Schafer, *Our Sonic Environment* 11).

In the end of her essay, Woolf laments that Anon is dead because of the birth of the printing press and the separation of the now silent audience and the isolated writer. As Brenda R. Silver notes in her commentary on "Anon" and "The Reader," "In both the notes and the essays themselves, not to mention her recent novel [*Between the Acts*], Woolf contrasts the communal aspects of early literature with the isolation of the individual writer who emerged in the Renaissance, and who was struggling in 1940 and 1941 to remain creative in a world where silence and emptiness were the norm" (Woolf, "Anon" 360). Yet in Woolf's time, auditory technologies such as the phonograph and wireless allowed the masses to listen to music communally while still within the privacy of the home. In the early twentieth century, the closest many came to participating in a chorus was as they listened to and sang along with phonograph recordings. While the phonograph revived the chorus for modern listeners, Woolf too crafted ways to make her characters and readers feel part of a chorus in her fiction. Indeed, I argue that Woolf is momentarily able to revive Anon in her own novels through onomatopoeia, which brings her characters temporarily together in a chorus through the shared aural experiences of a soundscape. Though Woolf concludes that the playwright and audience have been replaced by the novelist and reader, she combats the condition of the modern isolated artist by incorporating into her fiction sounds that embody the "impersonality" and "generality" associated with the voice of Anon. While maintaining her individual artistic vision, Woolf uses onomatopoeia to sound out common aural experiences, which rouse her characters—and reader—to feel momentarily part of an intimate chorus.

This chorus figures most centrally in *The Waves*, where the characters' interior monologues are put within quotations marks to suggest that they are spoken together. Beyond this larger formal chorus, however, characters listen to and are called to participate in the chorus of the soundscape. Bernard, since he brings the rest of the characters together in the last section of the novel, is usually the only one who names the chorus as such. As a child, he relates, "I hear . . . the chorus beginning; wheels; dogs; men shouting; church bells; the chorus beginning" (193); and later, at boarding school, he "lingers" to "listen" to the "rollicking chorus" of boys playing (237). In the last section of the novel, Bernard listens to and unites the chorus of characters, as he repeats parts from each of their roles within it:

> And I am so made, that, while I hear one or two distinct melodies, such as Louis sings, or Neville, I am also drawn irresistibly to the sound of the chorus chanting its *old*, chanting its *almost wordless, almost senseless song* that comes across courts at night; which we hear now booming round us as cars and omnibuses take people to theatres. (Listen; the cars rush past this restaurant; now and then, down the river, a siren hoots. (347, my emphasis)

The birds of the opening italicized sections often sing in chorus, though equally important is the "roar of London," the "boom" of the modern city that imposes itself on the characters' psyches.[8] This chorus, to which Woolf repeatedly points, is a mixture of human, natural, and modern city sounds; it is the modern version of Anon's chorus, as Woolf uses the same phrases verbatim in her later essay "Anon" to describe the "old," "almost wordless" and "almost senseless" song, which, she insists, is "not yet dead in ourselves" ("Anon" 398). There is an underlying conviction in *The Waves* that just by *listening* to the sounds of the real world—the shouts of people on the street, the waves of the sea, the motor of the omnibus, the songs of the birds—characters play their part in a chorus, temporarily affirming a sense of intimate connectivity that seems timeless in Woolf's depiction.

Although they are not conventionally considered onomatopoeia, the anonymous voices of the street become, in Woolf's fiction, permanent and repeating
fixtures of the London soundscape, calling characters to be part of the chorus.
We first encounter an "old blind woman" on the street in *Jacob's Room*, where
she sits "singing out loud, not for coppers, no, from the depths of her gay wild
heart—her sinful, tanned heart" (67). The voice of the old street woman goes
from being described in *Jacob's Room* to being rendered phonetically in *Mrs.
Dalloway*, which forces the reader to sound out the words on the page just as
one would with traditional onomatopoeia. The "frail quivering sound," "ee um
fah um so / foo swee too eem oo," is presented three times in the narrative
and momentarily connects Peter and Rezia through their shared experience
of hearing the incoherent song (87, 89). The narrator's description of the old
woman singing on the street as "the voice of no age or sex, the voice of an ancient spring spouting from the earth" with "so rude a mouth, a mere hole in the
earth" is reminiscent of Woolf's description of Anon, the poet, as "sometimes
man; sometimes woman," "liv[ing] a roaming life crossing the fields, mounting
the hills, lying under the hawthorn to listen to the nightingale," with "no place"
and "no name," "often ribald, obscene" (*Mrs. Dalloway* 87, 88, "Anon" 382, 383).
Like Anon, who sings "that flowers fade; that death is the end," the old woman
sings a song that could apply to anyone about the loss of a lover through death
("Anon" 398). Though "Anon" was written later than *Mrs. Dalloway*, there is an
undeniable kinship between Anon, the anonymous poet who connected with
the masses and with whom an audience could join in chorus, and the nameless
old woman on the street, who momentarily revives Anon for the characters of
the modern novel and textually connects Rezia, Peter, and Richard Dalloway.
Yet, although Rezia and Peter momentarily participate in the London chorus
by listening to her song, they fail to make complete sense of the old woman's
tune and ultimately remain separate, not harmonized, and consumed with their
personal tasks.[9]

Woolf strives, however, to bring the communal voice of Anon temporarily
into her narrative, as the reader's voice is slowed by the defamiliarized fragment, and the aural dimension of the text is brought to the forefront. As the
reader tries to make sense of "ee um fah um so / foo swee too eem oo," he or she
inevitably must pronounce the syllables and pay attention to sound rather than
linguistic meaning. The reader should be guided here by Bernard in *The Waves*,
where, in the last section, he calls for music instead of speech: "Here again there
should be music. . . . A painful, guttural, visceral, also soaring, lark-like, pealing
song to replace these flagging, foolish, transcripts—how much too deliberate!

how much too reasonable—which attempt to describe the flying moment of first love" (350). The old woman's song allows Woolf to represent a guttural and visceral voice that resists linguistic interpretation and brings the reader into Anon's chorus. The song of the woman on the street is detached from its source, in that the woman is never explored or explained in the novel; her role is similar to that of the figure of Anon, to connect the characters and reader momentarily in a shared attunement to the soundscape.

To complicate this notion of the chorus, however, complete choral harmonization is never achieved. While Woolf consistently brings together disparate sounds and demonstrates how her characters function within a soundscape, her characters are always already separate, no matter how much they struggle to be a part of the chorus. Indeed, in *To the Lighthouse* (1927), the narrator reflects on the ear's tendency to want to harmonize all sounds despite the impossibility of total harmonization. The sounds of the world are composed of,

> that intermittent music which the ear half catches but lets fall; a bark, a bleat; irregular, intermittent, yet somehow related; the hum of an insect, the tremor of cut grass, dissevered yet somehow belonging; the jar of a dorbeetle, the squeak of the wheel, loud, low, but mysteriously related; which the ear strains to bring together and is always on the verge of harmonising, but they are never quite heard, never fully harmonised. (212)

There is minimal attention to sound in *To the Lighthouse*, though the few instances of onomatopoeia such as the "bark," "bleat," "hum," "tremor," "jar," and "squeak" in the above quotation are in the "Time Passes" section of the novel, a distinction that clarifies Woolf's self-conscious usage of sound to achieve certain effects and contrasts. In this case, the careful attention to sound heightens the melancholic mood of the empty Ramsay home. Though Woolf's characters struggle to "belong" and "harmonise" with the sounds of the real world, it is a transitory unification, which in the end only highlights an inability to escape separateness. In *The Waves*, Susan, older and by herself, realizes, "The bird chorus is over, only one bird now sings" (242). Louis likewise remarks, "The roar of London . . . All separate sounds—wheels, bells, the cries of drunkards, of merrymakers—all churned into one sound, steel blue, circular. Then a siren hoots" (*Waves* 269). In the end, there is a sound that cannot be unified completely, and a character that is always separate from the chorus.

Prior to Woolf's diary documentation of war sounds and the writing of *Between the Acts* and "Anon," she portrays a chorus that *sadly* lapses into inevitable separation but wants ideally to harmonize and unify. In her last novel, however, there is a nuance in the relationship between the separated individual and the communal chorus, which hinges on a shift from lamenting separation to insisting on and desiring separation in order to combat completely succumbing to what Woolf called in her diary entry of September 5, 1938, "the herd impulse" (*Writer's Diary* 291).[10] Woolf's anxiety over communal feelings of nationalism and her disgust with a patriarchal civilization that produces war (detailed in *Three Guineas*) seem to lead her to a deeper investment in separation and individuality.[11]

Throughout *Between the Acts*, Woolf uses sound to call her characters (and readers) into the chorus, while simultaneously emphasizing individual auditory associations. For example, the "chuff, chuff, chuff" of the gramophone immediately sparks subjective reactions among the audience: "Some sat down hastily; others stopped talking guiltily. . . . Some finished their sentences" (76). Unsure if they should acknowledge the background noise of the machine, the audience members are divided on whether it merits their attention. Similarly, the ticks of the gramophone elicit subjective and individual interpretations from the characters, making Bartholomew Oliver mutter about "Marking time," his sister feel the present moment defying time and her old age, William Dodge think of beauty, and Isabella Oliver think of the future and her young age (82).

Michele Pridmore-Brown persuasively argues that in *Between the Acts*, although the playwright Miss La Trobe initially unites her audience by playing recordings of national songs and nursery rhymes, the noise of the gramophone eventually disturbs such absentminded reception by making the audience aware of the gramophone itself and its manipulation of its listeners (411–12). Yet, while the chuffs and ticks of the gramophone are sometimes interpreted subjectively by different characters, they simultaneously make the audience feel like they are in a "trance" and "held . . . together" (*Between the Acts* 82, 154). Like the "hoot hoot" and "tick tick" that "hail" Bernard and the characters of *The Waves* back to the mundane world, the gramophone noises pull people from their individual reveries, calling them back to the community, the audience, the chorus of which they are a part (*Waves* 332). In fact, it is the ticks and chuffs that reach the audience when the lyrics of the actual chorus of the pageant are "blown away" by the wind (*Between* 78). This paradox echoes a general condition of phonograph listening, which is both intensely personal, taking place in the privacy of the home, and a shared experience, generating the simultaneous consumption of mass-produced recordings.

The multitude of personal and communal associations allowed for by Woolf's onomatopoeia show that, for Woolf, unification does not preclude separation and individuality. In her essay on "traumatic reverberations" in *Between the Acts*, Judith Greenberg makes a similar claim for the resonant fragments of songs, poetry, conversations, and thoughts of the novel, a mix that "leaves its reader with the desire for unity intertwined with the reality of dispersity" (71). Though Greenberg's reading implies that the resonances of the novel are representative of repressed trauma rooted in disturbance and painful memories, Woolf's onomatopoeia, in contrast, allows her characters to make associations that are not limited to the traumatic. Furthermore, unlike the fragments of prose that Greenberg cites as spurring a "desire for unity" within a negative condition of separation, the sounds of Woolf's last novel hold the audience together while simultaneously insisting on fragmentation and personal interpretations. Thus, the onomatopoeia of *Between the Acts* both acknowledges and combats the communal obligations of patriotism by bringing Woolf's characters together momentarily into a chorus through their shared act of listening, while at the same time engendering a space in which to make a multiplicity of separate associations.

Throughout the novels thus far discussed, Woolf uses auditory perception to allow for a more open experience for her characters: they can be happily or oppressively included in an intimate chorus, or they can be happily or oppressively isolated by their individual associations with sounds, which are shaped not only by their subjectivity but by their literal positioning and the acoustic space. This stands in contrast to the function of visual perception in Woolf's fiction, which tends to encourage judgment and analysis. Similar to Richardson's *Pilgrimage*, both *The Years* and *Between the Acts* exemplify Steven Connor's understanding that "visualism signifies distance, differentiation and domination," while audition can potentially draw characters together ("Modern" 203–4). For instance, in Sara's noisy apartment in *The Years*, as Sara studies North's appearance, he thinks, "this feeling of the eye on the flesh, like a fly crawling—how uncomfortable it was" (310).[12] When he catches himself trying to sum up Sara, assuming from her disheveled appearance that men are not interested in her, North makes use of a visual metaphor to describe the inadequacy of such "snapshot" or "surface pictures" (314). In essence, he realizes that he is stereotyping his cousin based on her looks. Sound, on the other hand, can both disturb and create intimacy. When North once again unintentionally judges Sara, "crumpled in her chair" with her "shabby" dress, he feels disconnected from her, until he recites a poem aloud: "As he spoke the words out into the semi-darkness they sounded extremely beautiful, he thought, because they could not see each other, perhaps" (335). The act of observing is accompanied by judgment, while the act of listening is inclusive. Repeatedly in the novel, familiar, stereotyping streams of thought are set off course by sound.

The simplicity of this binary of vision and audition is collapsed, however, at the end of *The Years*, when the caretaker's children sing at Delia's party. The narrator reports that the children "[look] awkward and clumsy," and as Eleanor "glance[s] at their hands, at their clothes, at the shape of their ears," she deduces that they are of a lower class (422). The children, however, "[turn] their eyes" on the grown-ups, "star[ing] at them with a curious fixed stare as if they were fierce" (423, 422). Here, the hostility and judgment in the gaze of both parties is matched by the children's voices, which are interpreted by the adults as "so harsh; the accent . . . so hideous . . . so shrill, so discordant and meaningless" (424). There is a marked contrast between the children's "dignified" look and the "hideous noise" of their voices: "The contrast between their faces and their voices was astonishing" (424). While the image of the children fits with a certain anticipated stereotype of the humble and picturesque poor, the voices of the children force on the adults a more honest and intimate interaction with the children. Eleanor questions whether the sound was "Beautiful," and Maggie replies, "Extraordinarily," though "Eleanor was not sure that they were thinking the same thing" (424). Not only does the children's "Cockney accent" baffle and disturb the party, but it also sparks different ideas in the Pargiters, perhaps bringing to the surface ideological differences that they otherwise would prefer to repress (424). Thus, although Woolf, like Richardson, often indicates that the modern city brings different people together, collapsing the conventions of space and separation among classes through a shared soundscape, she also suggests that the intimacy of sound—particularly voice—can heighten social differences and prejudice without necessarily bridging this divide; similar to Miriam's essentializing criticism of certain class-inflected British dialects in *Pilgrimage*, the Pargiters hear only discord in the voices of the children.

In *Between the Acts*, characters likewise feel threatened when they are looked at by others. Using a similar bug metaphor as North from *The Years*, one character muses, "always some cold eye crawled the surface like a winter blue-bottle!" (176). Members of the audience of the town pageant consider themselves to be "caught and caged; prisoners; watching a spectacle," as the act of watching the pageant heightens their sense of alienation (179). They are disturbed when, at the end of the play, the performers use an assemblage of mirrors to catch the reflection of the audience so that it cannot escape "the inquisitive insulting eye" (186). Forced to see themselves on the stage, the audience members are embarrassingly caught in the roles that they perform every day. Aware of their own judging eyes as begrudging spectators, they cringe from the idea of being looked on themselves.

To counteract the uncomfortable and threatening eye in this scene, a "megaphonic, anonymous, loud-speaking affirmation" is heard from the bushes, and a voice "assert[s]" itself, saying, "All you can see of yourselves is scraps, orts and fragments? Well then, listen to the gramophone affirming..." (*Between the Acts* 186, 188, suspension points in original). Indeed, the gramophone and sounds of the play usually affirm and unite the spectators. The ticking noise of the gramophone "hold[s] them together, tranced," and the familiar songs played on it are "expressive of some inner harmony," which is able to "assemble" the audience members (82, 119, 118). As the music plays, the spectators seem to chant together, "Music wakes us. Music makes us see the hidden, join the broken" (120). When cows bellow just as the illusion of the play is failing, "it was the primeval voice sounding loud in the ear of the present moment" (140). In a similar vein, the narrator reveals that Lucy, a whimsical, religious character, sees disparate objects, "sheep, cows, grass, trees, ourselves," as "one" because they can make a "harmony—if not to us, to a gigantic ear attached to a gigantic head. . . . *All* is harmony, could we hear it" (175, emphasis in original). These moments show that for Woolf, though the eye/I has a tendency to dissect the world, alienating the observer, the ear can momentarily harmonize and unite listeners in a chorus. Whereas people may see themselves as fragmented, sound can make them feel whole, as vibrations pass through the entire body. Woolf uses the soundscape to allow for these communal and individual experiences for her characters, combatting the less flexible judgment that vision encourages. As this next section will show, however, there was some anxiety attached to the communal feelings that could be evoked through a shared soundscape, especially when they were dictated by the nationalism and patriotism of war.

A Fragmentation That Aestheticizes Sound: *Between the Acts* and World War II

It is interesting to note that as Woolf's wartime diary and essays increasingly reflect the sounds of World War II encroaching on her soundscape, Woolf began to use onomatopoeia to fragment and interrupt narrative—a different effect from the examples discussed in the first section of this chapter where onomatopoeia is syntactically worked into sentences. Woolf herself attests in her essay "The Leaning Tower," based on a talk given in 1940, that technological mediation and the proximity of war made it impossible for twentieth-century writers to ignore the sounds of war: "Today we hear the gunfire in the Channel. We turn on the wireless; we hear an airman telling us how this very afternoon he shot down a raider. . . . Scott never saw the sailors drowning at Trafalgar; Jane Austen never heard the cannon roar at Waterloo. Neither of them heard Napoleon's voice as we hear Hitler's voice as we sit at home of an evening" (131). In the same entries in which Woolf outlines her ideas for her "Common History book," she devotes even more attention to the "pop pop pop" of guns, the sounds of air raid sirens, the "roar" and "drone" of planes flying low, and the noise of bombs dropping (*Writer's Diary* 330, 331). Woolf meticulously describes the sound of the planes in her diary: "The sound was like someone sawing in the air just above us. . . . Hum and saw and buzz all around us. A horse neighed in the marsh"; "The air saws: the wasps drone; the siren"; "we hear the sinister sawing noise . . . which loudens and fades; then a pause; then another comes" (*Writer's Diary* 329, 331, 334). Her diary paints a picture of her and Leonard Woolf anxiously listening for planes, bombs, and guns, wondering whether the Germans had landed and whether they should "go to bed at midday," a euphemism for committing suicide (*Writer's Diary* 323).[13]

The sounds of bombs and sirens became a signal of the rising death toll and destruction, heightening one's perception of the minutiae of daily individual life, while at the same time uniting one more closely with the community sharing such life-threatening experiences. Woolf's sense of "community feeling"—the "us" and "we" of the above diary entries—was strengthened by the war, as she declares in her diary entry of April 15, 1939: "all England thinking the same thing—this horror of war—at the same moment. Never felt it so strong before. Then the lull and one lapses again into private separation" (*Diary* 5: 215). Woolf's attention to the invasion of the noise of war into the privacy of her home (even the most private of rooms, the bedroom) is similarly described in her essay "Thoughts on Peace in an Air Raid." Concluding that peace, rather than a weapon-defense system, is the only way to protect one from weapons, she writes, "It is a queer experience, lying in the dark and listening to the zoom of a hornet, which at any moment may sting you to death. . . . Let us think what we can do to create the only efficient air-raid shelter [peace] while the guns on the hill go pop pop pop and the searchlights finger the clouds and now and then, sometimes close at hand, sometimes far away, a bomb drops" (173). The sounds of bombs, air raids, and airplanes are one manifestation of the communal feeling Woolf sensed during World War II; as the English listened together to these sounds, they shared the experience of war.

Yet Woolf's ambivalence and constant self-analysis during the war reveals her wariness of such potentially patriotic feelings: "I don't like any of the feelings war breeds: patriotism, communal &c, all sentimental & emotional parodies of our real feelings. But then, we're in for it. Every day we have our raids. . . . I open my window when I hear the Germans. . . . Then the drone buzz booms away, rather like a dentist's drill" (*Diary* 5: 302). Written in July 1940, this diary entry oscillates between "I" and "we," illustrating Woolf's persistent notion of "private separation" in the midst of communal experience. A month later, Woolf writes, "When the 12 planes went over, out to sea, to fight, last evening, I had I think an individual, not communal BBC dictated feeling. I almost instinctively wished them luck" (*Diary* 5: 306). The hesitancy of this sentence and the trepidation with which Woolf approaches her mild patriotism once again reflect her ambivalence. Though Woolf affirms that her feelings are individual, these very feelings give her a sense of connection with her community, as she wishes the pilots luck. This ambivalent allegiance between the individual and communal is resolved, I would argue, in Woolf's use of real-world sounds. Onomatopoeia allows Woolf to infuse her narrative momentarily with the common, evoking the communal; these shared sounds, however, are also defamiliarized and particularized through the aesthetic form of her novels. As shown in the previous section, it is not just Woolf's characters that are both united and individualized through their interactions with sound; rather, Woolf herself is able to connect momentarily with her reader, while maintaining artistic control.

While listening for the "drone buzz booms" of war, Woolf was writing her most sound-oriented novel, *Between the Acts*, and her posthumously published essay "Anon," both of which reflect a growing preoccupation with the relationship of the dramatist and audience, whereby a "common life still unites them; but there are moments of separation" ("Anon" 389). As Woolf's exposure to auditory technologies and noise of war builds, the noises of her novels begin to fragment her narrative—a fragmentation that emphasizes the noises' status as interrupting sounds that are heard by all characters. As opposed to the examples from *Jacob's Room* and *The Years*, which signify within sentences and are among many details presented in a scene, the onomatopoeia of *Between the Acts* tends to stand alone and intrude on her narrative, demanding the reader's attunement to the noises' texture and resonance; sounds begin to disrupt semantic signification and draw attention to the acoustic qualities of words.

Woolf's readership would have been accustomed to appreciating sounds as meaningful in themselves through the practice of phonograph listening. As the phonograph shifted from its original intended purpose in business, where words merely had to be intelligible, to becoming a medium for music, fidelity became more important to listeners, who appreciated the particular tones of instruments and vocals (Thompson, *Soundscape* 137). The phonograph "introduced people to sounds that had been severed from architectural space, and it taught them to distinguish between desired sound signals and unwanted sounds or noises" (Thompson, *Soundscape* 236). As the sense of hearing was isolated and refined through the practice of phonograph listening, the public grew accustomed to the idea that sounds could be interesting and meaningful in and of themselves. In Schafer's words, sounds were granted "an amplified and independent existence" (*Our Sonic Environment* 90). This separation of a sound from its source allowed listeners to concentrate primarily on sound alone, isolating audition as an aesthetic experience.

Just as the phonograph brought an aesthetic appreciation to sound as such, repeated and fragmenting onomatopoeia draws the reader's attention to the texture, cadence, and acoustics of words as such. For instance, in *Between the Acts*, the "tick, tick, tick" and "chuff, chuff, chuff," which act like a choral refrain in the pageant as well as the novel, are read primarily for their sound rather than their meaning; they disrupt syntax and fail to signify for the reader in familiar ways. This onomatopoeia, as previously discussed, has a twofold effect: it allows the pageant spectators to make both personal and communal associations while keeping them momentarily unified; and it punctures the narrative with nonsensical noise, as the aural quality of the words "chuff" and "tick" are heightened through the defamiliarizing repetition (chuff, 11 times; tick, 6 times). This heightens the aurality of Woolf's prose, while acknowledging the limits of representation. Gillian Beer makes a similar claim about Woolf's "nonce words," "scurred" and "scrurred," in *Between the Acts*: "the mimesis comes close, and falls pleasurably short, encouraging the reader to try the sounds out with the inner ear, yet acknowledging also that we are reading words" (131). Woolf's onomatopoeia not only appeals to the inner ear of the reader but also has two seemingly contradictory effects: the realism of her novels is enhanced by references to the soundscape of everyday life, while the usual flow of her prose is defamiliarized and made poetic. Woolf herself proposes such a merger when she prophesizes that the novel of the future would "have something of the exaltation of poetry, but much of the ordinariness of prose" ("Narrow" 224).

We listen to this mixture of poetry and prose repeatedly in *Between the Acts*, where conventional syntax breaks down, and words begin to sound out for the reader. For example, Woolf disturbs the typical flow of prose to represent the sounds of birds in a tree: "The whole tree hummed with the whizz they made, as if each bird plucked a wire. A whizz, a buzz rose from the bird-buzzing, bird-vibrant, bird-blackened tree. The tree became a rhapsody, a quivering cacophony, a whizz and vibrant rapture, branches, leaves, birds syllabling discordantly life, life, life, without measure, without stop devouring the tree. Then up! Then off!" (209). In addition to the obvious onomatopoeia of *hummed, plucked, buzz,* and *whiz,* Woolf makes the words *life* and *bird* become onomatopoeic through repetition and breaking conventional syntax. This wordplay forces the reader to shift from reading for narrative to reading for sound. Daniel Ferrer similarly notices the "onomatopoeia, shout, [and] gestural language" of the quoted passage and remarks that "something is inscribed here which does not pass through the ordinary paths of signification" (121). As the typical flow of prosaic signification is disrupted by the alliteration, rhythm, rhyme, and onomatopoeia, a reader cannot help but get caught up in the sounds of the words.

The narrative is similarly disrupted when the pageant in *Between the Acts* ends, and the "Ding, dong. Ding" of church bells intrudes (199–201). Ellipses, located before and after the onomatopoeia, enhance the sense of fragmentation by creating silent gaps around the sound, concentrating the reader's attention on the alliteration and rhythm of the words. Such free-floating onomatopoeia not only fragments the narrative formally but also fragments the thoughts and communion of the characters. Though the sound triggers collective associations with the "cracked old bell" and "evening service," it still disrupts the once unified audience and forces the dispersal that the gramophone record heralds with the recurring pronouncement, "dispersed are we" (199). The fragmented thoughts of the dispersing audience indicate varying interpretations of Miss La Trobe's play, as well as a general confusion from the array of different cars that will take the audience members their separate ways (199–201).

This splintering of characters has already been established during the play in *Between the Acts,* when the narrator highlights a fragmentation that seems endemic to the "younger" generation. Woolf's narrator evokes the general mood of the elders in the community as they disapprove of one of the records that Miss La Trobe plays:

The rhythm kicked, reared, snapped short. What a jangle and a jingle! . . . What a cackle, a cacophony! Nothing ended. So abrupt. And corrupt. Such an outrage; such an insult; And not plain. Very up to date, all the same. What is her game? . . . O the irreverence of the generation which is only momentarily—thanks be—"the young." The young, who can't make, but only break; shiver into splinters the old vision; smash to atoms what was whole. (183)

Fusing form and content, Woolf builds on the traditional form of onomatopoeia to make her poetic prose take on the rhythm and beat of the jagged music. Such sounding out goes beyond a desire to present the soundscape of her characters, pushing the reader to engage with the acoustics of language. For it is nearly impossible to read this excerpt without listening to one's reading voice.

Shortly after this, the actors of the pageant reflect the audience in an assemblage of mirrors while reciting random lines from the pageant. The fragmentation that dominates this scene in both form and content implies that it is not just the "young" but an entire culture that has "smashed" what was "old" and "whole." A common trope of modernism, such fragmentation reflects the breakthroughs in science, psychology, and technology, not to mention two world wars, that made many feel that most if not all Victorian institutions were irrecoverably shaken. Yet noticing that this lament is instigated by the record being played, we can also historicize this fragmentation in the material conditions of the first phonograph recordings. As indicated by the record that Miss La Trobe plays, called "A Pot Pourri," a collection of "London street cries," early recordings often contained a hodgepodge of real-world sounds and performances (157). For example, Friedrich A. Kittler cites a recording that "promised Negro songs and dances" as well as the background noises of "pulling in the gang plank, . . . the steam engine, and . . . steamboat bell" (37). Even early demonstrations of the phonograph included "some combination of recitations, songs, music, and random noises" (Rubery 215). These phonographic collages assisted modernist writers in hearing sounds, music, and voices juxtaposed in fresh ways. Hence, the fragmented nature of the phonograph record engendered a new aesthetic that should be read as one among the many factors that helped to foster fragmentation in modernism.

The fragmented mix of poetry, sounds, pageant lines, character dialogue, newspaper stories, and free indirect discourse that Woolf presents in the narrative of *Between the Acts* points to an overall instability of representation, where readers are regularly left wondering which fragments are taken from outside sources and which material is particularly Woolf's invention. Woolf displaces the "real" by having a scripted pageant within a novel that depicts characters who often sound like they are reading scripted lines themselves. For instance: Isa repeats the clichés "in love" and "the father of my children" to herself (love, 14; father, 48, 207); different characters repeat the refrain of whether it would be wet or dry on the day of the pageant (22, 46, 62); and Mrs. Manresa acts her role as the "wild child of nature" and "a thorough good sort," making Giles her "sulky hero" (44, 108, 107). Ferrer writes of the novel, "the representative function of the narrative signs is continually short-circuited by the invasion of an underlying reality" (120). Similar to how the phonograph made the public question whether recorded sounds indicated a real presence, subverting the primacy of the source, Woolf's novel asks her reader to question what is real. While the chuffs and ticks seem more "real" than the fabrication of the pageant, the final curtain rising on Isabella and Giles Oliver at the end of the novel and the ultimate knowledge that the novel itself is a representation further displace the "real." Woolf repeatedly points to the fact that though the novel consists only of words, the author is in control of those words; with one simple sentence she can shape and change the world she has created for her characters. Woolf thus destabilizes representation throughout her last novel in order to assert her control as the artist.

Through her onomatopoeia, Woolf utilizes the medium of language to manipulate the sounds of the real world for her own aesthetic purposes. Just as the musician desires "to capture and control" the noises of the soundscape so that they can be used "not as sound effects but as musical instruments," Woolf's onomatopoeia in her later writing is an attempt to capture the soundscape and shape it into an aesthetic form (Cage 3).[14] The sound of the church bell, which signals communal associations for Miss La Trobe's audience at precisely the point they are dispersing, resonates with a church bell that Woolf herself recorded in a diary entry full of wartime bleakness from August 28, 1938, as she allows its "ding dong," tolling for the death of a community doctor, to break repeatedly into her thoughts and sentence: "Oh thank God, Ding dong—no, its [sic] begun again" (Diary 5: 164). The "ding dong" that interrupts her journal entry seems to be associated not only with the death of a community doctor but with the war and her observation that Leonard Woolf "is very black" (Diary 5: 164). In her diary, the bell prompts Woolf to wonder why they settled in a village, affiliating the bell with a sense of small-town closeness that is both comforting and unsettling. By representing the sound of the bell in her fiction, however, Woolf is able to manipulate the sound to her own purposes, as it fragments the thoughts and conversation of her characters. In Between the Acts, Woolf controls the associations that the bell can trigger. She has it bring her small-town characters momentarily together while simultaneously affirming their individual interpretations of the play and the separate homes they are about to retire to. While the artist, Miss La Trobe, did not create the incidental sounds of the gramophone that "tick" throughout her pageant, similar to the cows bellowing and the rain falling, she depends on the sounds of the real world to jolt her audience to attention and mend fragmentation. Similarly, Woolf represents these sounds in her novel to show how we are unified in a chorus through the soundscape we share yet can still maintain our individual revelries and associations with sounds. Not only is she able to shape the world around her through her onomatopoeia, she encourages her reader to sing out with her.

4

Turning Up the Volume of Inner Speech

Headphones and James Joyce's Interior Monologue

> In the headspace of earphone listening, the sounds not only circulate
> around the listener, they literally seem to emanate from points in the
> cranium itself, as if the archetypes of the unconscious were in conversation.
>
> R. *Murray Schafer, "The Music of the Environment"*

There is a certain affinity between Schafer's quotation above, which suggests that headphones made sound seem like it was coming from "the cranium it-self, as if the archetypes of the unconscious were in conversation," and D. H. Lawrence's sense of the stream of consciousness as "streaming through my brain, in at one ear and out at the other," going "round in my cranium, like Homer's Ocean, encircling my established mind" (*Psychoanalysis* 14). Schafer's description indicates that the sounds piped into one's ears through headphones could feel as though they were voices coming from the listener's consciousness; and both writers spatially depict the place where sounds are heard, either through headphones or from within, as a type of headspace. This chapter considers how the experience of headphone listening may have helped modernists conceive of inner speech as a commodified object. Just as headphones piped commodified voices on records and broadcasts into the listener's ears, modernists began to commodify inner speech by making it part of the novel. Just as headphones were bringing sounds from a variety of external sources into the privacy of one's headspace, modernists were creating interior monologues that were constructs of noise, music, and voices from the sound-scape, as well as a multitude of sources such as religious texts, advertisements, songs, journalism, and literature. Although I do not argue that there is a causal relationship between headphones and modernist stream of consciousness, I do propose that the development and widespread use of headphones makes a compelling historical context for understanding the development of stream of consciousness in the modernist novel.

Since James Joyce was so adept at crafting polyphonic interior monologues that sound out for the reader, this chapter focuses specifically on his representation of stream of consciousness. By historicizing Joyce's novels against headphone technology, I have two aims: first, to call attention to the auditory nature of stream of consciousness, which so easily lends itself to the metaphor of headphone listening; and second, to consider how the headphone's capacity to bring a cosmopolitan mix of sounds and voices into the headspace of listeners parallels Joyce's experiments in creating streams of consciousness that include a cosmopolitan collection of voices, noises, and texts.

Before headphones became a popular appendage to phonographs, telephones, and radios, they were used in medicine and telegraphy.[1] Invented in 1816, the stethoscope became a widely used tool in medical diagnosis, requiring that doctors use only their sense of hearing and shut out external sounds to discern the internal sounds of the body. This developing medical practice encouraged listening techniques that would become popularized with headphones and sound-reproduction technology such as: directing the listener's attention to sonic details, isolating the act of listening from the other senses (making it the only channel for information), and granting significance to sound as such, without privileging music and speech as the only sounds worth listening to.

Headphones became "ubiquitous" with phonograph parlors in the late nineteenth century, and later with home phonographs and radios; they "could appear in almost any situation, as much a symbol of connection to a common commodity culture and of that culture's integration into both domestic and public life as of anything specific about listening" (Sterne, *Audible* 173–74). Emily Thompson details how the earliest phonographs, telephones, and radios relied on headphones so that listeners could more easily decipher the weak recordings and transmissions from the noises of the machine (*Soundscape* 236–37). Thompson astutely observes that with the aid of "narrow tubes that carried the sound directly into their ears," "the room in which the listener listened played little role in shaping the character of the sound heard" (*Soundscape* 236). Listeners were cut off from their immediate soundscape and focused all their sensory attention through their ears. This allowed listeners to "transcend the 'immediate' acoustic environment to participate in another, 'mediated' linkage" (Sterne, *Audible* 158). This chapter contends that just as headphones enabled listeners to limit their soundscape to the sounds piped into their headspace, the fictional soundscapes of Joyce's characters are at times completely constructed through the interior monologues of their headspace; the reader can only rely on a character's inner speech for the narrative.

By cutting a listener off from an external soundscape and creating a mediated soundscape within the listener's headspace, headphones created what Sterne more generally calls a *private acoustic space* (*Audible* 155). Sterne shows how headphones and telephone booths both created a private listening space that heightened the public's awareness of sound as a commodity. Sterne clarifies, "Hearing tubes and audile technique construct an individuated, localized sound space, allowing the experience to be sold to a single individual" (*Audible* 163). I propose that as listening was directed to this inward acoustic space, the voice within one's head (inner speech) became differentiated, amplified, and more easily understood as an aesthetic object—even a commodity.

Headphones encouraged listeners to direct their sense of hearing to a voice, song, or noise that intimately reverberated within the private acoustic space of the listener's head rather than his or her external environment. While, as the artist and researcher Charles Stankievech reflects, this space is an "impossible space," since it cannot literally inhabit "the mass of the body," headphones still make one feel as though sound is "virtually located within the head" (56). This creation of an impossible virtual "space" within the head is what makes this technology such a fitting model for the stream of consciousness. The inner speech that modernists tried to record exists in the same headspace that headphones created. By making listeners use only their sense of hearing for comprehension and by creating a private acoustic space that could be commodified for an individual listener, headphones prefigured the modernist practice of attempting to make tangible and commodify the stream of consciousness—a voice constructed from various texts and noises and listened to within one's private acoustic space. As headphones brought voices and sounds that did not originate within the self into a listener's private acoustic space, the stream of consciousness began to be represented as an aesthetic object containing a mix of voices and sounds from both within and outside of the self.

With the professional use of headphones by telegraph operators in the 1890s, the collective use of "hearing tubes" in phonograph parlors at the turn of the century, and the insistence from advertisers in the 1920s that "your radio receiver set is no better than your head phones," we can assume that modernist writers were familiar with this auditory technology (White 109). While we cannot say for certain whether Joyce used headphones at home, we do know that he was an avid radio listener, picking up broadcasts from Ireland's Radio Eireann when he was in Paris, which gave him, as James A. Connor claims, "an immediate connection with home, with its tidbits of news, weather, drama, and poetry" (19). Jane Lewty helpfully imagines the type of radio that Joyce would have used to receive broadcasts from Ireland, a radio that was most likely of a certain quality:

> Of Joyce's listening, I imagine an incessant, restless switching of dials, calling for 2RN, which would invariably be barricaded by stronger frequencies. It is likely that Joyce had a three-valve, possibly five-valve, set with a radio-wave tuner (consisting of two coils and a variable condenser) as it was difficult to reach long-wave radio stations with a simple one-coil set. These developments were adapted into Dunham portable sets, Pye portables, and Lotus portables. If Joyce had no recourse to these more sophisticated models, he would spend considerable time adjusting a 1-valve set which demanded a regression to headphones. These mufflers exclusively fixed the wearer/listener on a sound edging its way down the ear canal, which then penetrated the tympanum. Noises from outer levels would impinge upon the operation, but this was largely an interiorized process, a suspension of other senses. (398)

Lewty effectively articulates the features of headphone listening that are most essential to the experience: the way in which sound is carried into the ear and headspace, fixating a listener's attention to sonic details and isolating one's sense of hearing, making it the dominant sense.

These same features apply to the experience of reading Joyce: as a reader of inner speech, one is asked to listen in on the sonic details of voice and aural interruptions that enter the stream of consciousness. Yet, more importantly, these features of headphone listening model the features of stream of consciousness, where a voice inside the head is fixed on and recorded as an aesthetic object. Just as advertisements for radio headphones in the *Wireless Age* from 1922 and 1923 consistently tout their brands as "highly sensitive" or "super sensitive," or as having "keen sensitiveness," Joyce too had a sensitive ear that, while practiced in picking up sounds from the radio, also picked up the ways in which internal and external soundscapes constitute inner speech (White 79, 4, 16).

After briefly reviewing the terms *inner speech*, *stream of consciousness*, and *interior monologue*, I will examine the interior monologue episodes of *Ulysses*, as well as the representation of audition and vision in the famously musical episode "Sirens." Yet, perhaps as an antidote to the solipsism of singular inner speech, Joyce also depicts what I call (in the second section of this chapter) *auditory cosmopolitanism*, as he strives to capture the many voices and sounds that interrupt and enter one's inner speech. In his desire to record as many voices and noises as possible, Joyce reminds one of the early radio listeners who were seduced by the "fetish of distanced listening"—a type of listening that "was both cosmopolitan (how *many* different places a listener could pick up) and exploratory (how *far* a listener could hear)" (Sterne, *Audible* 209, emphasis in original). If, as Brandes advertised of its Matched Tone headphones, "at least half of the interest of radio reception is in catching signals, the human voice, news and music from far-distant points," then headphones were marketed as an essential tool for listening closely to those far-off sounds (White 8). Just as headphones brought sounds from remote places into one's headspace, Joyce's representation of stream of consciousness reflects an interior space that is filled with voices, noise, texts, advertisements, and music that do not necessarily originate within the self.[2]

Recording Inner Speech: Limiting the Fictional World to the Stream of Consciousness

In his phenomenological study of voice and listening, Don Ihde maintains that one's inner speech is "linguistic thinking," a part of one's "auditory imagination" that is "an almost constant self-presence" (137). Not to be confused with Eliot's poetic sense of the auditory imagination, for Ihde, the auditory imagination simply refers to the sounds we imagine. Yet Ihde also recognizes that this inner speech can be "hidden" and "elusive" because it is always in the "background" and does not draw attention to itself as sound (137); unlike spoken speech, we only get "indirect 'glances' of inner speech" (139). Noting the way that inner speech can "jump" and "change key," Ihde (in a rare reference to the literary realm) argues that "stream-of-conscious writers" are able to "display this flow and associative 'play' of the interior" (140). Here, Ihde recognizes that modernist interior monologue most closely approximates inner speech, a "language which names, which familiarizes, which fits something into a scheme and thereby domesticates it" (142). Although this speech is elusive, modernists strove to make inner speech sound out through the reader's reading voice, often limiting the reader's exposure to a character's fictional world to only a voice inside the head, grappling with reality.

Literary critics such as Erwin Steinberg and Robert Humphrey stress that stream-of-conscious narratives must be primarily concerned with "the pre-speech levels of consciousness" (Humphrey 171). This idea makes sense when we consider William James's description of consciousness as "a stream, a succession of states, or waves, or fields . . . of knowledge, of feeling, of desire, of delibera-tion, etc., that constantly pass and repass, and that constitute our inner life" (43). For James, "fields of consciousness" can "contain sensations of our bodies and of the objects around us, memories of past experiences and thoughts of distant things, feelings of satisfaction and dissatisfaction, desires and aversions, and other emotional conditions, together with determinations of the will, in every variety of permutation and combination" (43). M. H. Abrams nicely adapts this psychological understanding to literature, defining stream of consciousness as "a special mode of narration that undertakes to reproduce, without a narrator's intervention, the full spectrum and the continuous flow of a character's mental process, in which sense perceptions mingle with conscious and half-conscious thoughts, memories, expectations, feelings, and random associations" (202). Al-though stream of consciousness can contain prespeech sensory experiences, I will focus this chapter on the "conscious and half-conscious thoughts" within the stream of consciousness, which will be interchangeably called inner speech and interior monologue.

Most definitions of interior monologue emphasize the vocal and rhythmic aspect of the technique, where "the character can hear himself in his mind's ear" (Steinberg, "Stream" 162). For example, David Lodge explains that in in-terior monologue, we "overhear the character verbalizing his or her thoughts as they occur," while Abrams declares that interior monologue "undertakes to present to the reader the course and rhythm of consciousness precisely as it occurs in a character's mind" (Lodge, "Stream" 43; Abrams 202). Each of these definitions emphasizes the auditory aspects of the "mind's ear," "overhearing," and "rhythm," while also indicating that there is an immediacy to interior monologue. The words are rendered on the page as they come to the charac-ter, sometimes making for irregular punctuation, grammar, and syntax. This also, however, enhances the auditory dimension of the form: rather than being a static visual picture, the stream of consciousness is an immediate voice heard in present time.

Realizing the limitations of their medium, however, modernist writers con-sistently struggled to bring the auditory nature of stream of consciousness into the experience of reading. In *The Waves*, for example, Virginia Woolf draws attention to the auditory nature of inner speech by using the narrative markers "he said" and "she said" and placing the interior monologues of her six char-acters within quotation marks. In *The Sound and the Fury*, William Faulkner presents three contrasting interior monologues, honing the reader's ear to dif-ferent voices and perspectives. Creating even more of a contrast, John Dos Passos, in his *U.S.A.* trilogy, shifts between fictional narratives, biographical stories, "Newsreel" sections constructed of newspaper clippings, and autobiographical "Camera Eye" sections. The interior monologues of these "Camera Eye" sections, which often include experiences where the author is being prompted to listen to music, a story, or the voice of another, are made more intimate and aural through their juxtaposition with the distanced third-person narrative form and journalist jargon of the other sections; they expose the inner speech of the writer and the thoughts that have created his perspective. These modernist novels are auditory narratives because these interior voices require a reader to listen to them, to eavesdrop on the private speech of the mind.

Among these modernists, however, James Joyce stands out in his tendency to incorporate voices, noise, and popular culture into the inner speech of his characters. In doing this, Joyce seems to be following his own sense of consciousness, which he describes in a letter as a "head . . . full of pebbles and rubbish and broken matches and bits of glass picked up 'most everywhere" (qtd. in Ellmann 512). In the interior monologues of *Ulysses*, critics have noted Joyce's inclusion of public discourse in the private consciousness of his characters. For example, Kevin Attell argues that "even in the smallest and most intimate section of interior monologue, where the narrative most nearly approaches the mechanics of a character's *cogito* or drives, the narrative representation reveals, under hermeneutic scrutiny, a vast network of determinate references and stylistic manipulations" (123). Vincent Sherry, similarly, in his comprehensive study of *Ulysses*, clarifies that by the "Proteus" episode, Stephen is "no longer a heroic solitary, pitting himself and his restricted meanings and narrowly drawn mannerisms against the energies of language, he is the center of a Bakhtinian dialogic; he is a node, a knot of linguistic energies charged by traditions equally literary and popular—a vortex-point through which the forces of the whole language are poured" (*Joyce* 90). Such linguistic forces are exemplified in Bloom, for whom, according to Sherry, the "autonomy of language—those resources of historically accrued meanings and socially determined usages outside the speaker's control" become an unconscious shaping force (*Joyce* 93). I would add, however, that it is not only historical and cultural discourses that shape the interior monologues of the characters of *Ulysses* but also their soundscape—the voices and noises that are overheard and swept up in their stream of consciousness.

This claim that Joyce represents inner speech as shaped by historical and cultural texts as well as one's soundscape may seem to challenge William James's assertion that each mind "keeps its own thoughts to itself," so that "no thought even comes into direct sight of a thought in another personal consciousness than its own" (226). Yet we can conceive of the stream of consciousness as constructed and shaped by external forces while still maintaining that one cannot penetrate the mind of another. While one can never know the thoughts of another, the overheard voices and sounds of a person's surroundings inevitably enter into and mix with that person's inner voice. The traits we typically associate with stream of consciousness—keeping a time that is not chronological or static (Henri Bergson's duration) and being limited to a character's inner world—can still be applied to this Joycean sense of stream of consciousness. The only difference is that the sounds one literally and imaginatively hears (cats meowing, songs sung, quotations remembered) are also represented within and influence the stream. Perhaps this does challenge Walter Pater's postulation that "experience, already reduced to a swarm of impressions, is ringed round for each one of us by that thick wall of personality through which no real voice has ever pierced on its way to us, or from us to that which we can only conjecture to be without" (60). However, as this chapter will show, for Joyce, the voices and soundscapes around his characters do more than pierce the wall of personality: they enter the self and become a part of the interior monologue. Although Joyce's representations of interior monologue remain an attempt to render the most private and impenetrable part of the human mind, they all the same are shown as absorbing the voices and noises of a character's soundscape and auditory imagination. This is why Joyce's specific form of interior monologue shares a kinship with headphone listening at the turn of the century: both allow external sounds to become interior sounds.

Although *A Portrait of the Artist as a Young Man* (1916) uses free indirect discourse rather than interior monologue, the reader can already gather that this character, Stephen Dedalus, is shaped by the voices, stories, and sounds of words that penetrate his sense of self. Young Stephen identifies with a playfully poetic story orally conveyed by his father about a "moocow" and thinks spelling sentences and nursery rhymes alike are "nice" and "beautiful" because of the way they sound (3, 6, 22). In his introduction to the novel, Seamus Deane notices the many references to hearing, from Stephen's desire to link the sounds of words with their meanings to his attention to the words of others such as the quotations of Newman and the speeches of Cranly and Davin (Deane xxv–xxvi). Deane asserts, "The aural dimension in *Portrait* is crucial because sound is physical and yet disembodied. It is through the ear that the talkative world of Dublin reaches Stephen's soul" (xxvi). While taste, touch, and sight are also represented in the novel, "the aural sense is finally more important" (Deane xxvi). In addition to using the sounds of language to understand himself and his environment, Stephen strives to hear "confused music within him ... one long-drawn calling note, piercing like a star the dusk of silence" (181–82). Although Joyce often ironically depicts Stephen caught up in his artistic ideals, sound and audition are nevertheless central to Stephen's development of his artistically in-clined inner voice.

This representation in *Portrait* of Stephen absorbing Dublin through the speech he hears is carried over to the reader in *Ulysses*, where Dublin is "overhear[d]" as we "read words that resonate in our mind, being transmitted as they are from what our eyes read to our 'mind's ear'" (Bénéjam 58). In *Ulysses*, Joyce "neither paints nor photographs [Dublin] for our guidance," choosing in-stead to show his characters listening to their soundscape, as he encourages the reader too to listen to the words on the page (Budgen 71). While we can indeed hear aural resonances throughout *Ulysses*, this tendency for the reader to "lis-ten" to the words on the page is particularly amplified when we read the interior monologues of the novel.

For instance, when we meet Stephen once again through the interior mono-logue of the "Proteus" episode in *Ulysses*, he is still musing about sound and sight, though instead of hearing a "voice from beyond the world" as in *Por-trait*, he simply wants to test how each sense works (*Portrait* 182).[3] This episode follows Stephen's interior monologue, which begins, "Ineluctable modality of the visible: at least that if no more, thought through my eyes. Signatures of all things I am here to read, seaspawn, the nearing tide, that rusty boot. Snotgreen, bluesilver, rust: coloured signs" (3, lines 1–4). Stephen follows the philosophical tradition of equating sight with knowledge and questions how we can be sure of the nature of what we see. If we can only decipher forms—not substance—with vision, how dependable is vision? Drawing on Aristotle's discussion in *On Sense and the Sensible*, which argues that a "body's" "translucent" qualities determine its color, Stephen identifies the colors within his line of vision and thinks of how they constitute his perception of objects (Aristotle, *On Sense* 5–6). He is the distanced reader of the world.

For contrast, Stephen closes his eyes to experience the world through only his ears, listening to his boots crushing shells: "Crush, crack, crick, crick" (3, line 19). With the onomatopoeia of this scene, the reader as well is asked to listen to Stephen's "boots crush crackling wrack and shells" (3, line 10). Distracted by his focus on sound, Stephen's inner speech becomes a little slurred and musi-cal, as he thinks, "You are walking through it howsomever" (3, line 11). More importantly, instead of "reading" the "signatures" of the visible world, Stephen is now "walking through it." This world of sound is one of touch: he feels himself moving through time and space and counts his steps; he listens to his step on the beach, which "sounds solid" (3, lines 12–13, 17). Separating his sense of hearing from his other senses, Stephen is able to pay greater attention to the sonic details of the present moment as it passes. Likewise, the reader is dependent on the reading voice, only able to listen in on Stephen's interior monologue to construct his fictional world. This causes the reader to pay keen attention to the sound of Stephen's inner speech and the interjecting soundscape.

This mode of perception is exciting because of its uncertainty, causing Stephen to exclaim, "Jesus!" as he jokingly feels he could walk off a cliff or "into eternity" (3, lines 14, 18). This moment of insecurity, which often accompanies the experience of an "acousmatic" sound that cannot be visually placed, is assuaged when Stephen falls into a rhyme, after which he remarks, "Rhythm begins, you see. I hear" (3, line 23). Punning on how "seeing" easily slides between literal vision and a metaphor for knowing, Stephen confirms that as a striving writer he hears above all else. As with the story of the boy with the gray-belted suit in *Portrait*, inner speech provides comfort and familiarity; language "fits something into a scheme and thereby domesticates it" (Ihde 142). Even after he opens his eyes, Stephen continues to concentrate predominantly on the language of his inner voice. Others on the beach ineluctably become poetic flow, as they walk "down the shelving shore flabbily, their splayed feet sinking in the silted sand" (3, lines 30–31). As in *Portrait*, Stephen is less interested in seeing the world than he is in listening to his own voice, embodying the charge of solipsism that has often been made against modernist characters.

Similar to how headphones "isolate[d] their users in a private world of sound," so that others could not hear what they heard and so that they could not hear their external surroundings, Stephen seems cut off in his own world of internal sounds (Sterne, *Audible* 87). The auditory inner "world" that is so essential to Stephen's development correlates with what Sterne describes as the "individuated, localized sound space" that headphones created and commodified. The close and detailed listening that headphones required of the isolated listener exemplifies Stephen's close listening for his inner voice, which isolates him from others. Moreover, Ihde clarifies that in speech, "what is ordinarily focal is 'what I am talking about' rather than the singing of the speech as a textured auditory appearance" (138). Yet Stephen is thoroughly engrossed in this "singing of speech." Though Ihde portrays inner speech as "hidden" and "elusive," Joyce implies that the writer must always be listening for it from within and paying attention to its phonic qualities (Ihde 137).

Although Molly is a singer rather than a writer, she also pays attention to the phonic qualities of language. Because she stays within the walls of her bedroom and avoids interaction with the larger world throughout the "Penelope" episode, the "individuated, localized sound space" of her interior monologue is enhanced. Only a few external sounds, such as a train, enter her interior monologue. By inhabiting Molly's private acoustic space and following the cadences and idiomatic expressions of her inner voice, the reader experiences what is perhaps the most aural episode of *Ulysses*. We are not asked to picture scenes but to listen in on Molly as she says "yes" to Bloom. Composed with only eight periods, this episode forces the reader to sound out Molly's inner speech with his or her reading voice in order to figure out when punctuation is needed. In her essay "About Punctuation," Dorothy Richardson justifies her own irregular use of punctuation, arguing that "in the slow, attentive reading demanded by unpunctuated texts, the faculty of hearing has its chance, is enhanced until the text *speaks* itself" (415, emphasis in original). With such a text, Richardson claims, the reader "finds himself *listening*" (415, emphasis in original). Without punctuation guiding the reader into immediate semantic meaning, the reader must make a conscious effort to listen to the words with his or her reading voice, so that he or she might hear where pauses are required to make meaning. This episode brings the acoustics of the narrative to the forefront, making Molly's inner speech a commodified listening experience for the reader.

The sparse punctuation, periodic repetition of "yes," and occasional onomatopoeia (such as "sweeeee theres that train far away pianissimo eeeee one more tsong," heard when Molly mixes her passing gas and the sounds of a train) all work to heighten the aurality of this episode (18, line 908). Because she is a singer, Molly's stream of consciousness consistently incorporates rhymes such as "Jesusjack the child is black" and "wherever you be let your wind go free" (18, lines 163, 909) and songs such as "To Never See Thy Face Again," "Oh Sweetheart May," "There Is a Flower that Bloometh," and of course "Love's Old Sweet Song" (18, lines 29, 229, 775, 874). This periodic infusion of musicality not only reminds the reader to keep sounding out the words on the page but also evokes Molly's voice as a singer. It is the reader's experience of listening in on this incredibly intimate voice that makes it feel like a voice overheard through headphones. Molly reveals private judgments and sexual thoughts that few characters of this time period would say aloud, as she considers "that old faggot Mrs Riordan" who probably "was pious because no man would look at her twice," asserts that Bloom "came somewhere," fantasizes about "seduc[ing]" "a young boy," and recalls Boylan's "tremendous big red brute of a thing" (18, lines 4, 11, 34, 85–87, 144). Just as headphones isolate one's sense of hearing, focusing all of one's sensory attention to the sounds heard in one's headspace, the reader's fictional world is limited to Molly's interior monologue. Our only sense of her world is through the inner speech that is listened to through the reading voice, as the rest of the fictional world slumbers. At no point in the novel are we more dependent on a sole voice, an aestheticized inner speech that is crafted to sound out in our own headspace.

Although not devoted to one character's interior monologue, the "Sirens" episode should be addressed, as it is most celebrated for its musical qualities. At the start of his explication of this episode, Stuart Gilbert recounts the musical gifts of Joyce as a singer and concludes that the episode "both in structure and in diction goes far beyond all previous experiments in the adaptation of musical technique and timbre to a work of literature" (241–42). While critics such as Margaret Rogers and Jack W. Weaver analyze the episode as a fugue, repeating certain elements throughout, and Zack Bowen reads the episode as a music-hall piece, I would like to examine the ways in which it represents auditory and visual perception.

After a list of sixty phrases and sentences that, in a fugue form, are repeated throughout the episode, we find ourselves with the barmaids Miss Douce and Miss Kennedy. They "[hear] the viceregal hoofs go by, ringing steel" and then go "all agog," straining to look at "the fellow in the tall silk hat," who in turn struggles to look back at them (11, lines 65, 69, 70). This sets the pattern for the rest of the episode, where the eye desperately tries yet never quite relays satisfactory information, while the ear is overwhelmed with sounds from all directions. For example, Miss Douce tries to examine her sunburn "askance in the barmirror," which is obscured with gilded letters, and gives up; whereas Miss Kennedy (reminiscent of Odysseus's men in the *Odyssey*) makes a futile attempt to "[plug] both two ears with little fingers" to avoid hearing Miss Douce's impersonation, which, when inevitably heard, causes "a giggling peal young goldbronze voices blended" (11, lines 118–19, 120–30, 158). Patrons come into the bar, asking the barmaids whether they have seen certain friends, and Miss Kennedy, reading the paper, replies in the negative, though she is "heard, not seen" (11, line 240). Further demonstrating the inadequacy of the eye, Blazes Boylan and Matt Lenehan catch only a quick glimpse of Miss Douce's leg, leaving their eyes hungry and "spellbound" (11, line 420). It is also significant that the waiter, who is "hard of hearing," is referred to as "bothered Pat," while the tapping of the blind piano tuner, who is an "exquisite [piano] player," is heard throughout the episode (11, lines 670, 288, 278). This saturation of sound offers a counterexample to the headphone effect of the interior monologue form. Whereas in the "Proteus" episode, Stephen can cut off the external environment and focus his attention on the prosody of inner speech, in the "Sirens" episode, characters cannot "plug" up their ears, and thus their perception is left skewed or incomplete.

Leopold Bloom, however, seems able to strike a balance. Unlike Stephen, Bloom's stream of consciousness is not so consumed with his inner speech that he cannot also connect to the city and people of Dublin; he is, as the next section of this chapter will show, the consummate cosmopolitan. Ihde describes the inescapable sound of inner speech as an "almost continuous aspect of self-presence," which can be interrupted only temporarily with noise and music (134). Such intrusions, according to Ihde, allow for "the penetration of sound into the very region of the 'thinking self'" (132). It should come as no surprise therefore that the "Sirens" episode is filled with noise and music that at one point or another penetrate Bloom's interior monologue. The "jingle jaunty jingle" of Boylan's car is interspersed into the narrative, along with a barrage of other sounds such as fragments of song lyrics played on the piano, the "clack[ing]" of the clock, the "clappyclapclap" of applause, and the "tap" of the blind piano tuner's cane (11, lines 245, 381, 756, 933). All these sounds comingle to construct Bloom's private acoustic space, redirecting or interrupting his inner speech. Discussing the proliferation of sounds in this episode, Hugh Kenner notes that "where every resource of onomatopoeia is bent upon musical effects and musicians' procedures, the balance between sound and sense is kept uneasy" (86). Though, as Kenner claims, the dominance of sound threatens to "subvert" one's understanding of the episode, it is also this subversion of rational and linear flow that gives us access to Bloom's flustered thoughts at this moment, which marks Boylan's approach to Molly (Kenner 86). Bloom eventually hears and sees Boylan's "jaunting car," but it is the sound of the car in particular that he cannot escape, reminding him of his wife's pending infidelity (11, line 302). Although Bloom can turn his eyes away from Boylan's car and avoid being seen by him, the sound trespasses where the visual cannot. By putting the reader into Bloom's private acoustic space, Joyce allows us to experience the noises that insinuate their way into his interior monologue—his thinking self.

As Bloom and the bar patrons listen to Simon Dedalus sing "M'appari" from the opera *Martha*, "they listened feeling that flow endearing flow over skin limbs human heart soul spine" (11, lines 668–69). In an episode that is full of superficial barroom chatter, the music creates the only moment of intense connectivity. Bloom considers how music relates to the sense of touch since it is the physical vibrations that are felt even after a song is done: "it's in the silence after you feel you hear. Vibrations" (11, lines 793–94). The echoed sound of blood pumping through the body is also noticed when the barroom patrons listen for the ocean in a "seahorn" (11, line 924). Seeing this, Bloom reflects, "Her [Miss Douce's] ear too is a shell. . . . The sea they think they hear. Singing. A roar. The blood it is" (11, lines 938–45). Throughout the episode, the reader is asked to focus attention on the ear, to listen not only to the singing and dialogue of the patrons but to Bloom's inner speech and bodily sounds. Bloom debates what is music and what is noise: the door "ee creaking" is noise, while the sound of Molly's "tinkling" is "chamber music," a pun on the title of Joyce's collection of poetry (11, lines 965, 981, 979). This episode ends with the sounds of Bloom farting, mixed with the far away sounds of the bar and tram, as he departs and averts his eyes to avoid looking at a prostitute. Once again, the eye can avoid what it wants to suppress, but noise and bodily sounds will be heard. As with the music heard at the bar, these bodily noises reaffirm the intimacy of sounds, which can both enter and escape the body. Just as the earliest use of headphones were in stethoscopes that amplified the sounds of the body, Joyce allows the reader to hear the bodily sounds that are typically private—shaping them into a commodified, aesthetic object (the novel). In this next section, we will see how headphones correlate with stream of consciousness in their shared capacity to bring cosmopolitan sounds from different cultures and classes into one's headspace.

The Auditory Cosmopolitanism of Interior Monologue

Reading famous examples of modernist writing such as Molly's monologue, one might view the modernist valuing of aesthetics and subjectivity to be antithetical to cosmopolitanism. Rebecca Walkowitz, however, convincingly argues that modernists such as James Joyce, Joseph Conrad, and Virginia Woolf participated in and influenced the project of *critical cosmopolitanism*. By critical cosmopolitanism, Walkowitz means a "type of international engagement" characterized by "an aversion to heroic tones of appropriation and progress, and a suspicion of epistemological privilege, views from above or from the center that assume a consistent distinction between who is seeing and what is seen" (2). Though Walkowitz's visual metaphor is only incidental, it nicely corroborates my analysis of vision and audition in the modernist novel. Modernists who are skeptical of modes of being that are based on a distanced, analytical, "objective" viewer of the world are more likely to demonstrate the style of cosmopolitanism that Walkowitz so astutely studies. In her chapter on Joyce, Walkowitz proposes that Joyce works against colonialism and racism through "a model of cosmopolitanism that values triviality, promiscuous attention, and what [she] call[s] 'canceled decorum'" (56). While Walkowitz insightfully traces these cosmopolitan traits in "Two Gallants," *Portrait*, and *Ulysses*, I will extend her research by considering what I call the *auditory cosmopolitanism* within the interior monologues of *Ulysses*.

My reading meshes with the "promiscuous attention" that Walkowitz identifies in *Portrait*, as she traces Stephen's purposeful distraction when he meets with a priest and rejects a vocation in the church. This diversion happens both within the fictional world, as Stephen hears a "trivial air" that is in direct contrast to the "hypocrisy of single-mindedness" represented by the priest and church, and on the level of the reader, who is likewise distracted "from evening breeze to trivial melody" (Walkowitz 65–66). These two levels are at work in the auditory cosmopolitanism of *Ulysses* as well. On one level, characters are distracted by the many sounds that enter their auditory field and become integrated into their interior monologue. These sounds can enter the stream of consciousness either through recollection or from a character's external environment. On another level, the reader, too, is distracted by the many fragments of sounds that intermingle on the page, keeping one from absentmindedly falling into plot. Yet, I see the foreign languages, texts, and plights of others that enter Stephen's and Bloom's interior monologues not merely as distractions that momentarily draw their attention away from the singular ideologies of race, religion, and nationalism; rather, these cosmopolitan sounds are the very materials that construct their interior monologues.

In the "Proteus" episode, Stephen's inner speech expands beyond a monolithic ideology by appropriating a barrage of different languages and discourses. This type of cosmopolitanism is best described as "the ability to stand outside of having one's life written and scripted by any one community, whether that is a faith or tradition or culture—whatever it might be—and to draw selectively on a variety of discursive meanings" (Hall 26).[4] We can discern this auditory cosmopolitanism within the first two paragraphs of Stephen's inner speech, which intermixes: an array of philosophical discourses, spanning from antiquity to the eighteenth century (Aristotle, Jacob Boehme, and the Church of Ireland Bishop of Cloyne George Berkeley, for example); German and Italian words; Scots dialect; a reference to Shakespeare; and a popular verse (3, lines 1–20). Later in the episode, Stephen recites a verse of seventeenth-century underworld cant (the secret language of thieves surveyed in Richard Head's *The Canting Academy* published in London in 1673 [Gifford 61]), sparked by a couple on the beach that he assumes to be gypsies, and recalls bits of French as he recollects his time in Paris. His usage of the slang of thieves and gypsies, in particular, directs his thoughts to sexuality and bawdiness, a train of thought that he checks with a phrase from Saint Thomas Aquinas (3, lines 381–85). The way in which Stephen integrates these fragments into his inner speech is auditory, as he repeats phrases in different languages and from various discourses (philosophical, religious, literary, underworld) within his mind's voice. As the reader struggles to pronounce the different languages and unfamiliar jargon, his or her attention is drawn to the aural texture of the words on the page. These fragments, however, are not ornamental side thoughts that serve Stephen's stream of consciousness; they *constitute* his stream of consciousness, making it take new turns and creating a cosmopolitan inner speech that transgresses the boundaries of Dublin and Irish culture.

Bloom's auditory cosmopolitanism, in contrast, is much subtler. Bloom's thoughts stay local and tend to focus directly on those around him. Being Irish and Jewish, Bloom already complicates any simplistic nation-state model for a character. This comes to the forefront with his occasional Yiddish—calling Denis Breen, in his mind, a "Meshuggah," for instance (8, line 314)—as well as with the talisman potato that Bloom carries, which suggests both a traditional post-funeral Jewish dish and the Irish potato blight (Gifford 71). As soon as we encounter Bloom, we are made aware of his sensitivity to stereotyping or essentializing another culture. When he sets out to buy his breakfast, he daydreams about "the east": "Wander through awned streets. Turbaned faces going by. Dark caves of carpet shops, big man, Turko the terrible, seated crosslegged, smoking a coiled pipe" (4, lines 88–90). After a sequence of such phrases, however, Bloom stops himself, thinking, "Probably not a bit like it really. Kind of stuff you read: in the track of the sun" (4, lines 99–100). Realizing that his revelry has been determined by popular pantomime (*Turko the Terrible*) and travelogues such as Frederick Diodati Thompson's *In the Track of the Sun: Readings from the Diary of a Globe Trotter* (1893), Bloom halts his thought and uses the phrase about the sun to transition to thinking about Arthur Griffith and Irish Home Rule. Here, what was initially conceived as foreign and exotic easily leads to local Irish history. Bloom recognizes the limitations of his knowledge and stops himself from narrating a story about a culture that he has never experienced firsthand.

Bloom attempts to imagine what it might be like to be a different person or even animal, and it is this empathetic impulse that makes his interior monologue cosmopolitan. Indeed, when we first meet Bloom, although we are told that he "ate with relish the inner organs of beasts and fowls," we also witness his stream of consciousness, which at first is focused on his own needs but then is distracted and absorbed by the repeated "Mkgnao!" of their cat (4, lines 1, 16).

Bloom dismisses people who assume that cats are "stupid" and decides that "they understand what we say better than we understand them" (4, lines 26–27). He wonders how the cat perceives him and understands that although he is taller, she could easily jump over him (4, lines 28–29). He appreciates her ability to mouse and lingers over questions such as why she might be affected by having her whiskers clipped and why her tongue is rough. As the reader experiences the cat sounds that Bloom hears and follows the attention that he pays to the cat, he or she gets a sense of Bloom as a character who does not assume his dominance but rather holds a healthy "suspicion of epistemological privilege" (Walkowitz 2). Bloom is willing to consider and be curious about different creatures.

Similarly, in "Lestrygonians" (episode 8), Bloom's interior monologue is distracted by seagulls. He tries to fool them into thinking he is throwing food for them by tossing a piece of paper, but, noticing their lack of attention, he thinks, "Not such damn fools. . . . Live by their wits" (8, lines 59, 61). The sight of them inspires Bloom to recite a rhyme, and the poetic form makes Bloom think of Shakespeare's use of blank verse, a recitation that is distracted when Bloom hears a woman selling apples. As he "gazes" on the shiny apples, Bloom's stream of consciousness is interrupted by "Wait. Those poor birds," which spurs him to buy cakes and feed the birds before moving on with his day (8, line 73). Later in the same episode, he sympathizes with animals that are slaughtered for meat: "Pain to the animals too. . . . Moo. Poor trembling calves. Meh" (8, lines 722, 724). This is a pattern within Bloom's interior monologue that is repeated when he considers the much more serious matter of Mrs. Purefoy's three days of labor in childbirth. His inner speech is repeatedly redirected toward her pain, as he exclaims within, "Poor Mrs Purefoy" and "Sss. Dth, dth, dth!" (8, lines 358, 373). He continues, "Three days imagine groaning in a bed with a vinegared handkerchief round her forehead, her belly swollen out. Phew! Dreadful simply! Child's head too big: forceps. Doubled up inside her trying to butt its way out blindly, groping for the way out. Kill me that would" (8, lines 373–77). Recognizing his own inability to cope with such pain, Bloom questions why no one has invented a way to lessen the pain for women in labor. But of more significance, Bloom's own hunger, which dominates most of this episode, is sidetracked as his stream of consciousness is pulled out of his own desires and needs. On one level, the reader is tuned into Bloom's interior monologue, listening to his thoughts and the sounds that interrupt and shape those thoughts, as if through headphones. Nonlinguistic sounds such as "Phew!" and "Dth" assure that the reader experiences the auditory narrative. On a deeper level, Bloom's interior monologue itself is reminiscent of one listening to a recording or broadcast with headphones, as his private acoustic space is infiltrated by the stories of others. Bloom's auditory cosmopolitanism comes through his receptivity to others, as well as through his way of letting them enter into his headspace and construct his interior monologue.

Though the pain of childbirth cannot personally affect Bloom, he questions the progress of a civilization that cannot do something to ease a woman's pain. This demonstrates Walkowitz's sense of cosmopolitanism as an "aversion to heroic tones of appropriation and progress" and skepticism of "views from above or from the center that assume a consistent distinction between who is seeing and what is seen" (2). Such an attitude is reinforced when Bloom later encounters a young blind man. In the midst of trying to avoid thoughts of Boylan and Molly, Bloom asks the young blind man if he needs help crossing the street. As he escorts the young man, Bloom reminds himself not to be "condescending" toward him, and he chides himself later for being surprised at the cleverness of the blind: "Look at the things they can learn to do. Read with their fingers. Tune pianos. Or are we surprised they have any brains. Why we think a deformed person or a hunchback clever if he says something we might say" (8, lines 1092, 1115–17). While he does not idealize the youth, noting that the "stains on his coat" indicate that he "slobbers his food," Bloom is attuned to the idea that the young man's other senses are sharper. Bloom likens the adolescent's hand to his own daughter's, wonders what his name is and what his idea of Dublin must be like, and questions how he might experience women and dreams. Each of these details within Bloom's interior monologue suggests an attempt on Bloom's part to get beyond generalizations, to identify with the young man on a personal level. Beyond his sympathy, which is repeatedly expressed through his inner speech with the exclamation "Poor fellow," Bloom tries to experience firsthand how one understands the touch of skin without seeing it (8, lines 1107, 1144). It is Bloom's interior monologue that leads him to this last act of compassion, where Bloom feels the skin of his own soft belly for a moment.

By showing how the pain of childbirth and the particularity of blindness enter into and shape Bloom's interior monologue, Joyce demonstrates how our inner speech can be attuned to an auditory cosmopolitanism that can act as a bridge between "who is seeing and what is seen" (Walkowitz 2). This resonates with Connor's understanding of an "auditory I" that, under the influence of turn-of-the-century auditory technologies and the noise of the modern soundscape, turned away from the "rationalized 'Cartesian grid' of the visualist imagination, which positioned the perceiving self as a single point of view, from which the exterior world radiated in regular lines" ("Modern" 206). This rational distanced vision "gave way to a more fluid, mobile and voluminous conception of space, in which the observer-observed duality and distinctions between separated points and planes dissolve" (Connor, "Modern" 207). Whereas the seeing self is separate from the perceived world, analyzing its surroundings through the distancing eye, the listening self is immersed in the perceived world through the sounds that reverberate through the ear and enter the body. Connor suggests that since we can hear many sounds at the same time and cannot turn our ears away from a sound as we can our eyes from a sight, the "self defined in terms of hearing rather than sight is a self imagined not as a point, but as a membrane; not as a picture, but as a channel through which voices, noises and musics travel" ("Modern" 207). As Bloom allows the sounds of his surroundings to enter his interior monologue, he becomes a channel that is tuned to the experiences of others. While the distance between subject and object can never be obliterated, Bloom's interior monologue is always taking the other into account by being curious about and humanizing the other. We consistently listen to Bloom's inner speech struggle to conceive of experiences that are outside his horizon of experience. Although Stephen's interior monologue exhibits a surface cosmopolitanism as it integrates different languages and discourses, Bloom's interior monologue demonstrates a deeper sense of cosmopolitanism in its attempts to identify with multiple subject positions and interests. Likewise, as the reader listens to Bloom's interior monologue through the reading voice, he or she allows Bloom's inner speech to inhabit his or her own headspace. Just as voices and music became commodified objects brought into the headspace through headphones, inner speech became a commodified object, crafted by modernists and brought into the headspace through the reading voice.

David Lodge describes the effect of interior monologue in *Ulysses* as "rather like wearing earphones plugged into someone's brain, and monitoring an endless tape-recording of the subject's impressions, reflections, questions, memories and fantasies, as they are triggered either by physical sensations or the association of ideas" ("Interior" 47). Perhaps Lodge found this metaphor to be so apt because headphones and the private acoustic space they created were gradually helping to shape the popular conception of *headspace*. Although one could argue that all reading that is tuned into the reading voice can be likened to the experience of listening to headphones, the fact of the matter is that we are usually encouraged not to pay attention to the sounds of words but rather to read primarily for meaning and content. The modernist interior monologue, conversely, directs the reader to listen to a voice within the head, to become attuned to its cadences, registers, and—what becomes most important for Joyce—the external sounds that are piped into the head, directing and integrating into the stream of consciousness.

In a recent article on the contemporary headphone user, Derek Thompson concludes, "In a crowded world, real estate is the ultimate scarce resource, and a headphone is a small invisible fence around our minds—making space, creating separation, helping us listen to ourselves" (par. 17). Although this "fence" pushes against the above notion of cosmopolitanism, Thompson's assertion that headphones relax us so that we can "listen to ourselves" is relevant to the above discussion. Could it have been much different for early twentieth-century users of headphones, who, after overcoming their fascination with hearing sound reproduced and brought into their private acoustic space, could then relax, enjoy the music, and allow their own insights to stream forward? Just as recorded, broadcast, and transmitted sounds entered one's private acoustic space through headphones, isolating listeners from their immediate external environment, modernist writers turned up the volume and transcribed the voices and noise within that same private acoustic space of the mind, making the demands of the external world secondary to inner speech.

5

Inner Speech as a Gramophone Record

Jean Rhys's Bohemian Voice and Popular Music

I still don't understand why I find popular music so enthralling. I'm not deaf to better things. But they fade away gently, gracefully, no haunting.

Jean Rhys, "Songs My Mother Didn't Teach Me"

If, as Bonnie Kime Scott states, "in the decades that coincided with the rise of modernism (1910–1920), records became a mass medium," then we must question how such mass production of music shaped modernist writing ("Subversive" 97). Jean Rhys attests to the power of popular music in an essay she began drafting in 1978, which, after five revisions, was to be possibly included in her autobiography, *Smile Please*. In the final version of the essay, titled "Songs My Mother Didn't Teach Me," Rhys recounts,

> I have been haunted by popular songs all my life. Walking to some tune in my head. Walking, talking to it, ("and for the ordering of her affairs to sing them too"). Not quite that but very nearly.
>
> Many people experience this I know but I wonder if they are, like me, possessed by it [last two words crossed out, replaced with an illegible word].
>
> Sometimes I think I can divide my life into neat sections headed by the songs I loved at the time. (vers. 5, p. 1)

Looking back at her life before, during, and after World War I, Rhys names the popular songs that "haunted" her, shaping the tempo of her thoughts and actions. Aside from her work in music halls, which familiarized her with popular songs, she mentions the phonograph as fulfilling her desire to hear certain songs repeatedly—a repetition that seems essential to such "possession." After hearing music that "excited [her] beyond measure," Rhys explains how she frequented "kiosks in Paris where for a small sum you could listen to a wide choice of records" ("Songs" vers. 5, p. 4). She continues, "I went from kiosk to kiosk always playing the Prince Igor dances and always the wild defiant music seemed to pour fresh life into me" (vers. 5, p. 4). Thus, it should come as no surprise that Rhys created characters who are inspired by and dance to popular recordings, who get songs stuck in their heads, and who ultimately feel that their own inner speech is a type of recording, repeating the same refrains.

When Rhys implies the lowly status of the popular music that "haunts" her, guiltily admitting that she was "not deaf to better things," she echoes George Gershwin's concern that mass recordings could "bastardize music and give currency to a lot of cheap things" (389). While Gershwin is somewhat optimistic, suggesting that the more the public listens to music, "the more they will be able to criticize it and know when it is good," John Philip Sousa feared that mass reproduction would eradicate local, amateur musicians, leaving in their place "a machine that tells the story day by day, without variation, without soul, barren of the joy, the passion, and ardor that is the inheritance of man alone" (Gershwin 389; Sousa 119).

Seconding Gershwin's and Sousa's wariness of the phonograph's commodification of music, Theodor Adorno, in a short essay called "The Curves of the Needle," laments the phonograph's "transition from artisanal to industrial production" (48). He argues that the technical improvements of recordings have resulted in a loss of "the subtlety of color and the authenticity of vocal sound . . . as if the singer were being distanced more and more from the apparatus" ("Curves" 48). As phonograph records became a mass-produced commodity, listening to popular recordings became associated with bourgeois leisure: "It is the bourgeois family that gathers around the gramophone in order to enjoy the music that it itself . . . is unable to perform" (Adorno, "Curves" 50). Adorno's association of the phonograph with the bourgeoisie continues throughout his essay and even becomes gendered, as he (like Rhys) discusses the popularity of the phonograph parlor in France, where "petit bourgeois girls" are "audience and object alike" ("Curves" 53). Yet, for Adorno, the female voice "easily sounds shrill" when recorded because it lacks the visualized female body, leaving the voice "needy and incomplete" ("Curves" 54). Here, as this chapter will show, Adorno echoes critics of Rhys's fiction, who thought that her interior monologues did not allow the reader to adequately picture her down-and-out female narrators. For both Adorno and these critics, the female voice must be attached to a body to be complete. As we will come to understand, this is exactly what Rhys subverts when she gives the reader the voices of her protagonists only through interior monologue.

Adorno continues his critique of the phonograph in his 1934 essay "The Form of the Phonograph Record," where, after an incredibly detailed description of a phonograph disc, he claims that the record "is the first means of musical presentation that can be possessed as a thing" (58). Unlike visual art that hangs on a wall, the record is a type of graspable "writing" that "absorbs into itself, in [a] process of petrification, the very life that would otherwise vanish" (Adorno, "Form" 59). For Adorno, as recordings were mass produced, there was a loss of intimacy and authenticity, a distancing between the artist and the listener. Yet, in his vivid description of the record, Adorno makes clear that this object is a permanent "thing" that captures the ephemeral voice through commodification ("Form" 58). Thus, ironically, while being recorded and reproduced reduced an artist's authenticity, the artist's "very life" was reified into the phonograph recording (Adorno, "Form" 59). The voice became a commodity.

In the same year that Adorno was writing "The Curves of the Needle," Jean Rhys published the short story "In a Café" in her 1927 collection *The Left Bank*. The story focuses on a man who captivates café patrons as he sings about "the *grues*," "the sellers of illusion of Paris" (14). The "peaceful atmosphere" of the Latin Quarter café is disturbed by the song's story of a prostitute who is compassionate and loving to her client but who is then treated as a disposable nuisance once this same man marries and becomes respectable (12). Noting that "Paris is sentimental and indulgent towards" the prostitute only "in the mass and theoretically"—not "practically or to individuals"—the narrator draws the reader's attention to the hypocrisy of the café listeners, who, similar to the male villain of the song, are attracted to the idea of the prostitute only when it suits them (14). When the song is done, there is "tumultuous" applause, as the patrons eagerly buy phonograph recordings of the song (15). Aside from the singer, the only dialogue presented in the short story comes from a female patron who, as she purchases the record, says "with calm self-assurance," "Give me two" (15). These bourgeois patrons, "stout business men" and "neat women in neat hats," mixed with "temperamental" types, who "wore turbans and drank *menthes* of striking emerald," are unsettled yet invigorated by how the song brings them closer to the underbelly of Paris; here, surely, is a song their mothers never taught them. Yet, just as the prostitute is only appreciated as part of a nonindividualized "mass," the mass-produced phonograph recording allows the patrons to appreciate the song from their position of bourgeois respectability, without risking their sense of "calm self-assurance."

Adorno's sense of the phonographic medium as producing a distanced and commodified yet vital voice offers insight not only into Rhys's "In a Café" but into much of her fiction. While the man singing in the café in person causes the women "to look into their mirrors" and the men to "thirstily" drink their beers and "look sideways," the recording can be purchased with "calm self-assurance" (Rhys, "In a Café" 14–15). In this case, the distance between the song's uncomfortable live performance and the recording allows the bourgeois patrons to possess the song about the prostitute as an object, bringing them closer to the alluring idea of "the *grues*," while keeping their distance from actual prostitutes. The way in which this popular phonograph recording embodies a vital connection with the singer while maintaining the distance of mass production makes it a fitting model for Rhys's interior monologues, which at times seem so intimate yet are perfected and crafted to be heard by the masses. Her readers, like the café patrons, appreciate the idea of the Parisian underbelly as a tantalizing commodity but not necessarily as part of their personal lives. Only a little over two pages, "In a Café" can thus function as a key to Rhys's interior monologues, which tapped into the bourgeois desire to purchase an "authentic" representation of the bohemian down-and-out life from a respectable distance.

Interestingly, Sousa's assessment of mass-produced recordings as "tell[ing] the story day by day, without variation, without soul," if taken out of context, might just as easily apply to the self-perception of Rhys's narrators (119). Indeed, one character warns herself against allowing "the cheap gramophone records starting up in [her] head, no 'Here this happened, here that happened'" (*Good* 15). Rhys's characters often feel looked down on, like a cheap commodity. Even Rhys's fiction was sometimes dismissed as dealing with unsavory subjects. In aligning her interior monologues with popular music, Rhys reflects on the ways in which the inner speech of her characters is mechanized and infiltrated by cultural, often antagonistic, voices. For Rhys, these multiple voices inject a negative internalization of bourgeois and gender stereotypes. Rhys, however, exploits these various voices to create and market a bohemian persona, which the reader accesses through the interior monologues of her short stories and her novels *Voyage in the Dark* and *Good Morning, Midnight*. Drawing on her own experiences in bohemian London and Paris, Rhys crafts lurid tales that, like the gramophone recording above, let bourgeois readers feel as though they are eavesdropping on a voice and tune that both repulses and entices them.

Several critics have noticed that Rhys's characters, particularly her first-person narrators, exhibit multiple voices within their interior monologues.[1] Gerald Guinness, for instance, remarks that "Rhys doubles the voice of a speaker, so that an inner voice answers an outer voice or communes with itself by means of a parenthesis" (91). Guinness argues that while this form can "give the effect of disorientation or strain" (92), making Rhys's characters seem "unhinged," it "can also generate a disconcerting and poetic effect—a sort of poetry of the crack-up" (93–94). Similarly, Maren Linett postulates that Rhys's first-person narratives "exemplify modernist fragmentation while intimating a deeper sense of pain and loss than most accounts of fragmentation acknowledge" (437). Linett astutely reads the fragmentation of the interior monologues of *Voyage in the Dark* and *Good Morning, Midnight* as rooted in trauma. While both Guinness and Linett offer compelling insights into Rhys's characters, I find that critics too easily associate the fragmentation of her narrative with mental disorders and psychological breakdown.[2] The fragmentation of Rhys's characters is on par with the fragmentation of Stephen Dedalus or of Leopold Bloom's interior monologue, though critics rarely suggest that James Joyce's characters are mentally unstable. Instead, I believe that if we examine Rhys's fragmented and multi-voiced interior monologues in the context of bohemian culture, a different story can be told about her first-person novels.

Bohemianism, first associated with down-and-out artists in Félix Pyat's 1834 essay "Les Artistes" and later popularized in Henry Murger's 1848 *Scenes of Bohemian Life*, was a term still in use by the early twentieth century. In his insightful analysis of Parisian bohemia from 1830 to 1930, Jerrold Seigel characterizes the world of bohemia as filled with "artists, the young, [and] shady but inventive characters," each of whom "shared—with the gypsies whose names they bore—a marginal existence based on the refusal or inability to take on a stable and limited social identity" (11). This vibrant community was able to congregate in certain neighborhoods, mainly Montmartre and later Montparnasse, where its members could enjoy inexpensive rent, cafés, and bars, each of which offered them uninhibited spaces to talk, drink, dance, sing, and live. Yet Seigel contextualizes the development of bohemia with the formation of the bourgeoisie, asserting that as "bourgeois progress called for the dissolution of traditional restrictions on personal development," bohemia functioned to test and to establish how far such a focus on individuality could be pushed (10). Hence, "Bohemia was not a realm outside bourgeois life but the expression of a conflict that arose at its very heart" (Seigel 10). This conflict between personal development and social cohesion and productivity is manifested in the diverse voices of Rhys's interior monologues, where internalized voices take turns encouraging characters to be selfish or accusing characters of being lazy and immoral. Rather than reading Rhys's fragmented interior monologues as representing mental trauma, within this context, I suggest that they reveal a dialectical tension between bourgeois and bohemian sensibilities.

By aestheticizing the interior monologues of her protagonists and predominantly focusing her artistic attention on their inner speech, Rhys makes the thoughts of her characters rather than their location and appearance dominant in her narratives. As this chapter demonstrates, this interior monologue thwarts the tendency of the male gaze to visualize and objectify the protagonists. The thoughts of Rhys's characters form a distinct voice, to which readers are asked to open themselves through the reading voice. One of the central ways that these interior monologues sound out is by incorporating popular songs that sometimes enhance a sense of overplayed cheapness and, at other times, have the power to encourage defiance and "pour fresh life" into her characters. As the music penetrates their interior monologues, it suffuses with and shapes its associative flow. Building on this observation, the next section will examine how these voices and quotations that penetrate the interior monologues of Rhys's first-person narrators are specifically crafted by Rhys to present a bohemian voice that was eagerly consumed by the reading public of the time. Just as popular recordings allowed the bourgeoisie to possess the commodified voice of the artist, Rhys's interior monologues allowed the bourgeoisie to possess the commodified voice of the bohemian.

Bohemia, Gramophone Recordings, and *The Left Bank*

Though few literary critics place much emphasis on the fact that Rhys frequented bohemian scenes, I believe that her immersion in this subculture had a greater impact on her writing than assumed.[3] Let us not forget that the complete title of her first collection of short stories was *The Left Bank: Sketches and Studies of Present-Day Bohemian Paris*. After the dissolution of her first affair as a young woman in London, Rhys frequented the Crab Tree Club, "the first of the great Bohemian nightclubs" founded by the famous bohemian figure Augustus John (Pizzichini 123). Once Rhys encountered the Parisian bohemian scene, she would refer to the Crab Tree as "a bad imitation of Montmartre"; however, during her time in London, "she practically lived there" (Pizzichini 124). When Rhys dated the artist Adrian Allinson, they spent time visiting the composer and music critic Philip Heseltine, who published under the name Peter Warlock. Heseltine was the model for D. H. Lawrence's minor "London Bohemia" character Halliday in *Women in Love* (Lawrence, *Women* 45), and he is characterized by Elizabeth Wilson in her study of bohemianism as one "whose artistic output was dwarfed by [his] bohemian lifestyle" (77). According to Lilian Pizzichini, Rhys "fell in love with" Heseltine when she heard him whistling the love duet from

Tristan and Isolde, and she began her lifelong habit of whispering her speech when she overheard Heseltine and others making fun of her accent (133, 135). Hence, two important points emerge from Rhys's time in London bohemia: she felt most attracted to and part of the bohemian scene, yet she still felt an outsider, partly due to her West Indian heritage.

This ambivalence is relevant to my reading of Rhys's interior monologues, which are of the bohemian world and yet distant from it. This allows Rhys to market the voice of the bohemian to a public that sought such lurid tales, while still maintaining a distance from the voice being presented. Just as a singer is distanced through and yet captured in a phonograph recording, Rhys produced a voice that is distanced through the form of her medium. Although "the subject matter of her novels was sufficiently intriguing to attract an almost prurient interest in the source of their inspiration," it was important to Rhys that readers understand her novels as "essentially works of the imagination which transcended [her] experience" (Wyndham 9).

Despite Rhys's desire that her life and art not be conflated, Ford Madox Ford, in his preface to *The Left Bank*, assures the reader that Rhys writes of bohemia from first-hand experience: "coming from the Antilles, with a terrifying insight and a terrific—an almost lurid!—passion for stating the case of the underdog, she has let her pen loose on the Left Banks of the Old World—on its gaols, its studios, its salons, its cafés, its criminals, its midinettes—with a bias of admiration for its midinettes and of sympathy for its law-breakers" (24). Advertising Rhys as an outsider from the West Indies, one who is intimate with jails, criminals, young saleswomen, and artists, Ford firmly locates Rhys within bohemia to promote the "luridness" of her stories. Although Ford explains in a self-deprecating tone that he "tried . . . very hard to induce the author of the *Left Bank* to introduce some sort of topography of that region," knowing the demands of "the book market," this suggestion only spurred Rhys to purge all references to location (25–26).

Ford's mention of "the book market" reminds us that Rhys entered bohemia just as it was being commodified and marketed to "eager consumers of stories of glamorous and sordid individuals, men and women of genius and eccentricity, who lived exciting lives and challenged the conventions" (E. Wilson 3). Wilson argues that while bohemia had become "a marketable commodity" as early as 1900, the modernist period saw an acceleration in such commodification, so that "by 1910 Montmartre was so over-run by tourists that there was a permanent relocation to Montparnasse," which was itself "transformed into a commercialized entertainment centre" by the end of World War I (E. Wilson 42,

43). By the 1920s, when Rhys wrote *The Left Bank*, there was a thriving tourist industry that ushered people to "bohemian" studios and cafés (Nicholson 235).

A 1927 review of *The Left Bank* attests to Rhys's success in tapping into this market for bohemian culture: "It is the far side of life to which she most often carries the people of her stories, the side of poverty, Bohemianism, unhappiness mixed with reckless freedom" (Rev. of *The Left Bank, Saturday* 287). Yet, after noting Ford's "generous introduction" to the collection, this same critic finds fault with Rhys's "little segments . . . tinged with a slightly hysterical sentiment," for being "so slight, so flashing, that their impression on the mind scarcely survives the reading"; this "indicates that Miss Rhys's vision of things has not yet clarified, though the tricks of her trade are already mastered" (287). The same year, a critic in the *Times Literary Supplement* goes so far as to draw a distinction between Ford's clarity and Rhys's haziness: "In his interesting preface Mr. Ford writes with easy authority about the particular qualities of Parisian Bohemianism, and his slightly consolatory air, as of a specialist called in suddenly for an important diagnosis, is distinctly pleasing. By comparison, Miss Rhys's sketches and short character studies seem almost tentative" (Rev. of *The Left Bank, Times* 320). Putting aside the gender stereotypes of associating femininity with "hysterical sentiment" or "tentativeness," we can see that this criticism is typical of modernists whose auditory narrative techniques give their works an immediate appeal to the ear rather than allowing them to paint a picture from a distanced "authoritative" point of view. More importantly, I suggest that Rhys purposely denies her readers a lasting impression, preferring instead that they listen to the voice of the bohemian woman. As I will later argue, by marketing a fragmented and alluring bohemian voice, Rhys is able to resist the voyeuristic gaze that so often objectified the female bohemian.

Although this chapter is mainly concerned with Rhys's use of interior monologue, the third-person narratives of *The Left Bank* establish Rhys's ideas about popular gramophone recordings and bohemian culture, which offer essential context when reading her novels. The way in which an artist is captured and possessed, not just through a recording but also through patronage, is explored in the short story "At the Villa d'Or" (1927), where Mrs. Valentine, an American millionaire, is a "patroness of the Arts, fond of making discoveries in Montparnasse and elsewhere" (75). A young singer, Sara, who lives with Mrs. Valentine and her husband, is beholden to perform for the wealthy couple in exchange for the "shallow but safe" comforts of their home (75). Even more intimate favors are suggested when the husband, "in a lower tone, grasping Sara's arm above the elbow," asks if she will take a trip to a casino with him while his wife plays

"La Bergère Légère" (a song about an elusive seducing shepherdess) on the Victrola in another room (77). Near the end of the short story, however, the patroness explains that sometimes she is "terrified" by the recorded voice of the phonograph when she considers "how strange it is that lovely music—and voices of people who are dead—like Caruso—coming out of a black box. Their voices—Themselves in fact" (78). In many ways, this affirms Adorno's observation that while a mass-produced recording offers a less authentic representation of the singer, it still "absorbs into itself, in [a] process of petrification, the very life that would otherwise vanish" ("Form" 59). Perhaps this terrifies the patroness because the phonograph clarifies what she does with artists: she collects them as objects of entertainment and stifles their freedom in the process. Rhys here draws a parallel between the way in which the phonograph uncannily captures the disembodied voice of the artist and the way in which artists like Sara are objectified when they must commodify their art to survive. This applies to Rhys's interior monologues, which commodify the bohemian voice for mass consumption.

Throughout her writing, Rhys is critical of the affluent who patronize the arts both because of their assumption that if they support an artist, they in some way own the artist—"Their voices—Themselves in fact"—and because most bohemian artists were averse to the financial preoccupations and bourgeois class that patrons represented. Focusing on modernist bohemian salons, Janet Lyon posits that there was a "negative critique of salons mounted by authors who themselves benefited from the artistic connections and symbolic capital that circulated through the site of the salon" (691). We see this disdain for the salon in Rhys's *Quartet* (1929), where it is associated with the exploitative patronizing of the Heidlers, characters loosely based on Ford Madox Ford and his wife. At one of their parties, H. J. Heidler is observed by the protagonist, Marya, "walking masterfully up and down the room to the strains of 'If you knew Suzie as I know Suzie' played on the gramophone" (60, 62). Once again, we see a gramophone recording, a 1920s hit about a woman who is proprietarily flaunted by the singer, connected with the way in which affluent patrons objectify the bohemian artists whom they support. Although Marya is not an artist, she still experiences this objectification, as she depends on the Heidlers' hospitality for survival and eventually becomes H. J.'s lover. Rhys's first-person narratives both parallel and voice what is silenced in these popular recordings, which tend to represent women only as sexual objects.

One of Rhys's characters in *The Left Bank* thinks to herself that English people "ask to be shocked and long to be shocked and hope to be shocked, but if you really shock them . . . how shocked they are!" ("La Grosse Fifi" 81, suspension points in original). Two short stories of the collection that use interior monologue echo this sentiment but direct it at the reader, who, like the Heidlers, uses money to buy tantalizing and amusing bohemian tales. In "Hunger," for example, a stream of consciousness is peppered with dashes and ellipses to mimic the hazy thinking of one who has not eaten in five days and ends by rebuking the reader: "I have never gone without food for longer than five days, so I cannot amuse you any longer" (44). This narrator is aware that her hardship is nothing more than entertaining fodder for her reader, who she assumes to be both judgmental and curious, repulsed and engrossed. Yet she denies her reader the lurid story that one might expect of a desperate woman: "I have been a mannequin. I have been . . . no: not what you think . . ." (43, suspension points in original). As the narrator directly addresses the reader, declaring "I tell you . . . I said" and making a "toast" to "Lost Causes," the reader cannot help but listen to the private tale of a bohemian woman (42, 44).

While the narrator of "Hunger" fends off the reader's desire to hear stories of prostitution, she also argues with a bourgeois "invisible and skeptical listener" who blames her for her poverty (42). Similarly, in the short story "Vienne" (1927), the female protagonist's knowledge that her husband's wealth does not come from a reliable (bourgeois) source is reflected in the voices that debate within her interior monologue: "a guardian angel" that "shriek[s]" in her head, revealing her "faults and failures" and advising her to "work" and "be quite different"; a voice that pities her; and one that "coldly" belittles her emotions, telling her, "Go to bed, woman" (109, 110). Here we have the three voices that often battle within Rhys's interior monologues: the narrator who pities herself, the bourgeois voice that encourages her to be an upstanding citizen, and a hardened and jaded voice that accuses her of being sentimental and weak. Underscoring these voices is the bohemian voice, encouraging her to be free, have fun, and appreciate beauty.

By including the judgmental bourgeois voice, Rhys holds a mirror to the reader's cultural assumptions. Just as the patron in "In a Café" buys the phonograph recording about a prostitute "with calm self-assurance," the reader is implicated in consuming the tales of these bohemian women. Whether it is the hungry woman living on her own or the woman living lavishly on the questionable profits of her husband, Rhys markets the voices of her bohemian protagonists to appeal to the public's desire to eavesdrop from a safe distance on the intimate voices of such characters. These voices embody the dialectical tension between the desire to be a respectable member of a community and the desire to be free to appreciate "the extraordinary beauty of life" (Rhys, "Hunger" 44). The bourgeois voice holds out for Rhys's single female characters the comfort and security of married life and the freedom from judgment and risk; yet it is this same secure position that creates a sense of distanced, critical superiority that the bohemian artist abhors.

Rhys's later first-person short story "Let Them Call It Jazz" (1962) brings these issues of the bohemian voice back to the medium of the phonograph recording and, like "In a Café," makes sense of the commodification of the bohemian voice through the marketing of a phonograph recording. This story, however, is exceptional for its narrator, a London immigrant from the West Indies who speaks in a patois, drawing the reader's attention to a distinct voice.[4]

The narrator, Selina, finds herself in Holloway Prison for throwing a rock through her neighbor's window—a response to their repeated complaints about her "abominable language," her "obscene" dancing, and the "dreadful noise" of her singing (169). Imprisoned for "want[ing] to sing," Selina loses her desire to live, until one day she hears a fellow inmate singing the "Holloway song" (172). Without even hearing the words, Selina feels that the "smoky kind of voice . . . could jump the gates of the jail easy and travel far, and nobody could stop it" (173). In this moment, the ability of sound to travel through and beyond walls is liberating. The melody prompts her to eat and gives her hope "that anything can happen" (173). Soon after she is released from prison and finds work as a seamstress, Selina is whistling the "Holloway song" at a party, when a man is smitten with the melody and turns it into a jazz song. When he sells the song and sends Selina some of the profits from the recording sales, she cries for two, perhaps contradictory, reasons: she "let them play it wrong," and worse yet, the "song was all [she] had," and now "it will go from [her] like all the other songs—like everything" (175). Selina feels that she was "*meant*" to hear the song (175, emphasis in original), and the misconstruing and marketing of the song tamper with her initial sense that the song had the power to make the "walls" of the prison "fall" (173).

This short story offers a compelling model for Rhys's writing about and marketing of the bohemian voice and life. While there are important differences between Selina and Rhys, and no easy connection can be drawn between the character and her creator, Selina's experience of having the song that saved her manipulated and sold as jazz shows Rhys's awareness of how, through the mass production of phonograph recordings, art is compromised by the marketplace. This is similar to the loss of "authenticity of vocal sound" that Adorno lamented with the industrialization of record making ("Curves" 48). The short story ends with Selina cynically yet comfortingly telling herself: "Even if they played it on trumpets, even if they played it just right, like I wanted—no walls would fall so soon. 'So let them call it jazz,' I think, and let them play it wrong. That won't make no difference to the song I heard" (175). While Rhys was encouraged by writers like Ford to promote her writing as an authentic voice of the "lurid" bohemian world, her fiction reveals how, in the process of mass marketing, that voice becomes a distanced piece of art. Rhys could "let them call it" an authentic bohemian voice, but the crafted interior monologue would always be distinct from the artist's inner speech.

The two third-person novels that Rhys published after her collection of short stories were both promoted as giving authentic pictures of bohemian women. A 1931 advertisement for *After Leaving Mr. Mackenzie* (1931), for example, quotes the writer Winifred Holtby, who testifies of Rhys, "She knows the left bank of the Seine, she knows the boarding houses of Bloomsbury and Bayswater; she knows poverty, the poverty that hides itself behind careful make-up and a flippant manner" (108). For her contemporaries, Rhys's first-hand knowledge of a particularly feminine poverty and hardness lent authenticity to her representations of bohemian women. Other critics, however, questioned why Rhys wasted her talents on such "profoundly depressing" characters (Rev. of *Good* 614). In a review that essentially summarizes "the peculiarly sordid" plot of *Postures* (1928) (published as *Quartet* in the United States in 1929), the reviewer concludes by relating Rhys's "method" to "the 'films'; a series of clearly cut impressions—set for the most part in the Quartier Montparnasse, a district in which the bourgeois element now struggles for the mastery with every promise of success" (Rev. of *Postures* 706). Rhys's third-person narratives offered critics clearer pictures of her characters, though they also seemed to give them a sense of superiority over her protagonists. One critic sums up *After Leaving Mr. Mackenzie* as "an episode in the life of a prostitute . . . a sordid little story" that "leaves one dissatisfied. It is a waste of talent" (Rev. of *After* 180). Despite the fact that prostitution does not explicitly enter the plot of the novel, it is assumed that the type of woman Rhys represents must be a prostitute—perhaps suggesting that the dissatisfaction here comes from the story not being sordid enough. In the next novel I discuss, *Voyage in the Dark*, the protagonist, Anna, moves into what one contemporary reviewer calls "half-hearted prostitution"—a life that is "pitiable" and "sordid" yet offers some "serenity and hope" (Rev. of *Voyage* 752). While the revulsion that some critics have for Rhys's characters reflects a general bourgeois disdain for the bohemian lifestyles that they embody, Rhys's insistence on giving these women distinctive voices in her interior-monologue novels, *Voyage in the Dark* and *Good Morning, Midnight*, forces the reader to lend an ear to her characters and let them enter the reader's "private acoustic space" (Sterne, *Audible* 155).

The "Two Tunes" of *Voyage in the Dark*

In a letter to Evelyn Scott, Rhys uses a musical analogy to describe the concurrence of the past and the present experienced by Anna Morgan, the protagonist and first-person narrator of *Voyage in the Dark*. After explaining that the novel has "something to do with time being an illusion," where "the past exists—side by side with the present," she continues, "I tried to do it by making the past (the West Indies) very vivid—the present dreamlike (downward career of girl)—starting of course piano and ending fortissimo" (Rhys, *Jean Rhys* 24). At one point titled "Two Tunes" by Rhys, *Voyage in the Dark* employs the immediacy of quick-paced stream of consciousness when the narrator is recalling the past and a distanced deadpan tone when she is reporting the present (Rhys, *Jean Rhys* 149). This is displayed at the very start of the narrative as Anna considers the distinction between the coldness of England and the warmth of her homeland, triggering a long list of sensory associations: "the smell of the streets and the smells of frangipani and lime juice and cinnamon and cloves, and sweets made of ginger and syrup, and incense after funerals or Corpus Christi processions . . . and the smell of the sea-breeze and the different smell of the land-breeze" (7–8). In contrast to these enticing smells and tastes, which are excitedly piled up between the repeated conjunction *and*, England is a sequence of "little grey street[s]," where "you were perpetually moving to another place which was perpetually the same" (8). The interweaving of these two tunes—one overflowing with variety and the other dulled with repetition—directs the reader's attention to the auditory nature of interior monologue, which shifts in tempo and tone throughout the narrative. Moreover, the negativity with which Anna depicts England establishes her skepticism of the assumed superiority of the colonial empire and her wariness of assimilation.

Several other voices, however, clamor to be heard within Anna's stream of consciousness. In the mere scope of one page, Anna's inner speech is taken over by an advertisement, a textbook description of Dominica, and a memory of the first time she saw England, which includes repeated lines from her stepmother, Hester. These voices reveal the forces that construct Anna's inner speech—her sense of self. The advertisement indicates the culturally constructed ideal feminine body type, as it advises, "No fascination without curves. Ladies, realize your charms" (17). Anna considers buying this product, "Venus Carnis," because it "makes your neck fat," which might give some warmth on "the damned cold nights" (17). The thought of the cold leads her to think of the latitude and longitude of Dominica, followed by a quoted textbook description of the island (17). These geographical and textbook representations of her homeland show her awareness of how Dominica is perceived by the dominant colonial power, England. While these paper representations have a power over her homeland— the island, Anna thinks, is "all crumpled into hills and mountains as you would crumple a piece of paper"—they also cannot ever fully represent her country (17). Unlike the reality of Dominica, which can never be contained on paper, the reality of England seems "smaller" and "meaner" than its literary representation (17). In a long sentence filled with dashes and bookended by ellipses, Anna expresses her disappointment with a country she has read about "ever since she could read":

> the streets like smooth shut-in ravines and the dark houses frowning down—oh I'm not going to like this place I'm not going to like this place I'm not going to like this place—you'll get used to it Hester kept saying I expect you feel like a fish out of water but you'll soon get used to it—now don't look like a Dying Dick and Solemn Davy as your poor father used to say you'll get used to it . . . (17, suspension points in original)

This internalized admonishment not to look sad is repeated later in the novel, as Anna thinks, "*It's soppy always to look sad*" (35, emphasis in original). As phrases from a multitude of sources repeat throughout Anna's stream of consciousness, the reader discerns dialectical tensions between England and the West Indies, the bourgeois and the bohemian.

This bourgeois-bohemian dialectic is deepened as Anna internalizes judgmental British voices. For instance, an earlier accusation from her landlady is replayed as inner speech when she first has sex with Walter: "'*Crawling up the stairs at three o'clock in the morning,*' she said. Well, *I'm crawling up the stairs*" (37, emphasis in original). Here, Anna's interior voice is shaped and determined by her landlady's accusation. As her affair with Walter is ending, she thinks, "Everyone says the man's bound to get tired and you read it in all the books. But I never read now, so they can't get at me like that, anyway" (74). Despite the fact that Anna realizes that such voices come from elsewhere, she still repeats this warning ("the man's bound to get tired") twice in her head (74). Evidently, even without reading books, Anna has internalized these bourgeois warnings against compromising "feminine" modesty through the influence of the people around her.

Discussing the bohemian figures Nina Hamnett and Viva King, Elizabeth Wilson concludes that their "sexual freedom and autonomy" could also be interpreted as "a search for an ever-elusive security and sexual fulfillment" (109). English bohemian women, in particular, were "to provide ambiance, atmosphere and sex, to entertain and at other times to keep out of the way" (E. Wilson 110). While Anna desires security, she ends up in the role of providing ambiance and sex. This bohemian position is affirmed when we learn that she is reading Émile Zola's *Nana* (1880), a novel that tracks a young bohemian woman's life from prostitution to a talentless theatrical rise to her eventual physical demise (punishment through smallpox). While their similar names, Anna and Nana, prompt the reader to parallel these women, the fact that we learn Nana's name before we learn Anna's allows her story to be a sort of blueprint for Anna's story. The book makes Anna "sad, excited and frightened," not because of the content but because of "the endless procession of words . . . the look of the dark, blurred words going on endlessly" (9). The commodified object of Nana's story, the very print of the novel, excites and frightens Anna. In this metatextual moment, Rhys suggests that the fate of women like Anna and Nana is often determined by the cultural stereotypes and expectations that are created by such commodification—of both the women themselves and the stories about them. The public's desire to hear such lurid stories makes for an "endless" supply of women who will internalize these narratives, mechanically following the plot that has been set out for them. Like Nana, Anna is physically punished for her sexual behavior by the end of the novel with her botched abortion, where it is hinted that Anna will keep "endlessly" repeating the same plot. I would argue, however, that it is the interior-monologue form that makes *Voyage in the Dark* more than just a commodified, stereotypical narrative; Anna's internal conflicts and voice complicate any simplistic reading of her story. While Anna internalizes the voices and texts around her, she is also a performer—both musically and sexually—and thus, at times, she enacts or even modifies these heard sounds.

We see such modification when Anna, during her first casual sexual experience, with a man named Carl, explains, "All that evening I did everything to the tune of *Camptown Racecourse*. 'I'se gwine to ride all night, I'se gwine to ride all day'" (154). Before they have sex, Carl corrects Anna's hopeful rewording of the song from "Somebody bet on the bay" to "Somebody won on the bay" (*Voyage* 155). Although Carl revealingly clarifies that "nobody wins," Anna insists on her own lyrics, telling him, "I'll sing it how I like" (155). This desire to be swept up in the melody of the tune, even distorting the words to match one's mood, elucidates how songs often function in Rhys's novels: they bring some happiness to characters, though they also block out the internal voice of reflection. Like the judgmental voices of the bourgeoisie, these songs infiltrate the stream of consciousness and shape Anna's thinking.

Anna self-consciously considers this modification of popular songs when she contemplates the words of "A Cigarette Song"—a music-hall song about a "heart-broken girl" who is encouraged to smoke cigarettes to forget her "despair," since crying will only age you and "injure your beauty with tears" (McLellan). Anna cannot recall the exact words of the song, and so she fills in her own more poetic version, which allows her stream of consciousness to free associate to the Caribbean Sea: "'And drift, drift / Legions away from despair.' It can't be 'legions.' 'Oceans,' perhaps. 'Oceans away from despair.' But it's the sea, I thought. The Caribbean Sea" (*Voyage* 105). Here, Anna makes a deliberate turn in her thinking toward her memories of home as a source of comfort. After this, Anna's interior monologue is taken over by a textbook-sounding description of the "Carib" people and their fierce resistance to and "extermination" by the British (105). The word that Anna first replaces with the militaristic "legions" and then "oceans," which leads her to the sea and memories of the Caribbean resistance, is (in the actual song) simply "right": "And drift, drift, drift right away from despair" (McLellan). As Anna writes desperate letters to Walter, she is warned by the overall message of the song, which "advise[s]" the jilted girl not to cry, die, or become a suffragette, but to realize that the "world doesn't care / For your private despair / And doesn't respect your regret" (McLellan). The best option, according to the popular song, is to smoke a cigarette and "sing, 'I don't care'" (McLellan). While Anna does adopt this attitude of flippant indifference, the misremembered lyrics reveal a desire to escape her misery by aligning with her homeland and resisting the infiltration of British bourgeois culture.

Just as Rhys recalls being "haunted" by popular music, the interior monologues of her characters are likewise "haunted" by popular songs, which the characters manipulate and revise to fit their own purposes. While buoying their spirits, music also aids in constructing their internalized voices. In the above lyrics, for instance, one can discern an originating influence from popular culture for the cynical voice that often interjects into Rhys's interior monologues. The voice of "A Cigarette Song," which warns a young woman that the "world doesn't care / For your private despair," is related to the voice repeatedly heard in *Good Morning, Midnight*, which parenthetically refers to the protagonist, Sasha, as "dear" or "dearie": "(They'll do that [leave her alone] all right, my dear)"; "(At it again, dearie, at it again!)"; and "(Let it pass, dearie, let it pass. What's it matter?)" (Rhys, *Good* 43, 61, 78). This modernist appropriation of popular culture into the stream of consciousness demonstrates how people consume popular culture and integrate it into their sense of self.

Yet, unlike the phonograph records that presented stereotypical songs about women and love, Rhys complicates the bohemian voice on which the reader eavesdrops. Within Anna's interior monologue, Rhys consolidates dialectical tensions between Anna's West Indian memories and her present downtrodden state in England, between bohemian and bourgeois sensibilities, between the colonized and colonizer. This denies the reader any simplistic, "authentic" colonial or bohemian narrative. We see this particularly in the original and revised endings of *Voyage in the Dark*, which depict Anna's monologue as a jumble of fragmented sentences from other characters and memories of her childhood. These internalized words play over and over in Anna's head without her control as she bleeds from her abortion. While Rhys originally wanted Anna to die, the revised ending leaves her fate open to interpretation, with Anna repeating the words from the doctor that she (like a record player stuck on the same song) will be "ready to start all over again in no time at all" (187). Aside from this major adjustment, however, there are minor changes in the role of music and the gramophone in the different endings that are worth exploring.

In her original ending, Rhys devotes more description to Anna's childhood memories, opening the last part of the novel with Anna as a child being told to stay still for a photograph. The original places an emphasis on vision and Anna's inability to control her body. She is told by the photographer and her mother to "smile" and "keep quite still," but her "hand shot up of its own accord," ruining the photograph ("Voyage [Original Version]" 382). As Anna remembers crying and her mother telling her that she is "ashamed" of her, the reader is left to connect this experience with Anna's sense of self and her present situation ("Voyage [Original Version]" 382). Prompted by female role models, Anna has tried to smile and visually appease the men in her life so that she can gain their approval and feel secure in their love, but their "love" never went beyond a visual objectification of her youth and beauty. Their idealized (and exoticized) picture of Anna is ruined when her body loses control, and she either cries or, in a more serious loss of control, becomes pregnant.

While both endings focus on her childhood memories of the Dominican Carnival, in the original ending, Anna explicitly acknowledges the sense of defiance inherent in Black Dominican music: "I knew what they were singing they were singing defiance to I don't know what but singing it all the same" ("Voyage [Original Version]" 386). Because Anna, as the daughter of a white former slave owner and a Creole mother, "objectifies race in her casual conversation" and is "still a colonial child in a racist society," she cannot share in the comfort and empowerment of such songs (Savory 59). Indeed, Anna perhaps cannot identify who the singers are defying because their songs would most likely be directed at colonizers like Anna's family. Yet Anna, in her position as a disempowered female in England, recalls their songs of defiance with a degree of understanding. In both versions, Carnival songs are internalized by Anna, creating an auditory cosmopolitanism within her interior monologue.

Anna also feels empowered by another song that she associates with the West Indies, "Connais-tu le Pays?" an aria from the opera *Mignon* (first performed in Paris in 1866). Anna avoids playing this record when she brings a client to her bedroom because it reminds her of her childhood French tutor, an "illegitimate poor old thing" who sang the song "in a thin quavering voice" (162). As they dance to popular tunes, Anna feels the dog from a framed picture titled *Loyal Heart* "star[ing] down at [them] smugly" (161). This observation is followed by a parenthetical side thought about "Connais-tu le Pays?": "(Do you know the country? Of course, if you know the country it makes all the difference. The country where the orange-tree flowers?)" (161). Clarifying through her interior monologue that she *does* know the country gives Anna the strength to voice her anger with her situation. Right after the parenthetical thought above, Anna states, "I can't stand that damned dog any longer," and she throws her shoe at it, breaking the glass frame. When her dancing partner warns that they are making "a row," Anna uncharacteristically replies, "It's all right. We can make as much noise as we like. It doesn't matter" (161).

This scene is significant in both form and content. In it, we once again hear the parenthetical commentaries that Anna maintains within her head, differentiating the voice that observes her present moment from a voice that recalls her past. More importantly, Anna identifies with the song "Connais-tu le Pays?" which is associated with the West Indies and a woman who is the offspring of a prostitute, reminding Anna of her childhood sense of never fulfilling her stepmother's ideal of a proper British lady. She takes refuge in the song, yet she refuses to let the song be cheapened by dancing to it with the man in her room. Similar to Selina in "Let Them Call It Jazz" as well as the masqueraders from Anna's memories, Anna keeps the song for herself. In a similar vein as the "Prince Igor dances" that Rhys recalls paying to hear in the Parisian kiosks in the 1920s, "the wild defiant music seem[s] to pour fresh life into" her ("Songs" vers. 5, p. 4).

Conversely, the picture of the dog above her bed, which advertises the "loyal heart" that is expected of both dogs and women within the home, gazes down at Anna in judgment as she plies her new trade. This image is referred to again in a memory in which Anna pleads for a "white-faced" man in her bed to "stop" having sex with her: she "lay looking at the dog in the picture *Loyal Heart* and watching his chest going in and out" (184). The picture becomes ironically conflated with the commodification of her body. If Anna cannot embody the "loyal heart" of domestic femininity, then she must play the other available stereotype of the whore.

Anna's memories of Carnival, the white-faced man, and the *Loyal Heart* picture crop up in both the original and revised endings of the novel, along with remarks made by her former lover, Walter, and a childhood memory of falling from a horse when she was not able to take her typical sidesaddle riding position. Each of these memories addresses issues of compromised modesty and the fear of transgressing that which is socially acceptable. These memories and Anna's present moment share one aspect: the people that are speaking either do not believe that she is listening or disregard her presence altogether, making her the object of their discussion and eclipsing any possibility of agency. For example, Anna remembers that when her father disparages that life in general is like Carnival, "a mask . . . with an idiot behind it," her stepmother tells him to be quiet because Anna is listening (184; "Voyage [Original Version]" 385). Her father, however, replies, "oh no she isn't . . . she's looking out of the window and quite right too" (184; "Voyage [Original Version]" 385). Although Anna is watching the colorful spectacle of Carnival, she is also being shaped by the words that enter her interior monologue. As these words are recorded and replayed in her mind, the bitterness that may have once been unclear to her as a child has now been clarified through her present situation and adult experiences.

In the revised ending, Anna's friend Laurie laughs with the doctor about how "you girls are too naïve to live," and once they stop, Anna sees a "ray of light" from "under the door like the last thrust of remembering before everything is blotted out" (187, 188). The novel then ends with Anna thinking about "starting all over again," repeating the demeaning words of the doctor (188). But in the original version, Anna only remembers the voices of the adults during Carnival, which "went up and down," while the voices of the doctor and Laurie in the present moment "sounded small like doll's voices" ("Voyage [Original Version]" 386, 389). Revealingly, the doctor's words do not take a place of prominence as they do in the revised version, where they enter Anna's interior monologue and usurp the ending of the novel. In the original ending, the diminutive sounds of the doctor and Laurie are offset by the sound of a gramophone, which is played at Anna's request. Both Mrs. Polo and the doctor assert that the gramophone is inappropriate, with Mrs. Polo first admonishing, "And her wanting the gramophone played. I never heard such a thing"; and the doctor later ordering, "Stop that gramophone" ("Voyage [Original Version]" 389). While we do not know what the gramophone plays, the music stopping is conflated with Anna's memory of the Carnival music stopping: "And the concertina-music stopped and it was so still so still and lovely like just before you go to sleep and it stopped and there was a ray of light along the floor like the last thrust of remembering before everything is blotted out and blackness comes . . ." ("Voyage [Original Version]" 389, suspension points in original). In this ending, Anna's interior monologue is likened to the gramophone record, which is reminiscent of the music of Carnival. When the music stops, Anna can have only one last image and then blackness. If, in Rhys's short stories, gramophone recordings are often associated with the bohemian female voice being exoticized and marketed, then it makes sense that Rhys has Anna die when a few socially empowered characters decide that the music is inappropriate. More importantly, the reader is not presented with a visual of Anna throughout her final ordeal. Deprived of an objectifying image, we are only given a voice, as we are forced to acknowledge and reckon with the memories, music, and voices that have brought Anna to this present moment.

Playing the Interior Monologue of *Good Morning, Midnight*

As with Anna's stream of consciousness, the first-person narrative of *Good Morning, Midnight* can be likened to a gramophone record, but this time, it is the narrator herself, Sasha Jenson, who explicitly makes the comparison. When walking through Paris, she twice warns herself not to allow her memories of time spent there to replay in her mind: "No trailing around aimlessly with cheap gramophone records starting up in your head, no 'Here this happened, here that happened'"; "The gramophone record is going strong in my head: 'Here this happened, here that happened. . . . '" (15, 17, suspension points in original). Here, the recording is not music, but the voice of the narrator, playing automatically through her stream of consciousness. Hence, at the start of the novel, Rhys alerts her reader to the auditory nature of Sasha's interior monologue, which, at times, can sound like a "cheap" popular recording that Sasha merely hears within her head.

I will return to the significance of gramophone recordings and music later in this discussion, but first, it is important to establish the ways in which Rhys uses rooms as metaphors for the private acoustic space of inner speech. The popularization of headphones gave modernists a spatial way of understanding the voice within the head, making inner speech into an aesthetic object that could incorporate disparate voices. Rhys uses hotel rooms and bathrooms as metaphors for private internal space because, like interior monologue, they are simultaneously private and public. While you can have moments of escape and privacy in hotel rooms and bathrooms, they are spaces that are only temporarily inhabited. They were someone else's private space before you and will be someone else's after you have gone. Rhys treats the interior monologue of her protagonists in much the same way. While her novels reflect the private inner thoughts of different women, they are commodified and sold for public consumption. More importantly, the interior monologues of Rhys's first-person narrators are a mixture of public, social voices that have been internalized, making their inner speech, like a bathroom or hotel room, not as private as they may at first seem.

Rhys clarifies the significance of these semiprivate rooms for Sasha's interior monologue by allowing them to speak within her mind. The novel opens not with a personal commentary by Sasha but with her imagining what the room asks her: "'Quite like old times,' the room says. 'Yes? No?'" (9). The generic hotel room that has always been a part of Sasha's life repeats this plea of old camaraderie later in the novel, but this time it ends with a definitive "Yes," indicating that Sasha really has no choice but to live in this room, just as she has no choice but to inhabit the internal space and voice within her. In another dialogue with the room, Sasha replies to the room's welcome, "There you are ... You didn't go off, then?" with "No, no. I thought better of it. Here I belong and here I'll stay" (39). The deictic *here* allows for some flexibility in how we interpret this line. Most explicitly, it refers to the hotel room. However, it also suggests Sasha's internal monologue, a voice that sounds out in an internal space that she cannot escape and which, like the hotel room, is both comforting and accusatory. By including the voice of the room in Sasha's interior monologue, Rhys invites the reader to interpret this literal place as a metaphor for the acoustic space within her mind, where internalized voices converse.

The rooms also indicate Sasha's sense of her station in life. Sasha has come to the point where she is more than familiar with rundown hotels with "dark rooms" and "red curtains" (12). As she takes a bath in the hotel, she hears a man asking the "patronne" for "a nice room" for "a young lady-friend" (33). Sasha can identify with this scenario, as the phrase runs through her mind repeatedly in the narrative: "Swing high. . . . Now, slowly, down. A beautiful room with bath. A room with bath. A nice room. A room"; "A room? A nice room? A beautiful room? A room with bath? Swing high, swing low, swing to and fro. . . . This happened and that happened. . . . And then the days came when I was alone"

(34, 142, suspension points in original). Echoing the gramophone recording in her head that mechanically recalls, "Here this happened. Here that happened," Sasha implies that she knows how the story about the "nice room" goes and what will be expected in exchange for it (15, 17). She has gotten used to the swinging unpredictability of her material existence, where she can sometimes afford, or finds herself offered, a "nice room" with a bath. Like the rooms that talk above, however, these rooms also suggest more than just Sasha's material conditions. They stand in for the expectations and excitement she may have once had for life, expectations that are continually readjusted. Now, for Sasha, "A room is a place where you hide from the wolves outside and that's all any room is" (38). She no longer expects a beautiful room, and her interior monologue likewise is no longer a naive and hopeful discourse.

In the quotations above, Sasha interweaves her own experiences of rooms with the title song of *Swing High, Swing Low*—a 1937 film about a woman who reluctantly falls in love with and is then jilted by a trumpet player in Panama. The lyrics of the song recommend music and "swinging" as a way to stay happy and relevant to those around you: "When your one and only / Complains that he's lonely and blue / A rhythmical campaign can do more than champagne / To see him through" (*Swing*). On the one hand, this is exactly what Sasha is doing for herself as she recites the permutations of the different types of rooms to the rhythm of the song. There is a comfort in this idea that fortune can change from high to low and that one must just follow the rhythms of life. On the other hand, the song seems to be speaking specifically to women and their roles in keeping men happy, perhaps distracting them with a little dance or song. Sasha has been through this routine and is done with such entertaining. She subtly connects how men barter rooms for sexual favors from women with the song's message of women being able to distract men from their "blues" by keeping their "swinging . . . up to date" (*Swing*). Rhys, however, subverts the message of the song by having Sasha use the tune herself as a way of dealing with her own shifts in fortune and of exposing how all rooms are essentially the same. She thinks, "But never tell the truth about this business of rooms, because it would bust the roof off everything and undermine the whole social system. All rooms are the same" (38). Whether one is "high" or "low," a room serves the same purpose. And if we return to rooms as metaphors for the private acoustic space of one's interior monologue, then Sasha is also drawing a connection among people as sharing the same linguistically constructed sense of self. The song itself is evidence of this, as it is a popular song, heard by many, which has become part of the fabric of Sasha's inner speech.

Throughout *Good Morning, Midnight*, overheard songs spark nostalgia or influence Sasha's mood depending on their emotional register. While Sasha is scornful of "the extremely respectable," who "think in terms of a sentimental ballad," she seems to identify with and find comfort in these very same ballads (42). The novel begins with Sasha recapping how she was brought to tears by a woman humming the song "Gloomy Sunday," which made her remember "something" (9–10). This song, composed by the Hungarian composer Rezső Seress in 1933, was rumored to cause listeners to commit suicide due to its melancholic tone (Patakfalvi-Czirják 146). An overheard song sparks positive thoughts in Sasha, however, when she wakes from a nightmare about a wounded man who claims to be her father as she is forced along by pointing fingers to an "Exhibition" (13). As Sasha overhears someone singing a waltz from the comedic opera *Les Saltimbanques*, the upbeat and happy lyrics make her think, "I believe it's a fine day," even after the disturbing visuals of her nightmare (13). Such an easy mood swing is again facilitated by music—this time, the repeated tune "Swing High, Swing Low"—when she recounts stepping out to "the air so sweet, as only it can be in Paris" after being humiliated and leaving her job with Mr. Blank (29–30). And her feelings of "defiance" are emboldened when she brings together a World War I song and a folk song, as she "drink[s] [her]self to death" (43): "Don't like jam, ham or lamb, and I don't like roly-poly"; "One more river to cross, that's Jordan, Jordan" (44). While Sasha sees her face as a "tortured and tormented mask" that she can "hang . . . up on a nail" or further obscure with a hat and "veil," singing gives her a way to announce her defiance to the world (43). Whereas her outward appearance allows people to judge her "face gradually breaking up" and is at best hidden by a costume, her voice actively expresses her dislike for the world and her identification with the downtrodden (43).

Popular songs transport Sasha to her past and often evoke emotions of youthful defiance and bohemianism. For instance, the memory of a younger Sasha being hungry in Paris and getting drunk with a man who speaks to her on the street is bracketed with the repeated line, "Walking to the music of *L'Arlésienne*" (86, 91). Written by Georges Bizet, this orchestral music was popularized from Alphonse Daudet's (less popular) 1872 play *L'Arlésienne*. This music is played in the café where Sasha and the man drink, and Sasha attests to its uncanny ability to trigger the memory: "I've just got to hear that music now, any time, and I'm back at the Café Buffalo, sitting by that man. And the music going heavily" (87). Although Sasha has not eaten a meal in weeks, she forgoes food at the café and instead "chews" over a letter that a woman has written to the man, asking for money for shoes (89). Much like the affluent who consumed the words and music of bohemia, this man is happy to "slum it" with Sasha until he finds out that she has her "own little story of misery" (90).

Yet far from being defeated by the incongruity of fortune, Sasha stresses that she does not mind when the man abandons her once he learns that she is hungry. Her interior monologue is insistent on a sort of insight that comes of hunger: "If you think I minded, then you've never lived like that, plunged in a dream, when all the faces are masks and only the trees are alive and you can almost see the strings that are pulling the puppets. Close-up of human nature—isn't that worth something?" (90). Although Sasha is not an artist, she echoes the sentiments of bohemian artists who saw their poverty as an important condition of their work and insights. As Elizabeth Wilson explains,

> while on the one hand the artist saw himself as a romantic genius elevated above the common run, on the other his fascination with the everyday, the obscure, the forbidden and the sordid contributed to the perception of the bohemian artist as one who deliberately went "slumming" or was filled with *"nostalgie de la boue."* This eventually led to a blurring of the very distinction between art and life. The bohemian identity came to be associated with the gutter, with low life and the forbidden. (24)

As we listen in on Sasha's interior monologue, she unselfconsciously fits within the myth of the bohemian artist. While she does not make a fuss over staying in a hotel where Verlaine and Rimbaud once stayed, she all the same makes a point of slipping this fact into her narrative (39). Rhys purposefully portrays Sasha as a bohemian, who makes her life into art but does not produce artwork that can be consumed. The artwork that is to be consumed is the novel's interior monologue itself—Sasha's bohemian voice.

The most significant musical scene of the novel is when Sasha's new artist friend Serge "puts on some béguine music, Martinique music, on an old gramophone" and dances for her wearing a West African mask that he made (92). The mask reminds Sasha of "peering" eyes that ask, "Who's your father and have you got any money, and if not, why not? Are you one of us? Will you think what you're told to think and say what you ought to say?" (92). She also hears the voice of a family member who once asked, "Why didn't you drown yourself in the Seine?" along with the overheard voice of a woman in a Parisian café, asking "Qu'est-ce qu'elle fout ici, la vielle?" (92). Conversely, the music triggers a memory of the West Indies: "I am lying on a hammock looking up into the branches of a tree. The sound of the sea advances and retreats as if a door were being opened and shut" (92). As Sasha's interior monologue is taken over by the lyrics of the Creole song, she is able to escape the judging questions of the mask and sing along with words that express a shared pain in love and youth. Similar to Anna's recollection of the masks and music of Carnival in *Voyage*, a contrast is affirmed between judging and malicious eyes and the exhilaration of the music.

The initial comfort of the music gives way to sadness, however, as it marks a lost youth and the ultimate inability of others to empathize with her as an outsider. This is indicated by the judgmental phrases that interrupt Sasha's interior monologue. She recalls comments made by the man who bought her drinks and abandoned her once he ascertained that she was hungry: "(*Have you been dancing too much?*) . . . (*Mad for pleasure, all the young people*)" (92, emphasis in original). Sasha's interior monologue is presented as an assemblage of the remembered voices of others; lyrics of the Martinique song, which Sasha translates within her interior monologue (93); and her own voice narrating the present moment and memory. This is a specifically bohemian voice because it articulates a dialectic of the socially outcast artist and the necessary bourgeois foil of outrage. Sasha's interior monologue demonstrates how "Bohemia and bourgeois were—and are—parts of a single field: they imply, require, and attract each other" (Seigel 5).

By marketing a fragmented and alluring bohemian voice, Rhys is able to resist the voyeuristic gaze that so often objectified the female bohemian figure. This objectification of vision is manifested in Sasha's nightmare of "an enormous machine, made of white steel," which has many "long, thin arms" with "an eye, the eyelashes stiff with mascara" at the end of each arm (187). Sasha reasons that once "Venus is dead; Apollo is dead; even Jesus is dead," heralding the end to love, art, and religion, "all that is left in the world is an enormous machine" (187). Although the eyes are "extraordinarily flexible and very beautiful . . . the grey sky, which is the background, terrifies" her (187). This feminine machine, with mascaraed eyelashes and thin arms, is reminiscent of the "automaton" Sasha calls herself at the start of the novel. The female eyes suggest the internalized masculine gaze, as Sasha continually inspects herself to make sure she looks respectable and attractive (10). But the machine also resonates with the internal "film-mind" and gramophone recordings that Sasha warns herself against, parenthetically reminding herself at one point, "For God's sake watch out for your film-mind. . . ." (176, suspension points in original). These appropriations of technology within the human body and psyche indicate the mechanically constructed idea of femininity, seen in film, heard on the gramophone, and popularized through the consumption of bohemian culture. Sasha understands parts of her stream of consciousness to be a construct of such media. This is implied by her identification with the exotic-sounding song that accompanies the machine: "the arms wave to an accompaniment of music and of song. Like this: 'Hotcha-hotcha-hotcha. . . . ' And I know the music; I can sing the song" (187, suspension points in original).

The next paragraph begins with Sasha separating herself from the cynical voice in her head and trying to silence the voice with drink: "I have another drink. Damned voice in my head, I'll stop you talking" (187). By objectifying this voice as "she," Sasha makes a conscious distinction among the voices within her head. While I do not suggest that one is authentic and the other a social construct, as all the registers of her interior monologue are constructs of language and culture, Sasha interprets the cynical voice as a "she" that oppresses the more sentimental side of herself. There is the "grimacing devil in [her] head," who "sings a sentimental song—'The roses all are faded and the lilies in the dust'" (175). This voice wants to be seduced by a gigolo, to feel young and loved once again. This is countered, however, by the experienced voice that can commiserate with the old Jewish banjo player in the painting that she purchases from her friend Serge. She replies to this musician, "I know the words to the tune you're playing. I know the words to every tune you've played on your bloody banjo. Well, I mustn't sing any more—there you are. Finie la chanson. The song is finished. Finished" (185). Singing at times is a metaphor for her youth and more free-spirited living; while at other times, music is reduced to an automatic gramophone recording, repeating "hotcha-hotcha-hotcha" (187). This tune, with its slightly exotic associations, is one that Sasha has been indoctrinated to sing.

It would be too simplistic to create a dualism in Rhys's work between vision and audition. Although vision is rarely represented in a positive light, as exemplified by the sinister eyes of the steel machine, Sasha's "film-mind," and the accusatory masks found in both *Voyage in the Dark* and *Good Morning, Midnight*, audition as well can foster automatic responses and clichéd understandings. Rhys herself writes ambiguously about popular music as both haunting and giving a rhythm to her life: "I have been haunted by popular songs all my life. Walking to some tune in my head. Walking, talking to it. I still don't know why I find cheap popular music so intransient" ("Songs" vers. 1, p. 1). Similarly, Sasha and Anna both use music to access a sense of defiance and comfort, making it one of the few channels for a momentary sense of fulfillment and expression. The inclusion of music also enhances the auditory nature of Rhys's interior monologues. Similar to the mixed responses to and function of popular phonograph recordings, Rhys's interior monologues are a mixture of inherited bourgeois judgments and attempts to express basic desires and bohemian impulses.

The interior monologue form gives these characters a voice that demands to be heard. As we read these voices, the inner speech of another penetrates our consciousness.

What do we get out of drawing attention to the auditory nature of stream of consciousness? Rhys shows how this voice inside the head is never a singular voice but one pieced together from other heard and read voices and songs throughout one's lifetime; once the stream of consciousness is made into an audible recordable object, it can be crafted and depersonalized by the artist. Moreover, this voice does not let the reader gaze on the female bohemian through visual descriptions of her body, clothing, and mannerisms. Instead, the internal voice of the protagonist enters the reader's headspace.

Ihde asserts that when we come across something unknown, it is our inner speech that helps us familiarize and come to know the thing: "The voice of language domesticates the World" (142). Rhys's and Joyce's interior monologues show us how their characters interact with the world and come to understand it. While vision often distances them from this world, encouraging judgment and analysis, sounds are incorporated into, influence, and construct the stream of consciousness. Likewise, when we are allowed to eavesdrop on this inner speech through the act of reading, the voice of the other is momentarily made less strange to us.

6

Turning Words into Sounds

Samuel Beckett's Repetition and the Tape Recorder

Beckett's sad yet humorous play *Krapp's Last Tape*, published almost ten years after his Trilogy (*Molloy, Malone Dies, The Unnamable*), centers on the prop of a tape recorder. The old Krapp listens to recordings of his younger self and records his voice once again, listing the small pleasures of his present life. The play consists mostly of recordings of Krapp's voice, edited and replayed in the context of Krapp's present time. As Krapp rewinds and replays an old recording titled "Farewell to Love" nearly three times, the audience becomes familiar with repeated fragments such as "Let me in," "Past midnight. Never knew such silence," and "But under us all moved, and moved us, gently, up and down, and from side to side" (60, 61, 63). The repeated playing of these slowed poetic lines, which are about Krapp floating in a punt with a lover he is about to leave, allows the audience to share in his remembrance of the piece (63). Though Krapp's recorded narratives are there to tell of what he has lost by sacrificing his "chance at happiness" for his artistic aspirations, there is simultaneously a sense of pleasure experienced by both Krapp and the audience in hearing the repeated story—a pleasure not unlike Krapp's bodily and acoustic reveling in the repeated word "spool" (63, 56). The repetition of the recording heightens our perception of the textured sounds of certain words, charging the fragment with an internally generated signification that carries through the play. This repetition draws our attention to the aesthetics of the recurring fragment, and yet we share in Krapp's frustration with his former self. The audience wonders whether, ironically, this love would have inspired Krapp to be a great writer, unlike the narcissistic "vision" that called for a solitary life.[1]

The mechanical reproduction of Krapp's voice through the apparatus of the tape recorder enacts a split between the voice of Krapp and the source of that voice, Krapp himself, to which an audience can visually attest. In Patrick Magee's portrayal of Krapp, the deep, full tone of the voice of his younger self contrasts so greatly with the present Krapp's raspy and high voice, one would think they were two different people. This sense of detachment between a character and the voice that speaks him is also found in Beckett's fiction. Although they do not make use of a literal tape recorder, Beckett's narrators repeat themselves just like Krapp, fixating on and repeating certain stories and words. Indeed, the narrators of Beckett's later novels and prose pieces listen to the voice that speaks them as if it was mechanically reproduced: "that is to say the same things recur. . . . It's mechanical" (*Texts for Nothing* 136). It is through this repetition, however, that the reader begins to appreciate the sounds of the words themselves, just as Krapp plays with the word *spool*.

While critics have addressed Beckett's repetition of themes, incidents, and characters, this chapter will explore Beckett's linguistic repetition.[2] Within Beckett's fiction, particularly from the Trilogy to his later short prose pieces, there is a proliferation of phrases such as "no matter," "I say it as I hear it," "little by little," and variations of "I can't go on, I'll go on," which are familiar to the reader because they have been repeated not only within each narrative but throughout Beckett's oeuvre. As the reader develops a growing sense of familiarity with such phrases, he or she shares in the pleasure and frustration that becomes associated with their mechanical-like reproduction. These paradoxical associations of pleasure and frustration relate to how Beckett's characters wrestle with a voice speaking a language that rings false in their ears yet is their only means to expressing a "self."

About the same time that Beckett was experimenting with a repetition that aestheticizes words, a French radio technician for the Parisian radio station Radio Television Français (RTF), Pierre Schaeffer, was using the new technology of the tape recorder to aestheticize everyday sounds. Although there is no evidence that Beckett heard *musique concrète*, he devoted a great deal of his time to listening to records and playing the piano. While Beckett preferred Haydn, Mozart, Beethoven, Chopin, Schumann, Brahms, and Schubert, he also was exposed to some modern composers such as Claude Debussy, Morton Feldman, Anton Webern, Paul Hindemith, Alban Berg, Béla Bartók, and Erik Satie (Debrock 69). Discussing Beckett's uncharacteristically easy collaboration with Feldman, Guy Debrock proposes that "he may have noted Feldman's fascination for sounds in themselves, a fascination not unlike Beckett's own for the sounds of words" (70). Schaeffer's work, too, was primarily about prompting listeners to appreciate everyday sounds not as byproducts of life but as sounds worth listening to in themselves.

Schaeffer recorded everyday sounds and manipulated them so that audiences would appreciate their acoustic qualities rather than hear them as referents to reality. He called this new art form *musique concrète* and defined it as "a commitment to compose with materials taken from 'given' experimental sound in order to emphasize our dependence, no longer on preconceived sound abstractions, but on sound fragments that exist in reality and that are considered as discreet and complete sound objects, even if and above all when they do not fit in with the elementary definitions of music theory" (14). Schaeffer's "symphonies," which strove to do away with traditional notation and instead compose with "sound fragments" from "reality," began in 1948 with multiple phonographs. However, his goal of making recorded sounds unidentifiable and thus appreciated in and of themselves was not completely realized until he began to experiment with the manipulating techniques of splicing, reversing, and looping offered by the tape recorder.

While Beckett may not have known about Schaeffer, Donald McWhinnie, a BBC producer who worked on Beckett's first radio play, *All That Fall* (written in 1956 and broadcast in 1957), visited Schaeffer's studio in the mid-1950s and encouraged the BBC to set up a similar studio; McWhinnie realized that "the solution to producing Beckett was to be found in the new technology of the tape machine" (Porter 441). The type of tape recording and manipulating that Schaeffer was doing opened a path for BBC producers to imagine how they might create a soundscape for Beckett's play that could evoke the real world without merely creating real-world sound effects. As Emilie Morin explains in her essay on Beckett's radio plays, "*Musique concrète* techniques afforded something very distinctive: namely, a partial freedom from causal alignments between a clearly-identifiable sound and a clearly-identifiable event, which proved germane to meeting the demands of Beckett's radio plays" (2). Daniel Albright similarly connects Beckett with Schaeffer, pointing out that Beckett "lived in the right country to investigate the possibilities of tape recording" (*Beckett* 87). Drawing on Beckett's use of the tape recorder in *Krapp's Last Tape* (as opposed to his mere mention of a phonograph in *Embers* in 1959), Albright concludes that "the tape recorder is Beckett's preferred sound-reproduction machine" (*Beckett* 87).[3] While these critics explore connections between the tape recorder, *musique concrète*, and Beckett's radio and stage dramas, I will demonstrate how this connection can be extended to his fiction. I consider how Schaeffer's goal of divorcing real-world sounds from their referents so that audiences could aesthetically appreciate their acoustic qualities parallels Beckett's goal of stripping words of their referents so that the reader can aesthetically experience the acoustic qualities of language. My hope is that as we come to understand Schaeffer's methods, goals, and anxieties, we can more deeply appreciate Beckett's narrative experiments with repetition, which were designed to let language fall into "disrepute" ("German" 172).

The art of splicing and looping magnetic tape allowed common sounds to be defamiliarized so that listeners could take pleasure in hearing familiar fragments of sound replayed in new contexts; however, with overuse and experimentation, such manipulation easily could seem too mechanical and obscure to listeners. We can discern this too in Beckett's fiction, where words and phrases are defamiliarized through repetition, both engendering a heightened pleasure for the sounds of words themselves and frustrating the conventions of plot and reading for meaning. Although the mechanical repetition of his characters may make their voices seem detached from them, part of their frustration is the recognition that their voices are indeed coming from themselves. On the one hand, this mechanically repeating voice is a source of pleasure, as it affirms existence and allows for some play with the texture and substance of sound, which can bring bodily joy; on the other hand, this mechanically repeating voice is frustrating in that it feels like an automatic foreign entity that is distanced from the narrator.

Just as music made from manipulated tape-recorded sounds sparked a general reevaluation of notation and melody, Beckett's repetition makes the reader reevaluate the function and use of language. As this chapter surveys his novels from *Watt* to the Trilogy, I trace a development in Beckett's fiction from using repetition to momentarily infuse language with a deeper significance and meaning to using it to cause language to be experienced as pure sound, dismissing the notion of a fictional reality to which words might refer. By apprehending the acoustic qualities of language, the reader affirms the existence of Beckett's narrators simply through their incessant vocalization. Such auditory narrative subverts the graphic/textual phenomenon of reading for meaning and redirects the reader's attention to the sounds of words. These radical experiments in form, I argue, are clarified and more deeply appreciated when read alongside the art of *musique concrète*, where, just as with Beckett's narrative, sound was to be appreciated not for its meaning but "for its own substance" (Schaeffer 13).

Repetition in Music and *Musique Concrète*

In his study of the philosophy of music, Peter Kivy asks why it is that "musical repeats" are central to what has come to be called "absolute music"—purely instrumental music of the late eighteenth and early nineteenth century. For example, if one were to extract the repetition from J. S. Bach's *Goldberg Variations*, the work would be cut in half. Kivy explains that such repeats "perform an obvious and vital function in that they are the composer's way of allowing us, indeed compelling us to linger; to retrace our steps so that we can fix the fleeting sonic pattern" (352). Far from feeling redundant, these musical repeats, which are each heard within a new context within the larger musical composition, give the listener the sense that "we are hearing different music; we are not going back but going on" (Kivy 340). In a dialogue about how the word *groove* suggests the repetitive rhythms of music (among other meanings), ethnomusicologists Charles Keil and Steven Feld consider why we get such pleasure from repetition in music: "We've got this developed cortex from watching the leaves flutter, tracking the animals, from grooving on reality and reveling in the repetition and redundancy of information with minor but frequent variations. *Slight* variations. Slight variations become magical, hypnotizing, mesmerizing. They give you deep identification or participatory consciousness. You flow into repetition" (23, emphasis in original). Just as Keil roots our affinity with the repetition of music to a more general repetition in life, it makes sense to think of language as a similar groove, anchored in repetition with slight variation. As I move to considering the mechanical repetition of *musique concrète*, it is important to keep in mind the "deep identification or participatory consciousness" that musical repetition engenders; it is precisely this participation that Beckett calls on in his textual repetition, which is sounded out by one's reading voice.

Yet, in Schaeffer's experiments with *musique concrète*, the musical repeat is taken to extremes, just as the typical repetition within language is taken to extremes within Beckett's narratives. Continuous mechanical repetition became essential for *musique concrète*, as Schaeffer came to realize that repetition made sounds less identifiable to listeners. For example, in 1948, Schaeffer composed *Études de bruits* from a wide range of recorded sounds:

> stokers on six locomotives with personal voices and buffers conducted by Schaeffer at the Batignolles depot (later combined with library samples of rolling wagon wheels); an amateur orchestra . . . tuning up to a clarinet call thus embellished with "fioriture" (later combined with Jean-Jacques Grunenwald's piano improvisations live at the studio); and Pierre Boulez on the piano in classic, romantic, impressionist, and atonal harmonizations of a given theme (later cut, reversed, and spliced). Closing the set, an ad libitum mix of objets trouvés gathered Balinese music, American harmonica, and French barge round Sacha Guitry's singing. (Palombini)

These musical compositions were not popular on a large scale, and Schaeffer's journals testify to his misgivings about the art. As he excitedly records six train engines on phonographs, relishing the different "voices" of each train (Schaeffer 11), he questions their musicality when he returns to the studio to work with them: "It's exciting, but is it music? Isn't the noise of buffers first and foremost anecdotal, and thus antimusical? If this is so, then there's no hope and my research is absurd" (12). Here, Schaeffer is most concerned that his recorded sounds are too "identifiable," so that a listener will consider them not music but mere references to the real world (6).

Schaeffer articulates this problem further: "So, every sound phenomenon (like the words of a language) can be taken for its relative meaning or for its own substance. As long as meaning predominates, and is the main focus, we have literature and not music. But how can we forget meaning and isolate the in-itself-ness of the sound phenomenon?" (13). Schaeffer discovers two ways to make sounds "unidentifiable" and thus a "musical element": "*Distinguishing* an element (hearing it in itself, for its texture, matter, color)" and "*Repeating* it. Repeat the same sound fragment twice: there is no longer event, but music" (13, emphasis in original). By trial and error, Schaeffer realized that a sound fragment, taken out of its larger context and repeated, loses its attachment to a real-world referent and instead is more likely to be heard purely as sound.

Heeding the parallel that Schaeffer draws between words and sound, as he suggests that "every sound phenomenon (like the words of a language) can be taken for its relative meaning or for its own substance," we can begin to listen to Beckett's repetition as a method for amplifying the substance of words. While recorded sound fragments and words are completely different mediums, the comparison reminds us to listen to the literature. Beckett's repetition asks the reader to listen to the texture of words and to place the event or fictional context in the background; in Schaeffer's words, the reader must "forget meaning and isolate the in-itself-ness of the sound phenomenon" (13). Beckett's texts create a world of self-referentiality, with each repeated phrase gesturing backward and forward to similar phrases, inviting the reader to experience these phrases as acoustic reverberations that sound throughout the Beckett canon. Though Beckett often modifies his repeated phrases, they still engender an uncanny sense of recognition in the reader, who, simulating the "deep identification or participatory consciousness" of musical repetition, can intuit that these words and phrases have been heard before (Keil and Feld 23). Beckett's auditory narrative, thus, sounds out through a repetition that draws the reader's attention to the sonic qualities of language, subverting their typical role in identifying a fictional reality.

Beckett's repetition and consistent attention to the acoustic qualities of words have led many critics to compare his prose to music and many composers to put his words to music.[4] In a collection of essays titled *Samuel Beckett and Music*, the editor Mary Bryden rightly attests, "Whether read aloud or silently, Beckett's careful words resemble elements of a musical score, coordinated by and for the ear, to sound and resound" (Introduction 2). Paying particular attention to Beckett's repetition, Charles Krance furthers this point, claiming that "Beckett music is structured primarily along patterns of reiterated permutations" (55). Yet, just as Schaeffer pushed against the very idea of what constitutes music, Beckett's fiction too pushes against the very idea of what constitutes a novel. It is for this reason that I find Schaeffer's *musique concrète* to offer a more suitable analogy for the effect of repetition in Beckett's fiction than does traditional music that uses notation. Similar to Schaeffer's realization that distinguishing and repeating recorded sounds would make them unidentifiable to listeners and thus appreciated in themselves, Beckett's repetition distinguishes words, displacing their conventional syntax so that words no longer identify a fictional reality but rather become simply sounds on a page.

Beckett himself draws a parallel between music and his goals as a writer in his often-quoted German letter of 1937 to Axel Kaun: "Is there any reason why that terrible materiality of the word surface should not be capable of being dissolved, like for example the sound surface, torn by enormous pauses, of Beethoven's seventh Symphony, so that through whole pages we can perceive nothing but a path of sounds suspended in giddy heights, linking unfathomable abysses of silence?" ("German" 172). This letter, where Beckett explains that the "goal" of the writer is to let language fall into "disrepute," to "bore one hole after another in it, until what lurks behind it—be it something or nothing—begins to seep through," was written a year after he finished *Murphy*, his last novel to focus predominantly on plot ("German" 172). Tellingly, Beckett's next novel, *Watt*, was his first to make extensive use of repetition. From the German letter of 1937 onward, a trajectory can be traced from *Watt* to the Trilogy and later prose pieces. As we read Beckett's prose, we struggle along with his characters as they try to penetrate "behind" language, to test whether "something or nothing," silence or music, can allow for an experience, an expression, a self, that is not "veiled" in language (171–72). I will argue throughout this chapter, however, that by the end of the Trilogy, Beckett's narrators and characters stop searching for an extralinguistic "something or nothing" and begin to use the art of repetition to infuse phrases, language itself, with an internally generated signification. Whereas *Watt*, as the following section will show, affirms a dualism of nonsense and meaning by juxtaposing linguistic loops and meaningful, poetic passages, by the end of the Trilogy, Beckett embraces language as it is, encouraging the reader to experience what Schaeffer calls the "in-itself-ness of the sound phenomenon" that repetition creates (13).

Listening for a "Whisper of That Final Music": *Watt*'s Loops

Following his proposal in the German letter that writing should contain sounds and silences similar to Beethoven's Seventh Symphony, *Watt* is Beckett's first novel in which words and phrases feel like they take on musical qualities. Indeed, Beckett's last novel to be written in English is filled with digressions that resemble magnetic tape loops. Beckett's narrator repeats phrases in long sequences so that their referential signification becomes subservient to their aural resonance. Consequently, words are listened to first and understood second. One of the first repeated loops of the novel relates to the voices that Watt hears in his head, a motif of the Trilogy:

> Now these voices, sometimes they sang only, and sometimes they cried only, and sometimes they stated only, and sometimes they murmured only, and sometimes they sang and cried, and sometimes they sang and stated, and sometimes they sang and murmured, and sometimes they cried and stated, and sometimes they cried and murmured, and sometimes they stated and murmured, and sometimes they sang and cried and stated, and sometimes they sang and cried and murmured, and sometimes they sang and cried and stated and murmured, all together, at the same time, as now, to mention only these four kinds of voices, for there were others. (29)

As with other loops in *Watt*, this sequence of possible combinations makes a mockery of clarification and the notion that more words yield a more complete explanation and comprehension of an idea. Language, as predicted in the German letter, falls into "disrepute" and becomes essentially alliterative and rhythmic sounds heard by one's reading voice.

We can better understand this effect of speech becoming musical through repetition by considering psychologist Diana Deutsch's "Speech to Song Illusion," an experiment where she played a recording of the looped spoken phrase "sometimes behave so strangely" for audiences. When asked to re-create what they heard, audiences overwhelmingly sang the phrase, showing that even though the phrase had been spoken, repeated looping made the speech be perceived as sung. For Deutsch, this affirms that "strong linkages must exist between speech and music" ("Speech to Song Illusion"). Similarly, as one progresses in reading

Beckett's loops, the reading voice begins to perceive the text as song. While Deutsch's experiment helps us to grasp how Beckett's loops, when read, become musical, Schaeffer's efforts to divorce sounds from their referents can aid us in grasping the deeper significance of Beckett's looping. By forgoing conventional syntax, Beckett disrupts the reader's tendency to read for meaning, and repeated phrases become pure sound; like the "slight variations" of the musical repeat, they "become magical, hypnotizing, mesmerizing" (Keil and Feld 23). Beckett manipulates language to make his reader experience it in a new way.

Beckett's loops become sounds detached from their referents because he employs one of Schaeffer's techniques for making real-world sounds less identifiable, what Schaeffer called "the closed groove" (32). To do this, Schaeffer "isolated a 'sound fragment' that has neither beginning nor end, a sliver of sound isolated from any temporal context" (32). By looping a fragment of sound and erasing any sense of a beginning or end, Schaeffer disrupted its contextual associations. For Schaeffer, this decontextualization and heightened appreciation of the formal aspects of sound are the key goals of *musique concrète*. Schaeffer claims that he is drawing on and refining a skill that we all have and can practice when listening to sounds: "the initial act in music is willed hearing, i.e., selecting from the chaotic hubbub of sounds a sound fragment that one has decided to consider. Here the memory acts as a closed groove: it retains, it records, it repeats. This fragment must be considered for all it contains: matter and form" (Schaeffer 66). *Musique concrète* mechanically creates closed grooves and strives to heighten the listener's attention to matter and form. By creating closed grooves from everyday noise, it makes us more aware of the sounds that we absentmindedly hear; it makes us "agile enough to hear" these sounds anew and to recognize the aesthetic qualities of these repeated sounds (Schaeffer 66).

In *Watt*, looped words are taken out of grammatical sentences, which typically imbue words with a sentence-level beginning and end and enhance the reader's tendency to read for meaning. "Slivers" of repeated words such as "and sometimes they" in the example above are decontextualized within the long sentence, encouraging the reader to listen to the words as pure sound. One becomes aware of the act of reading itself, and in this state of heightened perception, one finds oneself questioning the purpose of reading. What is the purpose of reading a page that merely repeats the same words in different patterns? Should not reading convey meaning and understanding? By this point, however, the text has already done something to the reader: it has made the reader question language.

Although Steven Connor is right when he suggests that reading *Watt* is a "slow and painful process," I feel that Beckett rewards his reader for going through the process (*Samuel* 31). Just as *musique concrète* encourages "willed hearing" over our typical absentminded reception so that a fragment is "considered for all it contains: matter and form," Beckett's loops make us stop and linger; they make us consider the matter and form of language itself (Schaeffer 66). Beckett's reader becomes accustomed to the looped fragments in *Watt* and begins to allow him- or herself to get caught in the rhythmic loops—to enjoy the aural resonance of the repetition and appreciate the texture of the sounds of words as such. Nevertheless, it is admittedly a slow indoctrination for the reader, just as it is for Watt.

The character Watt depends on the act of narration and naming to gain control over his tenuous situation in the service of Knott. He strives to understand quandaries by putting them into words, though he is also suspicious of words and their ability to refer to the things they name. For example, only when Watt exhausts the linguistic possibilities of the narrative does he lose interest in the belabored explanation of how dogs in the neighborhood are fed Knott's leftover dinner. At the end of a comprehensive explication, the narrator concludes, "he had turned, little by little, a disturbance into words, he had made a pillow of old words, for a head. Little by little, and not without labour" (117). Watt's struggle with words, like his desire to say for certain that the signifier "pot" is the same as the signified pot in Knott's kitchen, draws the reader's attention to the function of language and the way in which it can give us a sense of control over reality (81). Watt's drive to name and find meaning in events such as "the incident of the Galls father and son" mirrors the reader's drive to make sense of the digressions of the novel and to have the novel meet conventional expectations (80). The novel mocks and thwarts such generic expectations, gradually teaching the reader that plot is irrelevant and that language is meaningless when one attempts to represent the many possibilities of reality.

Still, the repetitive loops in *Watt* not only highlight the arbitrariness of language, they also demonstrate that Beckett's narrator is engaged in the project of making language signify beyond its problematic arbitrariness. As the reader progresses through the text, the looped phrases reduce language in certain passages to sound, while short passages that are not looped (sometimes only sentences that break the loop) become slowed and infused with meaning. For instance, there is a paragraph about Knott's footwear that repeats variations: "sometimes he wore on each a sock, or on the one a sock and on the other a stocking, or a boot, or a shoe, or a slipper, or a sock and boot, or a sock and shoe, or a sock and slipper, or a stocking and boot, or a stocking and shoe, or a stocking and slipper, or nothing at all" (202). After a page of this, the loop suddenly breaks, and the reader goes from being caught in the rhythmic repetition, in which words are appreciated aurally, to reading a slowed, beautiful, and meaningful passage:

> To think, when one is no longer young, when one is not yet old, that one is no longer young, that one is not yet old, that is perhaps something. To pause, towards the close of one's three hour day, and consider: the darkening ease, the brightening trouble; the pleasure pleasure because it was, the pain pain because it shall be; the glad acts grown proud, the proud acts growing stubborn; the panting the trembling towards a being gone, a being to come . . . and free, free at last, for an instant free at last, nothing at last. (202)

This passage stands out because it comes as an interlude between paragraphs that consist primarily of looped phrases. Though the sentiments of pleasure, pain, being, and freedom expressed in this passage are rare in the novel, the contradictions of the passage (young/old, ease/trouble, pleasure/pain) fall in line with the back-and-forth play with language found throughout the narrative. While these contradictions point to a linguistic confusion where "pain" and "pleasure" are interchangeable, and "free at last" becomes "nothing at last," they are still some of the few instances in which the narrator entertains such concepts. To assure a slowed reading, such passages are juxtaposed with long paragraphs of looped phrases that, in contrast, speed up the narrative of *Watt*. This back-and-forth movement between slowed passages and rhythmic loops, which mimics the literal back-and-forth movement of Watt's walk (one of several gestures that assure the reader that, though Watt moves, he stays in the same place), forces the reader to participate in the same play with language as does the protagonist.

This contrasting play with language in *Watt* allows Beckett to approach what he proposed in his German letter of 1937 with regard to the writer and language: "In this dissonance between the means and their use it will perhaps become possible to feel a whisper of that final music or that silence that underlies All" ("German" 172). In the dissonance between meaningless loops and slowed, meaningful moments of narration in *Watt*, Beckett tries to reveal something underneath language. There is a struggle for both Watt and the narrator to make language express emotions, conjure images, and communicate. As this next section will show, the Trilogy is the beginning of the undoing of this desire to "feel a whisper," and the beginning of a more complete dismissal of language, which paradoxically occurs through a complete resignation to the limitations of language. In other words, while the protagonist and the narrator of *Watt* cling to a desire that language, if played in the right way, will expose a "whisper of that final music or that silence," which reaches beyond language, the narrators of the Trilogy are in the process of resigning themselves to the idea that there is only language. In essence, the Trilogy narrators gradually teach the reader that language is nothing more than a collection of prerecorded phrases, yet it is in how we manipulate and mix these recorded phrases that we feel our existence. Beckett's later characters rely on the sounds of repeated phrases to affirm an existence that cannot be grasped by reading semantically. Just as Schaeffer's goal was to get his audiences to begin to appreciate the texture and acoustics of sounds in and of themselves, Beckett gradually asks his reader to appreciate words in and of themselves, for the pure pleasure of listening.

"I Shall Never Weary of Repeating It": The Trilogy

The repetition of Beckett's Trilogy is more spread out and less explicit than the obvious looped phrases of *Watt*. Rubin Rabinovitz helpfully calculates, "The three novels [in both the French and English translations] contain over 1500 sets of recurring elements with an average of three items in each set . . . this averages out to about eight items per page" (33). Though the narrators and characters of the Trilogy have different names—Moran, Molloy, Malone, Worm, Mahood, and the Unnamable—each voice is linked to the rest through the repeated phrases that they share, encouraging the reader to meld them into one voice. The stories of each narrator are both similar and different: the protagonists are usually tramps, though they differ in how incapacitated they are; they wear similar hats and coats, though their details differ; there is the similar location of a room where the protagonist is deprived of all except the ability to write and, sometimes, the necessities for survival. It is not only the repeated elements of plot, however, that create this uncanny sense of familiarity. Repeated figures of speech and phrases also trigger the reader's memory, as he or she recalls hearing such linguistic fragments before—in his or her own head during the reading process. Linguistic repetition helps the reader sustain a sense of continuity throughout narratives, which otherwise do not offer conventional plot progression. Take for example the following repeated phrases, which are particular to the Trilogy voice: "in the end" (32 times), "it's the end" (5 times), "to the end" (10 times), "come and go" (9 times), "come and gone, come again and gone again" (1 time), "comings and goings" (5 times), "more and more" (15 times), "more or less" (17 times), "little by little" (18 times), and "any old thing" (18 times). These regularly occurring fragments familiarize the reader with the preoccupations and rhetorical patterns of the Trilogy narrators, gradually indoctrinating the reader into the discourse of the text. As these stock phrases are looped throughout the Trilogy, as well as other Beckett texts, the reader begins to anticipate them just as she would recognize commonly exchanged figures of speech.

The repeated phrases, which the reader recites with the narrators, are recalled from the reader's memory, making them not just words read from a page but a "sonic pattern" we have come to know (Kivy 352). This sort of pleasurable anticipation is similar to the pleasure of repetition in music: as a refrain or motif repeats, the pleasure of its return builds for the listener. Just as repeated variations in music "give you deep identification or participatory consciousness," the repetition of the Trilogy makes certain phrases so familiar that the reader begins to anticipate and participate with the voices of the three novels (Keil and Feld 23).

Yet beyond these similarities with traditional music, Beckett's repetition is more akin to *musique concrète* in that, just as Schaeffer's goal was to make real-world sounds unidentifiable and thus appreciated for their own sake, Beckett's repetition in the Trilogy makes words lose their referentiality to a fictional world and thus become appreciated in and of themselves. We witness this in each subsequent novel of the Trilogy, where the convention of plot is exposed as merely a way to occupy language unselfconsciously. The narrators try to use words as if they could transparently relay stories and meanings beyond their internal referentiality, but they are ultimately left without stories to relay. In *Molloy*, the travels of Molloy and Moran invite interpretation as the reader tries to figure out the relationship between the two characters. *Malone Dies*, however, has no such plot conventions, only the bedridden Malone, who describes his room and meager belongings and tells stories, which, as he self-reflexively reminds his reader, are only recited to pass the time. Likewise, the physical bodies of the Trilogy narrators disintegrate with each succeeding novel. Molloy and Moran experience leg problems and physical pains, while Malone starts to lose feeling in his body altogether. By *The Unnamable*, the body completely loses its footing, so to speak, as the narrator eventually does away with the legless and armless Worm, the last character with a body, and repeatedly relays, "I don't feel a head on me" (412). Realizing that visual settings allow the narrative to fall back into familiar conventions of signification, the narrator excitedly asserts, "Balls, all balls, I don't believe in the eye either, there's nothing here, nothing to see, nothing to see with . . . No spectator then, and better still no spectacle, good riddance" (375).

This resolve is later shaken as the reader is left with only a voice marking time, and the narrator laments "if only there was a thing" (394). As plot and the physical bodies of the narrators break up, the reader begins to cling to the words, the repeated phrases, for a sense of progress and continuity. The skepticism toward vision that Martin Jay traces in French thinkers and writers, discussed in my first chapter, is exemplified by the end of the Trilogy, where vision is suspiciously regarded as facilitating the illusion that language simply refers to reality.

The eradication of a visual setting is partly what allows Beckett's narrative to achieve its auditory dimension. As the reader detaches words from their visual referents, the reading voice loses its focus on reading for meaning—what Michel Chion calls *semantic listening*, listening to a language or code to discern its message (28). Instead, the reader begins to partake in what Schaeffer calls *reduced listening*, a type of listening that Chion describes as "focus[ing] on the traits of the sound itself, independent of its cause and of its meaning. . . . Reduced listening takes the sound—verbal, played on an instrument, noises, or whatever—as itself the object to be observed instead of as a vehicle for something else" (29). Schaeffer believed that reduced listening could be facilitated through an acousmatic situation, in which one hears a sound but cannot see its source. Such a situation, in theory, "draws our attention to sound traits normally hidden from us by the simultaneous sight of the causes—hidden because this sight reinforces the perception of certain elements of the sound and obscures others" (Chion 32). Yet, Chion doubts Schaeffer's contention that acousmatic listening encourages a reduced listening, heightening one's attention to the acoustic texture of a sound over its identification, and argues instead that such listening initially prompts the opposite reaction, where one asks, "What's that?" (Chion 32). This initial reaction of questioning can also befall the reader of the Trilogy, but, just as Chion explains that "when we listen acousmatically to recorded sounds it takes repeated hearings of a single sound to allow us gradually to stop attending to its cause and to more accurately perceive its own inherent traits," a similar effect is achieved through the repeated phrases of the Trilogy (32). The overall effect of the repeated phrases and the gradual dismissal of any visual setting is to accustom the reader to a reduced listening of one's own reading voice, where words are perceived for their own inherent traits rather than for what they refer to.

The repetitions of the Trilogy can be grouped loosely into three categories: figures of speech; negations and affirmations; and phrases that are particular to Beckett's narrators, which usually refer to voice, silence, coming, going, and ending. The different types of repeated phrases and their many variations create a sense of automatic and formulaic thinking and speaking throughout the Trilogy. Like Krapp, who can only replay his prerecorded voice to get a sense of his past life, the narrators of the Trilogy are limited to the stored and familiar phrases that recur throughout the narrative. The narrators seem painfully aware that they can only choose from a limited source of prerecorded phrases to tell their stories and thoughts, and they often make reference to this problematic situation: "I have spoken of a voice giving me orders, or rather advice" (*Molloy* 169–70); "I have to speak, whatever that means. Having nothing to say, no words but the words of others, I have to speak" (*Unnamable* 314); "What I speak of, what I speak with, all comes from them" (*Unnamable* 324); "these voices are not mine, nor these thoughts" (*Unnamable* 347); and "the voice must belong to someone" (*Unnamable* 408). This collection of prerecorded speech, the voice of another, is the language that Beckett's narrators are born into and, of course, is the only one with which they can write and speak.[5] The narrators of the Trilogy struggle with the voices inside their heads, which seem to lead them away from silence and "self," and the reader partakes of this struggle as well. Before we consider the larger implications of Beckett's repetition, however, let us look more closely at the types of repeated phrases that he deploys.

The Trilogy narrators repeat several figures of speech, manipulating them slightly or repeating them verbatim. Though there are rarely any narrative markers for quotations (he said, she said), in their preoccupation with speech and voice, Beckett's narrators tirelessly use figures of speech that are permutations of the verb *to say*. For example: "that is to say" (62 times); "that is soon said" (6 times); "it's only fair to say" (*Molloy* 102; *Unnamable* 294, 316); "as the saying is" (8 times); "as one might say" (*Unnamable* 294); "as you might say" (*Malone* 220); "I must say" (9 times); "I must have said so" (*Malone* 221); "I must have said it" (*Unnamable* 402); "so to speak" (6 times); "so they say" (*Unnamable* 365); "so I said" (*Molloy* 87–88); and "so that I said" (*Molloy* 169).[6] These repeated phrases are usually set apart by commas, and the pauses before and after such fragments emphasize that they should be read as discrete units.

The hundreds of repeated phrases framed around the act of saying defamiliarize the conventional novelistic expectations of third-person and first-person narration, making the reader consistently aware that though the narrators of the Trilogy write in first person, they treat their narrating voice like a separate character. Just as Krapp's recorded voice seems like a different person to him, these mechanically repeated phrases feel detached from their speakers and create a distance between the narrators and the words that they use. A similar effect is also achieved through the repeated phrase "call that," which the narrators use to direct the reader's attention to words and their seemingly arbitrary act of naming: "Keep going, going on, call that going, call that on" (*Unnamable* 291); "To go on, I still call that on" (*Unnamable* 320); and "they call that living" (*Unnamable* 361).[7] Throughout the Trilogy, these repeated phrases remind the reader that thoughts are constituted by a language that is not inherent but always inherited.

Beckett's narrators also repeat figures of speech that are focused on the theme of time, highlighting the illusory assumption of the progression of time in a narrative. Like the other fragments, these phrases are usually set apart by commas, and they are perceived as previously heard units that cut into the narrative. Repeated fragments such as "from time to time" (50 times), "at the same time" (9 times), "for the time being" (5 times), "for a/the moment" (26 times), "after all" (17 times), "once and for all" (5 times), "the first time" (6 times), and "sooner or later" (13 times), among other variations, remind the reader that, like language, time is arbitrary. The narrators' self-consciousness about time draws the reader's attention to the present time of reading, as he or she comes back to familiar phrases and commiserates with the Trilogy narrators—yes, I have heard this before, and now here we are once again. The Trilogy narrators want nothing more than to stop the voice that speaks them, the voice that marks time: "decidedly it is the time for this to stop" (*Malone* 237); "Nevertheless I shall stop" (*Malone* 252); "I wonder if I shall ever be able to stop" (*Malone* 253); and "I can't stop it" (*Unnamable* 307). The repetition, however, is relentless; the voice keeps speaking. Paradoxically, the repeated phrases are also a way of stalling time, speaking yet staying in the same place. The reader does not progress through an advancing plot but rather progresses toward a feeling that everything has already been said before—a feeling that is accurate considering that the reader has most likely read at least half of the written matter on every page in another context, on another page of the Trilogy.

Similar to Schaeffer's attempts to instill a new appreciation for the substance of sounds in and of themselves by "tearing sound material away from any context, dramatic or musical, before giving it form," Beckett's auditory narrative works by tearing narrative away from contextual and dramatic settings, leaving the reader with only the sounds of the words (Schaeffer 38). These repeated phrases go from sounding pleasurably familiar to the reader (resonating in their comforting predictability) to sounding frustratingly meaningless through their mechanical overuse. Like *Watt*'s linguistic loops, which may seem to lack authorial control, the compulsive repetition of the Trilogy makes the reader question the narrative's capacity to signify beyond being a mix of prerecorded fragments.

Schaeffer faced a similar frustration in the reception of his compositions. The mechanical nature of his work—the fact that he was using recorded material rather than instrumental notes as the material of his compositions—made some (including Schaeffer) question its validity as an art. Considering audience reactions to his *Suite 14*, which combined manipulations of recorded noises and instruments, Schaeffer concludes that "distorting music right to the limit presented musicians with such a caricature of their art that they were really angry" (37). By detaching sounds or words from their everyday contexts, Beckett and Schaeffer both strove to produce a heightened attunement to the substance of their material. Yet such manipulations could frustrate one's expectations for how meaning is conventionally constructed through melody and plot. Similarly, "readymades" in modernist art such as Duchamp's *Bicycle Wheel* (1913), a sculpture of a bicycle wheel mounted on a stool, "generated consternation even among urbane, ostensibly liberated artists" (Gay 163).

The fluctuation between affirmations and negations in the Trilogy illustrates this oscillation between finding meaning through resonance and finding only meaninglessness and empty echoes. The ramblings of the narrators are punctuated with "yes" and "no," and the reader begins to anticipate regularly recited phrases like "Ah yes" (18 times), "yes indeed" (4 times), "no, no" (12 times), "no, not yet" (4 times), and "no matter" (46 times), along with the occasional "oh" (38 times) and "ah" (31 times).[8] Just as Schaeffer wanted fragments of sound to be heard as "discreet and complete sound objects," independent of their context, these phrases become recurring sounds that function more like looped backtracks than like sentences within a continuous story (Schaeffer 14).

In this dialectic of affirmation and negation, the speakers of the Trilogy question whether one can ever know anything through language. As they go back and forth between knowing and not knowing, they more often than not end with the repeated phrase, "I don't know," sampled as a sentence at least sixty-six times, as well as in other variations such as "I don't know how," "I don't know why," and "I don't know when" (at least 70 times). Yet, repeated phrases that gravitate around knowing, insisting in various ways that "I knew it well" (8 times), "you know" (9 times), and "that's all I know" (15 times) are also recited by Beckett's narrators. These affirmations and negations of knowledge contradict each other not only in content but in effect: at once, they lose meaning through overuse and become meaningful as they represent the need to depend on such worn out phrases for expression. In other words, these words are all that Beckett's narrators have, even if they are only used to sound out a formal back-and-forth movement between sounds. The reader comes to the Trilogy already familiar with overused sentences and phrases such as "I don't know," "that is to say," and "sooner or later," which allows Beckett to exploit a ready empathy in the reader for his characters' reliance on such figures of speech. Aware that such phrases have become meaningless through repeated use, the narrators of the Trilogy instead use them to highlight our shared dependence on these overused fragments, which in turn sparks a surprising sense of empathy and continuity between the reader and narrators.

The narrators of the Trilogy push themselves to go on, doubt their ability to go on, and doubt the value of going on. As with the silence, which begins with a literal silence between Moran and his son and ends with an internal, meta-phorical silence, the concept of going on begins with a literal question proposed by Molloy in reference to his sucking stones: "Do I have to go on? No" (*Molloy* 73).[9] The intermittent progress reports that document Molloy's ability to go on with his travels—"But before I go on" (*Molloy* 89), "I was able to go on" (*Molloy* 145)—become metaphoric and self-reflexive, as Malone encourages himself and questions his ability to narrate: "lets go on" (*Malone* 189); "I can go on" (*Malone* 189); "I shall try and go on all the same" (*Malone* 216); "So I wonder if I should go on" (*Malone* 251); and "Try and go on" (*Malone* 277). This question of going on becomes central in *The Unnamable*, as one of the first sentences of the novel demonstrates: "Keep going, going on, call that going, call that on" (291).

While permutations of the phrase "going on" permeate the Trilogy, a new variation in *The Unnamable* is that the narrator *must* go on: "That is to say I have to go on" (292); "But the discourse must go on" (294); "Unfortunately, I am afraid, as always, of going on" (302); and "I have only to go on" (335). The fear of going on and the inability to do so, mixed with the desire and necessity of going on, reach a crescendo by the end of the Trilogy. As we approach the end of *The Unnamable*, we hear a growing urgency and anxiety in the narrator: "I can't go on" (386); "let us go on" (387, 388); "I can't go on in any case. But I must go on. So I'll go on" (393); "impossible to stop, impossible to go on, but I must go on, I'll go on . . . in order to go on a little more, you must go on a little more, you must go on a long time more, you must go on evermore" (395); "I go on as best I can" (400); "I have to go on" (403); "it's a question of going on, it goes on" (404); "you must go on thinking too" (405); "to be able to go on" (408); "go on, go on again" (410); and "you must go on . . . you must go on, I can't go on, you must go on, I'll go on . . . you must go on . . . you must go on, I can't go on, I'll go on" (414). The above are the most obvious examples of the "going on" varia-tions, among several others that cannot fail to catch the reader's ear. We listen for patterns with our inner ear and find our own reading voices engaged in a type of reduced listening where words become sounds without a visual referent to guide the reader in making meaning.

Though Beckett's linguistic repetition initially reduces phrases to the level of sound, emptying them of signification, the cumulative effect of the repetition is one of heightened signification. This technique draws attention to the text as such and, in doing so, divests language of its power to create a fictional world that the reader can absentmindedly fall into. Yet, by showing the reader that language is just a sequence of repeated words, the Trilogy verifies that it can make meaning within the confines of its composition, through its own repetition; language is still the only means to going on. The unnamable narrator repeats himself to a frenzied frequency and allows the reader to take part in his inner argumentation, since, like him, his reader can predict the phrases that are to come, that must be said "as long as there are any" (*Unnamable* 414). Is it worth going on, reading and speaking, when the reader already knows the phrases that are to come? Does the reader have any choice but to go on?

In Christopher Ricks's published lectures, *Beckett's Dying Words*, he traces Beckett's relationship with dead words (clichés) and dead languages as well as his tendency to create characters that want "oblivion, extinction, irrecoverable loss of consciousness" (1). This convincing and illuminating exploration of death in Beckett's work, however, has a counterpoint: Beckett's writing equally questions what it means to be alive. If one is reduced to only hearing a voice inside a head, is this living? Though Beckett repeatedly renders voices as imprisoned in language and habit, having only illusions of a purpose in life, the end of the Trilogy affirms that one is alive as long as a voice speaks and the writer writes. The process of Beckett's repetition does something to language and the reader, which rehabilitates the otherwise bleak scenarios of his protagonists. Chion explains that Schaeffer's ideal of reduced listening "disrupts established lazy habits and opens up a world of previously unimagined questions for those who try it" (30). While a listener may at first try to guess the origins of the sounds that make up a *musique concrète* composition, he or she will eventually attend to "qualities of timbre and texture" (Chion 31). Hence, "reduced listening has the enormous advantage of opening up our ears and sharpening our power of listening" (Chion 31).

In the Trilogy, as repetition encourages reduced listening, our sense of language is opened up, so that words do not always have to be pinned to a visual referent but can be appreciated as sounds that simply affirm the existence of a narrator. For example, near the end of the Trilogy, the narrator, within a sentence that spans pages, is self-consciously trying to create a fictional setting while assuring the reader that there is no visual setting on which to hinge one's reading: "it's not I, that's all I know, no more about that, that is to say, make a place, a little world, it will be round, this time it will be round, it's not certain, low of ceiling, thick of wall, why low, why thick, I don't know, it isn't certain, it remains to be seen, all remains to be seen, a little world . . . no matter" (*Unnamable* 405). There is a cumulative effect here of repeated phrases such as "it's not I," "that's all I know," "no more about that," "that is to say," "I don't know," "it isn't certain," and "no matter," which have been repeated throughout Beckett's oeuvre. By the last novel of the Trilogy, such phrases gather an internally generated meaning, which affirms that even though language is a lame means to expression and self-knowledge, existence simply entails a voice making sound, regardless of whether that voice refers to a fictional world.

For Schaeffer, the goal of *musique concrète* was to make an audience listen to the sound of an everyday object without being able to identify it—to just appreciate a new form of sound that did not adhere to conventional notation and musical theory. Schaeffer contends that as sounds are decontextualized, repeated, and manipulated with the magnetic tape recorder, "the object forces us to listen to it, not by reference, but just as it is, in all the reality of its substance. As it doesn't say much, and certainly not what we would like it to say, once we have heard it, it makes us fall silent. In this silence we perceive more disturbances" (165). Both Beckett and Schaeffer perceive a somewhat disturbing silence with which one is left once the musical or linguistic sound is heard. Perhaps this is because if one truly appreciates the sounds of *musique concrète* or Beckett's auditory narrative, without attaching such sounds and words to real-world referents, then, once the sounds end, there is no residual meaning to which to cling. Once the experience of listening is done, there is no message left to hold onto.

Schaeffer and Beckett foster an appreciation for a new dimension of sound and language beyond our simplified polarization of music and noise, meaning and nonsense. Schaeffer took nontraditional sounds and manipulated them with a tape recorder so that they could be appreciated with a "sound eye, sensitive to the form and color of sounds" (Schaeffer 182). Instead of asking what instrument a sound came from or dismissing a sound as noise, Schaeffer hoped to compose a work of art that, through the mechanical reproduction of the tape recorder, could generate a new relationship between the listener and the sound—one that perhaps would "strike terror" or "arouse anguish" but that would also "extend into disturbing and profoundly hidden realms" (Schaeffer 165). Beckett's fiction also creates a new relationship between the reader and the text, which is sometimes filled with anguish and yet penetrates the reader's mind. In Beckett's

Trilogy, phrases that seem mechanically reproduced become substantial in and of themselves, creating their own meaning within the confines of the text.

In *The Unnamable*, the narrator repeatedly relays his submission to the voice that speaks him in mechanical terms: "I shall transmit the words as received, by the ear"; "I emit sounds, better and better it seems to me" (349, 353). Later, the narrator submits that a voice, "a transmission," is all that one needs to exist: "These millions of different sounds, always the same, recurring without pause, are all one requires to sprout a head. . . . The mechanism matters little, provided I succeed in saying, before I go deaf, It's a voice, and it speaks me" (351, 354). Shortly after this passage, the narrator is still thinking of his head as a type of mechanism, one that records and transmits words and phrases from the outside world and replays them within his inner monologue. He writes of his head, "It's a transformer in which sound is turned, without the help of reason, to rage and terror, that's all that is required, for the moment" (356). Later, the narrator's description of himself as a "tympanum," "thin as foil," "vibrating" between the "mind" and the "world," is reminiscent of an early phonograph (383).

The sense that language does not originate with the narrator but is mechanically reproduced through him reminds us of Krapp's tape recorder, which allowed him to edit and manipulate his own voice in ways that were unavailable with previous auditory technologies. The tape recorder, with its advanced capabilities for splicing and looping recorded sounds, aided artists like Schaeffer in aestheticizing noise. Likewise, Beckett's repetition aestheticizes words, turning them into sound. As the reader no longer reads to discern an event but rather listens for the sounds of the words themselves, the reader is able to experience the detachment between the words that speak us and the self that speaks. Similar to Schaeffer's proclamation that "while [*musique concrète*] revitalizes matter, it also presents itself as a sort of huge deterioration," Beckett causes language to deteriorate so that it can be revitalized for the reader (Schaeffer 65).

Afterword

In a neuroscientific study that claims that hearing is a "universal" sense that shapes the mind, Seth Horowitz writes, "The 1920s through the 1940s were the heyday of understanding how we perceive the acoustic world, and its most obvious contributions were arguably not the wealth of scientific papers but rather the ability to actually use sound to create worlds through popular media" (171). Experiencing the creation of worlds through phonograph recordings, broadcasts, talkies, and tape-recorded montages, often piped straight into one's headspace through headphones, helped the public (modernist writers included) conceive of auditory perception as a sense that could potentially create intimate connections yet that could also connect a listener with cosmopolitan or bohemian worlds that were not necessarily part of one's everyday life. Hearing sounds mechanically reproduced detached them from their assumed visual connection with an origin, freeing sounds for artistic manipulation. Discerning the mechanical noises of auditory technologies and hearing noises recorded and appropriated into musical compositions encouraged listeners to expand their sense of notational music and become close listeners to the textures and qualities of the soundscape.

This study has shown how these gradual and small changes in auditory perception may have prompted modernist writers to take up the challenge of making their narratives auditory. For the novel could always create fictional worlds, which readers could envision in their imagination, but modernists now needed to compete with auditory technologies that could also create noisily appealing fictional worlds. This is perhaps what motivated them to create such sonic novels—novels that make the reader not just envision but listen to a narrative.

Just as auditory technologies brought the public into experiences that were conducted through the ear, the modernist novel too brought readers into an aural experience. They did this by creating auditory narratives that consistently represent characters listening to prosody, music, and noise, and by asking their reader to become attuned to the words on the page through onomatopoeia, interior monologue, and repetition. Unlike their representations of vision, which often entail characters analyzing and judging one another from a distance, their representations of sound bring characters and the reader into a vibrational sympathy. Rather than a distanced picture that leaves the reader with a clear message, these modernist novels beckon the reader to share in a character's soundscape, to hear the voices, music, and noises that a character hears, and even to listen in on the inner speech of a character. Such a positive rendering of and engagement with audition reflects a larger cultural shift in the modernist period, from a presumed reliance on vision as the primary means of knowing to a growing skepticism of vision. As Viet Erlmann clarifies, "In one bold stroke, Heidegger had reconfigured philosophy's relationship with its other in ways that defy the stability of Cartesian representation and instead involve resonance, oscillation, and vibration: in short, acoustics" (333–34). This shift from ocularcentrism to a consideration of acoustics or, at the very least, a questioning of the eye's superiority brought on by visual technologies that made the public more aware of the limitations of the naked eye, contributed to an atmosphere in the early twentieth century that recognized the potential power of the ear as a bridge to the world. This movement, along with the auditory technologies developed and popularized during the period, created a heightened awareness of auditory perception as a way to connect with the other.

The goal of this study has been to encourage the reader to become receptive to the arousal of the inner ear that the modernist novel so often elicits. These novels draw attention to language as sound: not a transparent medium of communication but textured rhythmic patterns that we communally chant and listen to together. Modernists often ask their readers to slow down in their reading and to listen actively and closely. The type of listening required of these novels resonates with Barthes's description of the activity: "to listen is to adopt an attitude of decoding what is obscure, blurred, or mute, in order to make available to consciousness the 'underside' of meaning" ("Listening" 249). This is perhaps why the novels of this study are aligned with the modernist movement, where there is a sincere drive to record the seemingly insignificant details of life, the psychological oscillations of the mind, and heightened moments—epiphanies—in the ordinary. While vision lends itself to grand spectacles and detached analysis, listening can potentially lead one to deciphering the unseen, an "'underside' of meaning" that modernists intuited. Even with Beckett, who straddles modernism and postmodernism, we hear a desire to amplify the notion that language, while arbitrary and mechanical, still unites humans in our sameness and can be manipulated to create an internal sense of meaningfulness. By calling on the reader's ear, modernists fulfill what Woolf called "the prevailing sound of the Georgian age": "we hear all round us, in poems and novels and biographies, even in newspaper articles and essays, the sound of breaking and falling, crashing and destruction" ("Mr. Bennett and Mrs. Brown" 334). Celebrating the breaking of literary conventions, as well as of the dominant ideologies of patriotism, sexism, and classism, modernists made music from the noises crashing around them.

Notes

Introduction

1. I have in mind here the criticism of Georg Lukács, Lionel Trilling, and Daniel Bell. Specifically, in "The Ideology of Modernism" (1955), Lukács argues that modernism fails to show the dialectical nature of human history that is shown in nineteenth-century realism. While such realism is able to fuse the general and the particular, modernism gives only the particular and subjective.

2. Picker draws evidence from: Charles Dickens's *Dombey and Son* (1846–48), examining communication among his characters as well as Dickens's own desire to communicate his work through readings; the reactions of Victorians to street noise; the role of speech and silence in George Eliot's *Daniel Deronda* (1876); and the depiction of the phonograph in the fiction of Sir Arthur Conan Doyle and Bram Stoker's *Dracula*. Though there are not many studies that look at sound and nineteenth-century literature, an interesting exception is Mark M. Smith's *Listening to Nineteenth-Century America*. Though Smith presents an insightful aural history of nineteenth-century America, he admits that "for reasons that have to do with the nineteenth-century preoccupation with visuality, the rise of print culture, and the long shadows cast by these developments, it seems fair to say that a good deal of historical work interprets the past principally, if unwittingly and implicitly, through historical actors' eyes" (6).

3. As Sarah Gleeson-White writes in a footnote in a *PMLA* article, "literary sound has been somewhat neglected" in scholarship (97n1). She cites me, along with Tim Armstrong, Sarah Wilson, Philipp Schweighauser, and Kata Gellen as exceptions to this trend. Armstrong, Wilson, and Gellen have each published insightful articles in *Modernism/modernity* that examine, respectively, poetry and the player piano, Gertrude Stein and the radio, and architectural acoustics and German literature. For examples of studies on modernism and visual culture, see Murray Roston's *Modernist Patterns*, Karen Jacobs's *The Eye's Mind*, Michael North's *Camera Works*, Laura Marcus's *The Tenth Muse*, Maggie Humm's *Modernist Women and Visual Cultures*, Johanna Drucker's *Theorizing Modernism*, and Rebecca Beasley's *Ezra Pound and the Visual Culture of Modernism*.

4. While I do not devote a chapter to the telephone, it has appeared in several modernist works: the narrator of Marcel Proust's *In Search of Lost Time* (1913–27) is amazed by what the telephone can reveal within a person's voice, Franz Kafka uses the telephone in *The Trial* (1925) and *The Castle* (1926), and telephones are important to the plots of some novels by Elizabeth Bowen. I also do not devote a chapter to the wireless or radio

because its influence on modernism has been so well documented. For example, the collections *Broadcasting Modernism* (Cohen, Coyle, and Lewty), *Broadcasting in the Modernist Era* (Feldman, Mead, and Tonning), and *Wireless Imagination* (Kahn and Whitehead) look at fiction and poetry in relation to the radio. Monographs such as Melissa Dinsman's *Modernism at the Microphone*, Todd Avery's insightful *Radio Modernism*, and Timothy C. Campbell's *Wireless Writing in the Age of Marconi* also examine the radio in the modernist period. Other important contributions to the field include Michael Coyle's essay on T. S. Eliot's BBC broadcasting and Sarah Wilson's article on the radio as "a powerful formal model" for Gertrude Stein's writing (261).

5. For more on Stein's repetition and the phonograph, see my essay "The Phonograph and the Modernist Novel."

6. See Margaret Fisher's *Ezra Pound's Radio Operas* and Robert Hughes and Margaret Fisher's *Cavalcanti* for more on Pound's radio operas, musical training, composing, and theorizing.

Chapter 1. The Modernist Soundscape: Ocularcentrism and Auditory Technologies

1. The term *soundscape* was first described and analyzed by the Canadian composer R. Murray Schafer in his 1969 volume *The New Soundscape*. In general, Schafer's work warns against an absentminded acceptance of noise in our modern soundscape and calls for a greater consciousness in acoustic design. His understanding of the soundscape is explained in more detail in my chapter on Virginia Woolf.

2. For more on anti-noise societies and their growth in the early twentieth century, see Karin Bijsterveld's *Mechanical Sound*.

3. Even futurist painting had an aural dimension. Pointing out that Umberto Boccioni's painting *The Street Enters the House* (1911) was later retitled by a critic as "The Noise of the Street Penetrates the House," Vincent Sherry perceptively describes the significance of sound in the painting: "The artist has torn the objects from the eyes' linear distance and placed them in the ears' circumambient plane, letting them move into and through the woman as though they were acoustic sensations, whose effects are more immediate, invasive, and physically dense than those of eyesight" (*Ezra Pound* 14). Sherry's enlightening study of Ezra Pound and Wyndham Lewis demonstrates how they valued the eye's associations with a distanced, rational clarity and an individualized, hierarchical worldview over the empathetic and democratic inclinations of the ear. While Pound and Lewis may have aligned themselves with thinkers who praised the eye's ability to differentiate and objectify reality, I will show that this was not the case with modernists such as Woolf, Joyce, Richardson, Rhys, and Beckett.

4. Antheil was supposed to compose an electric opera that used the "Cyclops" episode of *Ulysses* as libretto and was to include, "twelve electric pianos hooked to a thirteenth which played the master roll; on this would be recorded also drums, steel xylophones, and various blare instruments" (Ellmann 558).

5. For more on the relationship between nineteenth-century literature and photog-

raphy see: Jennifer Green-Lewis's *Framing the Victorians*, Nancy Armstrong's *Fiction in the Age of Photography*, and Daniel A. Novak's *Realism, Photography, and Nineteenth-Century Fiction*. Jay likewise concludes that "Nineteenth-century realist fiction . . . called on the author's visual acuity to create its effect of represented reality, the novel's 'holding a mirror to nature,' in Stendhal's famous phrase" (*Downcast* 173).

6. Unlike Danius and Jacobs, Jay attributes this "crisis" to: first, a loss in the hierarchal distinction between *lux* (human visual perception) and *lumen* (the mind's eye or divine light); second, a growing skepticism of visually defining oneself against or as a reflection of the other; and third, an anxiety engendered by the obscurity, shadow, and unrepresentativeness of baroque vision ("Rise" 318). Though North quotes Jay, he does not view this historical period as one of crisis. Similar to my own argument, North claims that these technologies inspired modernist artists to represent the world in new ways, making "it impossible for any of the arts to take their own representational routines for granted" (31).

7. Steven Connor differs from these theorists in observing that, while auditory openness may be positive in many ways, it can also be threatening to the subject (214). There is a need to organize and control sound, which can be overwhelming and disorienting, particularly in ego formation (220).

8. Arendt clarifies, "Metaphors drawn from hearing are very rare in the history of philosophy, the most notable modern exception being the late writings of Heidegger, where the thinking ego 'hears' the call of Being" (111).

9. Although Edison, David Edward Hughes, and Nikola Tesla each contributed to the development of wireless technology in important ways, wireless broadcasting is usually attributed to Marconi, who patented his invention (which was used for ships to send telegraphs wirelessly) in 1896. Initially a medium for Morse code, broadcasting quickly advanced, so that by 1908, phonograph records were being heard from the Eiffel Tower by the American radio pioneer Lee De Forest.

10. For examples of erotic telephone advertisements, see Sterne, *Audible* 171.

11. Matthew Rubery explains how the phonograph was considered beneficial because it could be used to record novels for the blind or to save people from the strain of reading: "The economics of publishing cylinders and discs would supposedly expedite America's transition from a reading to a listening nation" (227). Although phonographs could only record for about three minutes and did not have the technological ability to record books until the 1930s, this excitement shows that the public was thinking of the novel as an auditory experience.

12. Electronic instruments such as the theremin (1920), the Electrophone (renamed the Sphaerophon) (1924), the Ondes Martenot (1928), and Thaddeus Cahill's Telharmonium, also known as the Dynamophone, expanded the public's sense of what constituted a musical sound.

13. For a vivid description of Varèse's New York premiere of *Poème électronique*, see Thom Holmes's *Electronic and Experimental Music*.

14. For more on Satie and bohemianism, see Steven Moore Whiting's *Satie the Bohemian*.

15. Sterne references Schafer as well as Pierre Schaeffer, Barry Truax, and John Corbett, who claim that reproduced sounds infer a visual lack (*Audible* 20).

16. Oberlin Smith laid out the basic ideas for magnetic tape recording as early as 1878, and Valdemar Poulsen demonstrated the first magnetic tape recorder, which he called "The Telegraphone," in 1900 at the Paris World Exhibition. In 1938, the German electronics group Allgemeine Elektricitäts-Gesellschaft introduced the first commercially viable tape recorder, which they called the Magnetophon K4. Magnetic tape recorders were primarily used in the military, until they began to be widely used in the sound-recording industry in the 1940s.

17. For more on the specific relationship between the phonograph and the modernist novels of Woolf, Joyce, and Gertrude Stein, see Frattarola, "The Phonograph and the Modernist Novel."

Chapter 2. Music and the Prosody of Voice: Dorothy Richardson and the Transformation from Silent Film to the Talkie

1. Rick Altman explains how early sound film technicians, in an attempt to match the scale of an image and its sound, played with "sound localization through speaker placement," strategically adding loudspeakers in theaters and trying to make sounds emit from the correlating action on the screen (48). When recording film in the late twenties, microphones were often hidden within props so that they could get close enough to amplify a speaker, or a single microphone would be attached to a camera (Altman 53). While this arrangement helped to align the image and sound scale, as an actor farther from the camera would sound farther away in the audio recording, it also caused problems if characters turned away from the camera or the studio had different acoustics from the imagined space of the film (Altman 52–53). By the early thirties, however, microphones became lighter and could be suspended above a scene by a mobile boom (Altman 53). By the mid-thirties, technological improvements made it so that, rather than being created from the incidental sounds picked up in a shoot, sound tracks could be "constructed" "to provide a clean, clear, continuous sound record, oblivious to image scale but attuned to dialogue intelligibility, story continuity, and freedom of action" (Altman 53–54). Altman tracks an interesting shift here from technicians trying to match the scale of sound and image to valuing dialogue intelligibility, a valuing that is "modelled on theatrical intelligibility" (63). This resonates with Richardson's argument that the speech of the talkie did not feel natural but rather overly enunciated.

2. Although I have not come across evidence that Richardson was an avid radio listener, one might also consider whether the practice of using "distinct and stereotypical dialects and accents" on radio programs at the time—which allowed listeners to aurally discern different races, ethnicities, classes, and genders—influenced Richardson's keen ear for prosody (Hilmes 359).

3. For example, see David Trotter's *Cinema and Modernism*, John McCourt's edited collection *Roll Away the Reel World*, Laura Marcus's *The Tenth Muse*, and Susan McCabe's *Cinematic Modernism*. One notable exception to these predominantly visual-oriented

studies of film and modernism is Sarah Gleeson-White's "Auditory Exposures." P. Adams Sitney's survey of modernist film and literature *Modernist Montage* is particularly relevant for this study, as it establishes how vision and visual experience are problematized in both film and literature of the period. A consequence of such a troubling of vision, I would argue, is a heightened attention to sound and auditory experience.

4. For examples of critics who analyze Richardson's fiction within a visual context, see Elisabeth Bronfen's *Dorothy Richardson's Art of Memory* and Susan Gevirtz's *Narrative's Journey*. The one exception is David Stamm's insightful *A Pathway to Reality*, which examines vision, musical allusion, silence, and synesthesia in *Pilgrimage*.

5. Martin Miller Marks explains that in the early silent period of film, "cue sheets provided a series of suggestions for music to be used in accompaniment, 'cued' to the titles and action of the screen" (6).

6. Though it is not the focus of his analysis, Stamm too notices that Miriam has a "seismographic awareness of all of the shades of expression in other people's voices" (5).

7. It would be reasonable to question whether Richardson was against the talkies because she saw them as a threat to the novel—the traditional medium for characters and narrative—or whether she was anxious about their mass appeal. This, however, was not the case. In one of her film columns, she dismisses H. G. Wells's prediction that film will replace literature, arguing instead that film will create "a new form" of "film literature" that will attract new readers ("Almost" 191). She also defends the lowbrow "Movie" and satirizes critics who deplore the movie as catering to an audience's desire for "stock characters" and a "happy ending" ("Thoroughly" 178, 179).

8. For more on the film industry's complicated attempts to court female spectators to promote film as a respectable leisure activity, see Shelley Stamp's *Movie-Struck Girls*.

9. Since Richardson was an avid viewer of film, early representations of women in film undoubtedly influenced her fictional representations of women. Though Mulvey rightly sees women in early Hollywood film as passive, Richardson in her fiction radically works against such representations by focusing thousands of pages on Miriam.

10. Radford deals with this most thoroughly, arguing that Miriam in the first three novels "is identified and identifies herself with the father, with the masculine position" (70).

11. As Hypo looks at her, Miriam analyzes the different parts of her body "with her own eyes opened by Amabel," her close companion (*Dawn's* 231). Referencing this scene, Radford points out that Miriam's "appreciation of her body is mediated by the gaze of others, which is in turn constructed in relation to cultural icons of female beauty" (128). Taking a different point of view, Bluemel, in her examination of Richardson's representations of female sexuality, argues that "Miriam hopes to put herself into the active position of the subject who gazes rather than the position of the body that is gazed upon" (55). While these discussions of the male gaze are of great significance, what is most relevant to my argument is that Miriam finds herself the object of Hypo's gaze and becomes critical of his way of looking.

12. For example, there are detailed references to the bells of Saint Pancras in the second volume of *Pilgrimage* (21–23, 96, 145, 322, 362, 405), third volume (35, 329, 436) and final volume (204).

Chapter 3. Recording the Soundscape: Virginia Woolf's Onomatopoeia and the Phonograph

1. Although most of the sources cited in this introduction to the phonograph are not British, I am working from the understanding that the sense of surprise and the nuanced perception of noise fostered by the phonograph were similarly experienced among Western listeners.

2. Bonnie Kime Scott refers to a letter from Eliot to Woolf, as well as Woolf's diary, both of which suggest that when Eliot visited Woolf, they played popular jazz records he had brought ("Subversive" 102–3).

3. For more on Woolf and classical music, see Emma Sutton's excellent study *Virginia Woolf and Classical Music*.

4. For a summary of critics who have discussed Woolf and sound, particularly in her later work, see Rishona Zimring's "Suggestions of Other Worlds" (131). For a comprehensive review of Woolf's references to and thoughts about music, see Joyce E. Kelly's "Virginia Woolf and Music."

5. Melba Cuddy-Keane also links Woolf's representations of communal aural experience with auditory technology more generally and with avant-garde music. Cuddy-Keane recommends a new terminology to address the significant role of the auditory in literature, adopting the term *diffusion* to describe the "emission of sound from its source," and the term *auscultation* to describe the act of listening to a sound ("Virginia" 70, 71).

6. For example, Woolf's sentences, especially in the opening italicized sections, lull and lap, and the reader gets a sense of the movement of the repeatedly described waves: "*Gradually as the sky whitened a dark line lay on the horizon dividing the sea from the sky and the grey cloth became barred with thick strokes moving, one after another, beneath the surface, following each other, pursuing each other, perpetually*" (*Waves* 179, emphasis in original). We hear the waves not only in the last phrases set apart by commas, each containing five to six syllables, but in the alliteration and assonance of paired words such as "sky whitened," "line lay," "horizon dividing," "become barred," and "thick strokes." Stewart holds that Woolf is able to resist "the high style of the fathers" of the English canon through "textual resistance, a thickening or impedance of syntax, an intrusion of the phonic into the scriptive" (261).

7. There are too many references to sounds to cite them all. The most common examples of onomatopoeia in the novel are: the "roar" of London (95, 223, 241, 268–69, 299–302); the "hoot" of car horns and sirens (223, 292, 305–7, 383, 419), the "twitter" (7, 59, 218) and "chatter" (90, 114, 116) of birds; the "coo" (76, 77, 115, 176, 186) and "croon" (273, 427) of pigeons; the "boom" of guns (287–88); and the "rattle" of all sorts of things—people, windows, and carts (147, 154, 167, 175, 186, 206, 313, 316, 339, 386).

8. On the Virginia Woolf Web page, a computerized count of the frequency of words in *The Waves* shows that the words *roar, roared, roaring,* and *roars* appear thirty-two times throughout the novel ("Waves").

9. J. Hillis Miller asserts that the old woman is singing a translation of the words put to Richard Strauss's "Allerseelen," a song about "the day of a collective resurrection of

spirits" (64). Similar to my argument that sounds momentarily unify characters, Miller reads the song as heralding the gathering of characters at Clarissa's party and as a resurrection of their memories of one another.

10. It is of interest to note that Woolf read Freud's *Group Psychology* in December 1939, making a note in her diary, "I read Freud on Groups" (*Diary* 5: 252).

11. Alex Zwerdling finds that while critics often notice that Woolf's novels "move towards a climactic moment of unification," they ignore Woolf's "sense of the pervasiveness of human isolation" (321). Whereas I see Woolf's leanings toward separation in *Between the Acts* as a positive insistence on individuality, Zwerdling holds that the novel has only moments of unification and a predominantly negative tone of isolation.

12. Zimring agrees that in *The Years*, "Woolf uses sound to reveal the limitations of the visual" (135). While Zimring and I both see sounds in *The Years* as connecting characters, we differ in that Zimring generally interprets the aural intrusions, particularly in the "Present Day" modern urban setting, as disruptive, sparking a desire for silence and unity that must be counteracted through a newly conceived creativity (exemplified by Sara Pargiter, the artist figure of the novel, and the singing children at the end of the novel).

13. The fact that two of Woolf's homes (at 37 Mecklenburg Square and 52 Tavistock Square), in addition to Vanessa Bell's studio, were bombed between 1940 and 1941, shows the extent to which the war impacted Woolf's life.

14. Cage opened his 1937 talk "The Future of Music: Credo" with, "Wherever we are, what we hear is mostly noise. When we ignore it, it disturbs us. When we listen to it, we find it fascinating. The sound of a truck at fifty miles per hour. Static between the stations. Rain. We want to capture and control these sounds, to use them not as sound effects but as musical instruments" (3).

Chapter 4. Turning Up the Volume of Inner Speech: Headphones and James Joyce's Interior Monologue

1. Although early users of this technology called them *headsets*, I use the term *headphones* for consistency.

2. Most critical studies of Joyce and sound have focused on Joyce's musical references and forms, onomatopoeia, and phonetic punning in *Ulysses*, as well as the way in which *Finnegans Wake* repeatedly refers to and is formally influenced by the radio. For more on Joyce and music, see Sebastian D. G. Knowles's edited collection *Bronze by Gold*, Jack W. Weaver's *Joyce's Music and Noise*, and Derek Attridge's *Joyce Effects*. For discussions of the relationship between *Finnegans Wake* and the radio, see Harry Levin's *James Joyce* and James A. Connor's "Radio Free Joyce."

3. In his survey of the musical elements of this episode, Jack W. Weaver points out that, as with much of *Ulysses*, "verbal compounds suggest musical notes linked together by ligatures in dyads, triads, and tetrads" (58–59). Though I am more concerned with Stephen's view and experience of auditory perception in this episode, Weaver's analysis confirms that Joyce's writing appeals to the ear.

4. This definition puts aside negative stereotypes of cosmopolitanism such as: "cosmo-crats," a label developed by John Micklethwait and Adrian Wooldridge that can be understood as "a new global economic elite" (Vertovec and Cohen, "Introduction" 6); "aesthetic cosmopolitanism," which includes those who travel to consume the exotic fares of foreign cultures (Vertovec and Cohen, "Introduction" 7); and historical associa-tions of cosmopolitanism (found in Homer's *Odyssey*, mid-nineteenth-century Ameri-can culture, and the nationalism or totalitarianism of the Soviet Union, Nazi Germany and Fascist Italy) for those without roots or national attachment (Vertovec and Cohen, "Introduction" 5–6).

Chapter 5. Inner Speech as a Gramophone Record: Jean Rhys's Bohemian Voice and Popular Music

1. For example, Nancy Harrison discusses how, in *Voyage in the Dark*, Anna "is, al-ways, self-consciously, addressing someone, even if it is nominally herself, even if it is the reader or whoever may be listening" (68). Harrison calls this "unspoken dialogue" and notes "three levels or kinds of conversation" that work in "counterpoint" (68, 82, 83). As with my study, Harrison's musical terminology and analysis of unspoken dialogue draw the reader's attention to the auditory nature of Anna's inner speech.

2. See Elizabeth Abel's "Women and Schizophrenia," where Abel uses R. D. Laing's theory of the divided self to examine the sense of separation between the body and mind in Rhys's characters, and Anne B. Simpson's *Territories of the Psyche*, which argues that, in *Good Morning, Midnight*, we must listen to Sasha as an analyst would to hear the repressed trauma of her father's molestation.

3. In her study on bohemian life, Virginia Nicholson lists Rhys in her appendix of "Dramatis Personae" and briefly references Rhys's short story "Hunger" and her drink-ing habits as examples of bohemian culture (187, 274). Yet most critics only mention her bohemian associations in passing. For examples, see Helen E. Nebeker's *Jean Rhys* and Elaine Savory's thorough *The Cambridge Introduction to Jean Rhys*.

4. In her perceptive essay on the patois of the narrator, Kristin Czarnecki specifies that Selina "is also mulatto, a Martiniquaise immigrant" (20).

Chapter 6. Turning Words into Sounds: Samuel Beckett's Repetition and the Tape Recorder

1. In directing *Krapp's Last Tape*, Beckett paid considerable attention to how the tape recorder should be held and touched, wanting the actor to show Krapp concentrating on the act of listening. In his notebook for a production at the Schiller-Theater Werkstatt in Berlin, Beckett questions whether, when listening to the recorded recollection of the woman on the punt, the actor's "left hand on the switch of the tape-recorder" can "be-come (how?) 'Meine Hand auf ihr' ['my hand on her']" (Beckett, *Theatrical* 88). Beckett emphasizes the physical presence of the tape recorder, treating it almost as a human presence on the stage.

2. For an analysis of repetition in Beckett, see Steven Connor's *Samuel Beckett*, Rubin Rabinovitz's "Repetition and Underlying Meaning in Samuel Beckett's Trilogy," and Bruce Kawin's *Telling It Again and Again*, which has a chapter on Beckett and Gertrude Stein. Critics who study repetition in Beckett have often alluded to Freud's reference to a child's game of "fort/da." For more on this reading, see S. E. Gontarski's essay "Molloy and the Reiterated Novel" and Angela B. Moorjani's *Abysmal Games in the Novels of Samuel Beckett*.

3. Beckett's familiarity with the tape recorder is evidenced not just by *Krapp's Last Tape* but by the fact that the BBC gave him a tape recording of his first radio play, *All That Fall* (Maude 63). On a rare occasion, Beckett also allowed Martin Esslin to tape-record him reading *Lessness*—one of the few recordings of Beckett reading his work (Esslin 150).

4. To name a few examples: Brigitta Weber made Beckett's play *That Time* into a German opera; Marcel Mihalovici adapted *Krapp's Last Tape* into an opera called *Krapp*; Heinz Holliger staged *Come and Go* and *What Where* with musical scores; Morton Feldman wrote a musical score for *Neither*; Roger Reynolds's *A Merciful Coincidence* uses text from *Watt*; Lucian Berio's *Sinfonia* uses text from *The Unnamable*; and Giacomo Manzoni's *Parole de Beckett* uses a mix of Beckett texts. See Mary Bryden's edited collection *Samuel Beckett and Music* for more on these compositions.

5. The notion of one's speech as imposed from outside of one's self should be understood from within the larger discourses of psychoanalytic and post-structuralist theory, particularly Lacan's statement that "in the unconscious is the whole structure of language" (147), and Derrida's claim that "From the moment that there is meaning there are nothing but signs. We *think only in signs*" (108, emphasis in original). My suggestion that Beckett's narrators experience language as the voice of another is also informed by Roland Barthes's essay "The Death of the Author," in which he describes the author as a "scriptor" and all writing as a fabric of quotations. While Barthes' is a general theory that can be applied to all literature, however, Beckett's repetition needs to be distinguished as a specific technique whereby he keeps a sequence of familiar phrases in circulation to show his reader how language, within the context of his work, can be seen as quotation. Barthes's focus on the reader as the site of meaning is also helpful in understanding how Beckett's repetition ultimately affects his reader.

6. The tracking of repeated phrases was done by hand rather than by computer, so all the counts I give here must be assumed to be approximations. When there are more than three citations for a phrase, I note the number of times that I was able to document it rather than list all the page numbers.

7. This phrase is used in various permutations at least twenty-three times in the Trilogy, most of which fall in *The Unnamable*.

8. Within the Trilogy, "no" can be found at least 267 times, and "yes" appears at least 175 times.

9. The phrase "go silent" is repeated at least thirty times in *The Unnamable* and has an even greater variety of permutations. Silence is introduced to the reader of the Trilogy with the literal silence between Moran and his son in *Molloy*: "All was silent" (128); "The silence was absolute" (158). This eventually leads to a desire in Malone for internal

silence in *Malone Dies*: "Then that silence of which, knowing what I know, I shall merely say that there is nothing, how shall I merely say, nothing negative about it" (221); "and to the long silence that has silenced me, so that all is silent. And if I ever stop talking it will be because there is nothing more to be said" (236). Silence does not become a dominant preoccupation of the narrator, however, until *The Unnamable*, when the narrator states from the beginning, "I shall never be silent. Never" (291) and "I cannot be silent" (294). *The Unnamable* does away with plot and goes straight to the heart of what the first two novels of the Trilogy wrestle with: the desire to "go silent" in order to put an end to the voice that only takes one further away from the "self," and the conflicting drive to keep the voice going.

Works Cited

Abel, Elizabeth. "Women and Schizophrenia: The Fiction of Jean Rhys." *Contemporary Literature* 20.2 (1979): 155–77. Print.

Abrams, M. H. "Stream of Consciousness." *A Glossary of Literary Terms.* 6th ed. Fort Worth: Harcourt, 1993. 202–3. Print.

Adorno, Theodor. "The Curves of the Needle." 1928. Trans. Thomas Y. Levin. *October* 55 (1990): 48–55. *JSTOR.* Web. 9 Feb. 2008.

———. "The Form of the Phonograph Record." 1934. Trans. Thomas Y. Levin. *October* 55 (1990): 56–61. *JSTOR.* Web. 9 Feb. 2008.

Adorno, Theodor, and Hanns Eisler. "Composing for the Films." Cox and Warner 73–75.

After Leaving Mr. Mackenzie. Advertisement. *Times Literary Supplement,* 12 Feb. 1931: 108. *TLS Historical Archive 1902–2006. Cengage Learning.* Web. 21 Feb. 2012.

Rev. of *After Leaving Mr. Mackenzie,* by Jean Rhys. *Times Literary Supplement,* 5 Mar. 1931: 180. *TLS Historical Archive 1902–2006. Cengage Learning.* Web. 21 Feb. 2012.

Albright, Daniel. *Beckett and Aesthetics.* Cambridge: Cambridge UP, 2003. Print.

———, ed. *Modernism and Music: An Anthology of Sources.* Chicago: U of Chicago P, 2004. Print.

Altman, Rick. "Sound Space." *Sound Theory, Sound Practice.* Ed. Rick Altman. New York: Routledge, 1992. 46–64. Print.

Antheil, George. Letter to Nicolas Slonimsky. 1936. Albright, *Modernism and Music* 71.

Arendt, Hannah. *The Life of the Mind: The Groundbreaking Investigation on How We Think.* San Diego: Harvest, 1978. Print.

Aristotle. *Metaphysics.* Trans. W. D. Ross. *ProQuest eLibrary.* Web. 15 Aug. 2015.

———. *On Sense and the Sensible.* Trans. J. I. Beare. Internet Classics Archive. Web. 25 Feb. 2009.

Armstrong, Nancy. *Fiction in the Age of Photography: The Legacy of British Realism.* Cambridge: Harvard UP, 1999. Print.

Armstrong, Tim. "Player Piano: Poetry and Sonic Modernity." *Modernism/modernity* 14.1 (2007): 1–19. Print.

Attell, Kevin. "Of Questionable Character: The Construction of the Subject in *Ulysses.*" *Joyce Studies Annual* 13 (2002): 103–28.

Attridge, Derek. *Joyce Effects: On Language, Theory, and History.* Cambridge: Cambridge UP, 2000. Print.

Avery, Todd. *Radio Modernism: Literature, Ethics, and the BBC, 1922–1938.* Farnham: Ashgate, 2006. Print.

Ball, Hugo. "Dada Manifesto." 1916. *Flight Out of Time: A Dada Diary by Hugo Ball.* Ed. John Elderfield. Berkeley: U of California P, 1996. 219–21. Print.

Barthes, Roland. "The Death of the Author." *Image-Music-Text.* Trans. Stephen Heath. New York: Noonday, 1989. 142–48. Print.

———. "The Grain of the Voice." *Image-Music-Text.* Trans. Stephen Heath. New York: Noonday, 1989. 179–89. Print.

———. "Listening." *The Responsibility of Forms: Critical Essays on Music, Art, and Representation.* Trans. Richard Howard. Berkeley: U of California P, 1985. 245–60. Print.

Beasley, Rebecca. *Ezra Pound and the Visual Culture of Modernism.* Cambridge: Cambridge UP, 2010. Print.

Beckett, Samuel. "German Letter of 1937." *Disjecta: Miscellaneous Writings and a Dramatic Fragment.* Ed. Ruby Cohn. New York: Grove Press, 1984. 170–73. Print.

———. *Krapp's Last Tape. Collected Shorter Plays.* New York: Grove, 1984. 53–63. Print.

———. *Malone Dies.* 1956. Trans. Samuel Beckett. *Three Novels.* New York: Grove, 1965. 179–288. Print.

———. *Molloy.* 1955. Trans. Patrick Bowles and Samuel Beckett. *Three Novels.* New York: Grove, 1965. 7–176. Print.

———. *Texts for Nothing* (1–13). Trans. Samuel Beckett. *The Complete Short Prose, 1929–1989.* Ed. S. E. Contarski. New York: Grove, 1995. 100–154. Print.

———. *The Theatrical Notebooks of Samuel Beckett: "Krapp's Last Tape."* Ed. James Knowlson. Vol. 3. New York: Grove, 1992. Print.

———. *The Unnamable.* 1958. Trans. Samuel Beckett. *Three Novels.* New York: Grove, 1965. 291–414. Print.

———. *Watt.* New York: Grove, 1953. Print.

Beer, Gillian. *Virginia Woolf: The Common Ground.* Ann Arbor: U of Michigan P, 1996. Print.

Bell, Daniel. *The Cultural Contradictions of Capitalism.* New York: Basic Books, 1996. Print.

Bénéjam, Valérie. "The Acoustic Space of *Ulysses.*" *Making Space in the Works of James Joyce.* Ed. Valérie Bénéjam and John Bishop. New York: Routledge, 2011. 55–68. Print.

Benjamin, Walter. "The Work of Art in the Age of Mechanical Reproduction." *Illuminations: Essays and Reflections.* Ed. Hannah Arendt. Trans. Harry Zohn. New York: Schocken, 1968. 217–51. Print.

Berard, Carol. "Recorded Noises—Tomorrow's Instrumentation." *Modern Music* 6.2 (1929): 26–29. Print.

Bijsterveld, Karin. "The Diabolical Symphony of the Mechanical Age." Bull and Back 165–89.

———. *Mechanical Sound: Technology, Culture, and Public Problems of Noise in the Twentieth Century.* MIT P, 2014. ProQuest Ebook Central. Web. 11 Jan. 2018.

Bluemel, Kristin. *Experimenting on the Borders of Modernism: Dorothy Richardson's Pilgrimage.* Athens: U of Georgia P, 1997. Print.

Bowen, Zack. *Musical Allusions in the Works of James Joyce.* Albany: State U of New York P, 1974. Print.

Bronfen, Elisabeth. *Dorothy Richardson's Art of Memory: Space, Identity, Text.* Manchester: Manchester UP, 1999. Print.

Brøvig-Hanssen, Ragnhild. "Recording Aesthetics in the New Era of Schizophonia." *Material Culture and Electronic Sound.* Ed. Frode Weium and Time Boon. Washington: Smithsonian Institution Scholarly P, 2013. 131–57. Print.

Bryden, Mary. Introduction. Bryden, *Samuel Beckett and Music* 1–5.

———, ed. *Samuel Beckett and Music*. Oxford: Clarendon, 1998. Print.

Bucknell, Brad. *Literary Modernism and Musical Aesthetics: Pater, Pound, Joyce, and Stein*. Cambridge: Cambridge UP, 2001. Print.

Budgen, Frank. *James Joyce and the Making of "Ulysses," and Other Writings*. Oxford: Oxford UP, 1972. Print.

Bull, Michael, and Les Back, eds. *The Auditory Culture Reader*. Oxford: Berg, 2003. Print.

Cage, John. *Silence: Lectures and Writings by John Cage*. Hanover: Wesleyan UP, 1961. Print.

Campbell, Timothy C. *Wireless Writing in the Age of Marconi*. Minneapolis: U of Minnesota P, 2006. Print.

Caughie, Pamela L, ed. *Virginia Woolf and the Age of Mechanical Reproduction*. New York: Garland, 2000. Print.

———. "Virginia Woolf: Radio, Gramophone, Broadcasting." Humm, *Edinburgh* 332–47.

Cavarero, Adriana. "Multiple Voices." Sterne, *Sound Studies* 520–32.

Childs, Peter. *Modernism*. London: Routledge, 2007. ProQuest Ebook Central. Web. 3 Jan. 2018.

Chion, Michel. *Audio-Vision: Sound on Screen*. Trans. Claudia Gorbman. New York: Columbia UP, 1994. Print.

Clements, Elicia. "Transforming Musical Sounds into Words: Narrative Method in Virginia Woolf's *The Waves*." *Narrative: The Journal of the Society for the Study of Narrative Literature* 13.2 (2005): 160–81. Print.

Cocteau, Jean. Excerpt from *Cock and Harlequin*. 1918. Albright, *Modernism and Music* 324–27.

Cohen, Debra Rae, Michael Coyle, and Jane Lewty. *Broadcasting Modernism*. Gainesville: UP of Florida, 2009. Print.

Comolli, Jean-Louis. "Machines of the Visible." *The Cinematic Apparatus*. Ed. Teresa De Lauretis and Stephen Heath. New York: St. Martin's, 1980. 121–42. Print.

Connor, James A. "Radio Free Joyce: Wake Language and the Experience of Radio." *Sound States: Innovative Poetics and Acoustical Technologies*. Ed. Adalaide Morris. Chapel Hill: U of North Carolina P, 1997. 17–31. Print.

Connor, Steven. "The Modern Auditory I." *Rewriting the Self: Histories from the Renaissance to the Present*. Ed. Roy Porter. New York: Routledge, 1997. 203–23. Print.

———. *Samuel Beckett: Repetition, Theory and Text*. Oxford: Blackwell, 1988. Print.

Conrad, Joseph. "Preface to *The Nigger of the 'Narcissus*.'" *The Norton Anthology of English Literature*. Ed. Stephen Greenblatt et al. 8th ed. Vol. 2. New York: Norton, 2006. 1887–89. Print.

Cox, Christoph, and Daniel Warner, eds. *Audio Culture: Readings in Modern Music*. New York: Continuum, 2004.

Coyle, Michael. "T. S. Eliot on the Air: 'Culture' and the Challenges of Mass Communication." *T. S. Eliot and Our Turning World*. Ed. Jewel Spears Brooker. New York: St. Martin's. 141–54. Print.

Cuddy-Keane, Melba. "Modernist Soundscapes and the Intelligent Ear: An Approach to Narrative through Auditory Perception." *A Companion to Narrative Theory*. Ed. James Phelan and Peter J. Rabinowitz. Malden: Blackwell, 2005. 382–98. Print.

———. "Virginia Woolf, Sound Technologies, and the New Aurality." Caughie, *Virginia Woolf and the Age* 69–96.

Czarnecki, Kristin. "Jean Rhys's Postmodern Narrative Authority: Selina's Patois in 'Let Them Call It Jazz.'" *College Literature* 35.2 (2008): 20–37. Print.

Danius, Sara. *The Sense of Modernism: Technology, Perception, and Aesthetics*. Ithaca: Cornell UP, 2002. Print.

Deane, Seamus. Introduction. *A Portrait of the Artist as a Young Man*. By James Joyce. New York: Penguin, 1964. vii–xliii. Print.

Debrock, Guy. "The Word Man and the Note Man: Morton Feldman and Beckett's Virtual Music." Oppenheim 67–82.

DeMarinis, Paul. "On Sonic Spaces." *Sound: Documents of Contemporary Art*. Ed. Caleb Kelly. Cambridge, Massachusetts: MIT P, 2011. 73–75. Print.

Derrida, Jacques. Excerpt from *Of Grammatology*. *Critical Theory Since 1965*. Ed. Hazard Adams and Leroy Searle. Tallahassee: Florida State UP, 1986. 94–119. Print.

Deutsch, Diana. "Speech to Song Illusion." *Diana Deutsch*. UC San Diego, n.d. Web. 13 Jan. 2015.

Dillingham, William B. "Eavesdropping on Eternity: Kipling's 'Wireless.'" *English Literature in Transition, 1880–1920* 55.2 (2012): 131–54. *Project Muse*. Web. 1 June 2016.

Dinsman, Melissa. *Modernism at the Microphone: Radio, Propaganda, and Literary Aesthetics*. London: Bloomsbury, 2015. Print.

Dolar, Mladen. "The Linguistics of the Voice." Sterne, *Sound Studies* 539–54.

Donald, James, Anne Friedberg, and Laura Marcus, eds. *Close Up 1927–1933: Cinema and Modernism*. Princeton: Princeton UP, 1998. Print.

Drucker, Johanna. *Theorizing Modernism: Visual Art and the Critical Tradition*. New York: Columbia UP, 1996. Print.

Dunn, Leslie C., and Nancy A. Jones. Introduction. *Embodied Voices: Representing Female Vocality in Western Culture*. Cambridge: Cambridge UP, 1994. 1–13. Print.

Edison, Thomas. "The Perfected Phonograph." *North American Review* 146.379 (1888): 641–50. *JSTOR*. Web. 9 Jan. 2015.

———. "The Phonograph and Its Future." 1878. Taylor, Katz, and Grajeda 29–37.

"Edison's Phonograph In Paris." *New York Graphic*, 8 June 1878. Rutgers University, The Thomas Edison Papers. *TAED* MBSB10664X. Web. 9 Jan. 2015.

Eisler, Hanns. "An Old and New Music." 1925. Albright, *Modernism and Music* 339–41.

Eliot, T. S. "The Music of Poetry." 1942. *On Poetry and Poets*. New York: Farrar, 2000. 17–33. Print.

———. *The Use of Poetry and the Use of Criticism*. 1933. London: Faber, 1964. Print.

Ellmann, Richard. *James Joyce*. New and rev. ed. New York: Oxford UP, 1982. Print.

Epstein, Josh. *Sublime Noise: Musical Culture and the Modernist Writer*. Johns Hopkins UP, 2014. Print.

Erlmann, Viet. *Reason and Resonance: A History of Modern Aurality*. New York: Zone, 2010. Print.

Esslin, Martin. "Martin Esslin on Beckett the Man." *Beckett Remembering—Remembering Beckett*. Ed. James and Elizabeth Knowlson. London: Bloomsbury, 2006. 146–51. Print.

Faulkner, Anne Shaw. "Phonographs and Player Instruments." *National Music Monthly*, August 1917: 27–29. Rpt. in Taylor, Katz, and Grajeda 129–33.

Feldman, Matthew, Henry Mead, and Erik Tonning. *Broadcasting in the Modernist Era*. London: Bloomsbury, 2014. Print.

Ferrer, Daniel. *Virginia Woolf and the Madness of Language*. Trans. Geoffrey Bennington and Rachel Bowlby. London: Routledge, 1990. Print.

Fisher, Margaret. *Ezra Pound's Radio Operas: The BBC Experiments 1931–1933*. Cambridge: MIT P, 2002. Print.

Flint, Kate. "'Seeing is Believing?': Visuality and Victorian Fiction." *A Concise Companion to the Victorian Novel*. Ed. Francis O'Gorman. Malden: Blackwell, 2005. 25–46. Print.

———. "Sounds of the City: Virginia Woolf and Modern Noise." *Literature, Science, Psychoanalysis, 1830–1970: Essays in Honour of Gillian Beer*. Ed. Helen Small and Trudi Tate. Oxford: Oxford UP, 2003. 181–94. Print.

Ford, Ford Madox. Preface. *The Left Bank & Other Stories*. By Jean Rhys. London: Jonathan Cape, 1927. 7–27.

Forster, E. M. *Aspects of the Novel*. 1927. San Diego: Harcourt, 1985. Print.

———. *Virginia Woolf*. 1941. London: Folcroft, 1971. Print.

Frattarola, Angela. "The Phonograph and the Modernist Novel." *Mosaic: An Interdisciplinary Critical Journal* 43.1 (2010): 143–59. Print.

Friedberg, Anne. "Introduction: Reading *Close Up*, 1927–1933." Donald, Friedberg, and Marcus 1–27.

Fromm [Glikin], Gloria. "Dorothy M. Richardson: The Personal 'Pilgrimage.'" *PMLA* 78.5 (1963): 586–600. Print.

Gallo, Rubén. "Jean Cocteau's Radio Poetry." Perloff and Dworkin 205–18.

Gay, Peter. *Modernism: The Lure of Heresy from Baudelaire to Beckett and Beyond*. New York: Norton, 2008. Print.

Gellen, Kata. "Hearing Spaces: Architecture and Acoustic Experience in Modernist German Literature." *Modernism/modernity* 17.4 (2011): 799–818. Print.

Gershwin, George. "The Composer and the Machine Age." 1933. Albright, *Modernism and Music* 386–89.

Gevirtz, Susan. *Narrative's Journey: The Fiction and Film Writing of Dorothy Richardson*. New York: Peter Lang, 1996. Print.

Gifford, Don. *"Ulysses" Annotated: Notes for James Joyce's "Ulysses."* Berkeley: U of California P, 1988. Print.

Gilbert, Stuart. *James Joyce's "Ulysses": A Study*. New York: Vintage, 1955. Print.

Gitelman, Lisa. *Scripts, Grooves, and Writing Machines: Representing Technology in the Edison Era*. Stanford: Stanford UP, 1999. Print.

Gleeson-White, Sarah. "Auditory Exposures: Faulkner, Eisenstein, and Film Sound." *PMLA* 128.1 (2013): 87–100. Print.

Gontarski, S. E. "Molly and the Reiterated Novel." *As No Other Dare Fail: For Samuel Beckett on His 80th Birthday by His Friends and Admirers*. Ed. John Calder. New York: Riverrun, 1986. 57–65. Print.

Goodman, David. *Radio's Civic Ambition: American Broadcasting and Democracy in the 1930s*. New York: Oxford UP. *Oxford Scholarship Online*, May 2011. Web. 8 Jan. 2015.

Rev. of *Good Morning, Midnight*, by Jean Rhys. *New Statesman and Nation*, 22 Apr. 1939: 614. Print.

Graves, Robert. *Good-Bye to All That*. 1929. Rev. 2nd ed. New York: Doubleday, 1985. Print.

Greenberg, Judith. "'When Ears Are Deaf and the Heart Is Dry': Traumatic Reverberations in *Between the Acts*." *Woolf Studies Annual* 7 (2001): 49–74. Print.

Greene, Richard. *Edith Sitwell: Avant Garde Poet, English Genius*. London: Hachette, 2011. Print.

Green-Lewis, Jennifer. *Framing the Victorians: Photography and the Culture of Realism*. Ithaca: Cornell UP, 1996. Print.

Guinness, Gerald. *Here and Elsewhere: Essays on Caribbean Literature*. Río Piedras: Universidad de Puerto Rico, 1993. 85–118. Print.

Hall, Stuart. "Political Belonging in a World of Multiple Ideas." Vertovec and Cohen, *Conceiving Cosmopolitanism* 25–31.

Halliday, Sam. *Sonic Modernity: Representing Sound in Literature, Culture and the Arts*. Edinburgh: Edinburgh UP, 2013. Print.

Harrison, Nancy R. *Jean Rhys and the Novel as Women's Text*. Chapel Hill: U of North Carolina P, 1988. Print.

Heidegger, Martin. *Being and Time*. Trans. John Macquarrie and Edward Robinson. New York: Harper, 1962. Print.

Hilmes, Michelle. "Radio and the Imagined Community." Sterne, *Sound Studies* 351–62.

Holmes, Thom. *Electronic and Experimental Music: Pioneers in Technology and Composition*. New York: Routledge, 2002. Print.

Horowitz, Seth. *The Universal Sense: How Hearing Shapes the Mind*. New York: Bloomsbury, 2012. Print.

Hubert, Philip. G., Jr. "What the Phonograph Will Do for Music and Music-Lovers." *Century Magazine* May 1893: 152–54. Rpt. in Taylor, Katz, and Grajeda 39–44.

Hughes, Langston. *The Collected Poems of Langston Hughes*. Ed. Arnold Rampersad. New York: Vintage, 1995. Print.

Hughes, Robert, and Margaret Fisher. *Cavalcanti: A Perspective on The Music of Ezra Pound*. Emeryville: Second Evening Art, 2003. Print.

Humm, Maggie, ed. *Edinburgh Companion to Virginia Woolf and the Arts*. Edinburgh: Edinburgh UP, 2010. Print.

——. *Modernist Women and Visual Cultures: Virginia Woolf, Vanessa Bell, Photography, and Cinema*. New Brunswick: Rutgers UP, 2003. Print.

Humphrey, Robert. "The Results." Steinberg, *Stream-of-Conscious* 170–77.

Ihde, Don. *Listening and Voice: Phenomenologies of Sound*. 2nd ed. Albany: State U of New York P, 2007. Print.

Jacobs, Karen. *The Eye's Mind: Literary Modernism and Visual Culture*. Ithaca: Cornell UP, 2001. Print.

James, Richard Schmidt. *Expansion of Sound Resources in France, 1913–1940, and Its Relationship to Electronic Music*. Diss. U of Michigan, 1981. Ann Arbor: UMI, 1997. Print.

James, William. *The Principles of Psychology*. Vol. 1. New York: Dover, 1950. Print.

Jay, Martin. *Downcast Eyes: The Denigration of Vision in Twentieth-Century French Thought*. Berkeley: U of California P, 1994. Print.

——. "The Rise of Hermeneutics and the Crisis of Ocularcentrism." *Poetics Today* 9.2 (1988): 307–26. Print.

Joyce, James. *A Portrait of the Artist as a Young Man*. New York: Penguin, 1964. Print.

———. *Ulysses*. Ed. Hans Walter Gabler. New York: Vintage, 1986. Print.

Kahn, Douglas. "Introduction: Histories of Sound Once Removed." Kahn and Whitehead, *Wireless Imagination* 1–29.

Kahn, Douglas, and Gregory Whitehead, eds. *Wireless Imagination: Sound, Radio, and the Avant-Garde*. Cambridge: MIT P, 1994. Print.

Katz, Mark. *Capturing Sound: How Technology Has Changed Music*. Berkeley: U of California P, 2004. Print.

Kawin, Bruce. *Telling It Again and Again: Repetition in Literature and Film*. Champaign: Dalkey Archive, 2015. Print.

Keil, Charles, and Steven Feld. "Dialogue 1: Getting into the Dialogic Groove." *Music Grooves*. Chicago: U of Chicago P, 1994. 1–31. Print.

Kelly, Joyce E. "Virginia Woolf and Music." Humm, *Edinburgh* 417–36.

Kenner, Hugh. *Ulysses*. Rev. ed. Baltimore: Johns Hopkins UP, 1987. Print.

Kipling, Rudyard. "Wireless." *Scriber's Magazine* 32.2 (1902): 129–42. *Unz Review*. Web. 21 June 2016.

Kittler, Friedrich A. *Gramophone, Film, Typewriter: Writing Science*. Trans. Geoffrey Winthrop-Young and Michael Wutz. Stanford: Stanford UP, 1999. Print.

Kivy, Peter. "The Fine Art of Repetition." *The Fine Art of Repetition: Essays in the Philosophy of Music*. Cambridge: Cambridge UP, 1993. 327–59. Print.

Knowles, Sebastian D. G., ed. *Bronze by Gold: The Music of Joyce*. New York: Garland, 1999. Print.

Krance, Charles. "Beckett Music." Oppenheim 51–66.

Lacan, Jacques. *Écrits: A Selection*. Trans. Alan Sheridan. New York: Norton, 1977. Print.

Lacey, Kate. *Listening Publics: The Politics and Experience of Listening in the Media Age*. Malden: Polity, 2013. Print.

Lastra, James. *Sound Technology and the American Cinema: Perception, Representation, Modernity*. New York: Columbia UP, 2000. Print.

Lawrence, D. H. *Psychoanalysis and the Unconscious*. 1923. London: Secker, 1928. *Internet Archive*. Web. 15 Jan. 2015.

———. *Women in Love*. New York: Dover, 2002. Print.

Rev. of *The Left Bank*, by Jean Rhys. *Saturday Review of Literature*, 5 Nov. 1927: 287. Print.

Rev. of *The Left Bank*, by Jean Rhys. *Times Literary Supplement*, 5 May 1927: 320. *TLS Historical Archive 1902–2006. Cengage Learning*. Web. 21 Feb. 2012.

Levenson, Michael. Introduction. *The Cambridge Companion to Modernism*. Ed. Michael Levenson. Cambridge: Cambridge UP, 1999. 1–8. Print.

Levin, David Michael. *The Listening Self: Personal Growth, Social Change and the Closure of Metaphysics*. London: Routledge, 1989. Print.

Levin, Harry. *James Joyce: A Critical Introduction*. New York: New Directions, 1960. Print.

Lewty, Jane. "Joyce and Radio." *A Companion to James Joyce*. Ed. Richard Brown. Malden: Blackwell, 2011. 390–406. Print.

Linett, Maren. "'New Words, New Everything': Fragmentation and Trauma in Jean Rhys." *Twentieth-Century Literature* 51.4 (2005): 437–66. *MLA International Bibliography*. Web. 20 Jan. 2012.

Lodge, David. "Interior Monologue." *The Art of Fiction*. London: Penguin, 1992. 46–51. Print.

———. "The Stream of Consciousness." *The Art of Fiction*. London: Penguin, 1992. 41–45. Print.

London, Kurt. *Film Music: A Summary of the Characteristic Features of Its History, Aesthetics, Technique and Possible Developments*. Trans. Eric S. Bensinger. New York: Arno, 1970. Print.

Lukács, Georg. "The Ideology of Modernism." 1955. *Realism in Our Time: Literature and the Class Struggle*. New York: Harper, 1971. 17–46. Print.

Lyon, Janet. "Sociability in the Metropole: Modernism's Bohemian Salons." *ELH* 76 (2009): 687–711. Print.

Magee, Patrick, perf. *Krapp's Last Tape*. By Samuel Beckett. Dir. and adapt. Donald McWhinnie. British Broadcasting Company, London, 1972. Video recording.

Marcus, Laura. "Introduction, Continuous Performance: Dorothy Richardson." Donald, Friedberg, and Marcus 150–59.

———. *The Tenth Muse: Writing about Cinema in the Modernist Period*. New York: Oxford UP, 2008. Print.

Marinetti, F. T. "Destruction of Syntax—Imagination without Strings—Words-Freedom." 1913. *Futurism and Futurisms*. Ed. Pontus Hulten. New York: Abbeville Press, 1986. 516–19. Print.

Marks, Martin Miller. *Music and the Silent Film: Contexts and Case Studies, 1895–1924*. New York: Oxford UP, 1997. Print.

Martin, Michèle. *"Hello, Central?": Gender, Technology, and Culture in the Formation of Telephone Systems*. Montreal: McGill-Queen's UP, 1991. Print.

Maude, Ulrika. *Beckett, Technology and the Body*. Cambridge: Cambridge UP, 2009. Print.

McCabe, Susan. *Cinematic Modernism: Modernist Poetry and Film*. Cambridge: Cambridge UP, 2009. Print.

McCaffery, Steve. "Cacophony, Abstraction, and Potentiality: The Fate of the Dada Sound Poem." Perloff and Dworkin 118–28.

McCourt, John, ed. *Roll Away the Reel World: James Joyce and Cinema*. Cork: Cork UP, 2010. Print.

McLellan, C. M. S. "A Cigarette Song." New York: Chappell, 1907. *Frances G. Spencer Collection of American Popular Sheet Music*, Baylor University, 11 July 2011. Web. 25 May 2012.

Miller, J. Hillis. *"Mrs. Dalloway*: Repetition as the Raising of the Dead." *Critical Essays on Virginia Woolf*. Ed. Morris Beja. Boston: Hall, 1985. 53–72. Print.

Moholy-Nagy, László. "Production—Reproduction: Potentialities of the Phonograph." Cox and Warner 331–33.

Moorjani, Angela B. *Abysmal Games in the Novels of Samuel Beckett*. Chapel Hill: U of North Carolina Dept. of Romance Languages, 1983. Print.

Morin, Emilie. "Beckett's Speaking Machines: Sound, Radiophonics and Acousmatics." *Modernism/modernity* 21.1 (2014): 1–24. *Project Muse*. Web. 5 Apr. 2014.

Mulvey, Laura. "Visual Pleasure and Narrative Cinema." *Film and Theory Criticism: Introductory Readings*. Ed. Leo Braudy and Marshall Cohen. 6th ed. New York: Oxford UP, 1975. 837–48. Print.

Nancy, Jean-Luc. *Listening.* Trans. Charlotte Mandell. New York: Fordham UP, 2007. Print.

Nebeker, Helen E. *Jean Rhys: Woman in Passage.* Phoenix: Acacia, 2009. Print.

Nicholson, Virginia. *Among the Bohemians: Experiments in Living 1900–1939.* London: Penguin, 2003. Print.

North, Michael. *Camera Works: Photography and the Twentieth-Century Word.* Oxford: Oxford UP, 2005. Print.

Novak, Daniel A. *Realism, Photography, and Nineteenth-Century Fiction.* Cambridge: Cambridge UP, 2008. Print.

Oppenheim, Lois, ed. *Samuel Beckett and the Arts: Music, Visual Arts, and Non-Print Media.* New York: Garland, 1999. Print.

"The Painterly Image in Poetry: Overview." *Norton Anthology of English Literature,* Norton Topics Online, n.d. Web. 11 Nov. 2008.

Palombini, Carlos. "Musique Concrète Revisited." *Electronic Musicological Review* 4 (1999): n. pag. Web. 3 Apr. 2000.

Patakfalvi-Czirják, Ágnes. "'Gloomy Sunday': The Hungarian 'Suicide Hymn' between the Myths and Interpretations." *Made in Hungary: Studies in Popular Music.* Ed. Emília Barna and Tamás Tófalvy. New York: Routledge, 2017. 146–58. *ProQuest Ebook Central.* Web. 6 May 2018.

Pater, Walter. *The Renaissance in Selected Writings of Walter Pater.* Ed. Harold Bloom. New York: Columbia UP, 1974. Print.

Perloff, Marjorie, and Craig Dworkin, eds. *The Sound of Poetry/The Poetry of Sound.* Chicago: U of Chicago P, 2009. 205–18. Print.

"The Phonograph." *Scientific American,* 30 Mar. 1878. Rpt. in *Music in America 1860–1918: Essays, Reviews, and Remarks on Critical Issues.* Ed. Michael J. Budds. Hillsdale: Pendragon, 2008. 161–62. Print.

Picker, John M. *Victorian Soundscapes.* Oxford: Oxford UP, 2003. Print.

Pizzichini, Lilian. *The Blue Hour: A Life of Jean Rhys.* New York: Norton, 2009. Print.

Porter, Jeff. "Samuel Beckett and the Radiophonic Body: Beckett and the BBC." *Modern Drama* 53.4 (2010): 431–46. *Project Muse.* Web. 8 Jan. 2014.

Rev. of *Postures,* by Jean Rhys. *Times Literary Supplement,* 4 Oct. 1928: 706. *TLS Historical Archive 1902–2006. Cengage Learning.* Web. 21 Feb. 2012.

Pound, Ezra. "The Tradition." *Literary Essays of Ezra Pound.* New York: New Directions, 1968. 91–93. Print.

Pridmore-Brown, Michele. "1939–40: Of Virginia Woolf, Gramophones, and Fascism." *PMLA* 113 (1998): 408–21. Print.

Rabinovitz, Rubin. "Repetition and Underlying Meaning in Samuel Beckett's Trilogy." *Rethinking Beckett: A Collection of Critical Essays.* Ed. Lance St. John Butler and Robin J. Davis. New York: St Martin's Press, 1990. 31–67. Print.

Radford, Jean. *Dorothy Richardson.* Bloomington: Indiana UP, 1991. Print. Key Women Writers Series.

Remarque, Erich Maria. *All Quiet on the Western Front: A Novel.* 1929. Trans. Arthur Wesley Wheen. New York: Random House, 2013. *Google Books.* Web. 12 Jan. 2015.

Rhys, Jean. "At the Villa d'Or." Rhys, *Collected* 73–78.

———. *The Collected Short Stories.* New York: Norton, 1987. Print.

———. *Good Morning, Midnight.* 1938. New York: Norton, 2000. Print.

———. "Hunger." Rhys, *Collected* 42–44.

———. "In a Café." Rhys, *Collected* 13–15.

———. *Jean Rhys Letters 1931–1966.* Ed. Francis Wyndham and Diana Melly. London: Deutsch, 1984. Print.

———. "La Grosse Fifi." Rhys, *Collected* 79–93.

———. "Let Them Call It Jazz." Rhys, *Collected* 158–75.

———. *Quartet.* 1929. New York: Norton, 1997. Print.

———. "Songs My Mother Didn't Teach Me." 19 July 1978. TS. McFarlin Library, University of Tulsa, Oklahoma. Print.

———. "Vienne." Rhys, *Collected* 94–124.

———. *Voyage in the Dark.* 1934. New York: Norton, 1982. Print.

———. "Voyage in the Dark Part IV (Original Version)." Scott, *Gender of Modernism* 381–92.

Richardson, Dorothy. "About Punctuation." Scott, *Gender of Modernism* 414–18.

———. "Almost Persuaded." Donald, Friedberg, and Marcus 190–92.

———. "Autobiographical Sketch." *Authors Today and Yesterday: A Companion Volume to Living Authors.* Ed. Stanley J. Kunitz. New York: Wilson, 1933. 562–64. Print.

———. *Backwater.* 1916. Richardson, *Pilgrimage*, vol. 1, 189–346.

———. "Captions." Donald, Friedberg, and Marcus 164–65.

———. "The Cinema in the Slums." Donald, Friedberg, and Marcus 180–81.

———. *Clear Horizon.* 1934. Richardson, *Pilgrimage*, vol. 4, 271–400.

———. "Continuous Performance." Donald, Friedberg, and Marcus 160–61.

———. "Continuous Performance VIII." Donald, Friedberg, and Marcus 174–76.

———. *Dawn's Left Hand.* 1931. Richardson, *Pilgrimage*, vol. 4, 131–267.

———. *Deadlock.* 1921. Richardson, *Pilgrimage*, vol. 3, 11–229.

———. "Dialogue in Dixie." Donald, Friedberg, and Marcus 193–96.

———. *Dimple Hill.* 1938. Richardson, *Pilgrimage*, vol. 4, 403–552.

———. "The Film Gone Male." Donald, Friedberg, and Marcus 205–7.

———. "The Front Rows." Donald, Friedberg, and Marcus 172–74.

———. *Honeycomb.* 1917. Richardson, *Pilgrimage*, vol. 1, 349–490.

———. "The Increasing Congregation." Donald, Friedberg, and Marcus 170–71.

———. *Interim.* 1920. Richardson, *Pilgrimage*, vol. 2, 291–453.

———. *March Moonlight.* 1946. Richardson, *Pilgrimage*, vol. 4, 555–658.

———. "Musical Accompaniment." Donald, Friedberg, and Marcus 162–63.

———. "Narcissus." Donald, Friedberg, and Marcus 201–3.

———. *Pilgrimage.* 4 vols. London: Virago, 1979. Print.

———. *Pointed Roofs.* 1915. Richardson, *Pilgrimage*, vol. 1, 15–185.

———. *Revolving Lights.* 1923. Richardson, *Pilgrimage*, vol. 3, 233–396.

———. "A Tear for Lycidas." Donald, Friedberg, and Marcus 196–201.

———. "The Thoroughly Popular Film." Donald, Friedberg, and Marcus 177–79.

———. "A Thousand Pities." Donald, Friedberg, and Marcus 166–68.

———. *The Trap.* 1925. Richardson, *Pilgrimage*, vol. 3, 399–509.

———. *The Tunnel.* 1919. Richardson, *Pilgrimage*, vol. 2, 11–287.

Ricks, Christopher. *Beckett's Dying Words.* Oxford: Clarendon, 1993. Print.

Rogers, Margaret. "Decoding the Fugue in 'Sirens.'" *James Joyce Literary Supplement* 4.1 (1990): 15–20. Print.

Roston, Murray. *Modernist Patterns: In Literature and the Visual Arts.* New York: New York UP, 1999. Print.

Rubery, Matthew. "Canned Literature: The Book after Edison." *Book History* 16 (2013): 215–45. *Project Muse.* Web. 5 Apr. 2014.

Russolo, Luigi. *The Art of Noises.* 1916. Trans. Barclay Brown. New York: Pendragon, 1986. Print.

Sacks, Oliver. "The Power of Music." *Brain: A Journal of Neurology* 129.10 (2006): 2528–32. *Oxford Academic.* Web. 6 June 2014.

Savory, Elaine. *The Cambridge Introduction to Jean Rhys.* Cambridge: Cambridge UP, 2009. *Cambridge Books Online,* June 2012. Web. 1 Dec. 2014.

Schaeffer, Pierre. *In Search of a Concrete Music.* 1952. Trans. Christine North and John Dack. Berkeley: U of California P, 2012. Print.

Schafer, R. Murray. "The Music of the Environment." Cox and Warner 29–39.

———. *The New Soundscape: A Handbook for the Modern Music Teacher.* Scarborough: Berandol, 1969. Print.

———. *Our Sonic Environment and the Soundscape: The Tuning of the World.* Rochester: Destiny, 1977. Print.

Schwartz, Hillel. "The Indefensible Ear: A History." Bull and Back 487–501.

———. "Noise and Silence: The Soundscape and Spirituality." Inter-Religious Federation for World Peace Conference. Seoul. 20–27 Aug. 1995. *Noise Pollution Clearinghouse Online Library,* n.d. Web. 8 Aug. 2012.

Schweighauser, Philipp. *The Noises of American Literature, 1890–1985: Toward a History of Literary Acoustics.* Gainesville: UP of Florida, 2006. Print.

Scott, Bonnie Kime, ed. *The Gender of Modernism: A Critical Anthology.* Bloomington: Indiana UP, 1990. Print.

———. "The Subversive Mechanics of Woolf's Gramophone in *Between the Acts.*" Caughie, *Virginia Woolf and the Age* 97–113.

Seigel, Jerrold. *Bohemian Paris: Culture, Politics, and the Boundaries of the Bourgeois Life, 1830–1930.* Baltimore: Johns Hopkins UP, 1986. Print.

Sheppard, Richard. *Modernism—Dada—Postmodernism.* Evanston: Northwestern UP, 2000. Print.

Sherry, Vincent. *Ezra Pound, Wyndham Lewis, and Radical Modernism.* New York: Oxford UP, 1993. Print.

———. *Joyce: "Ulysses."* New York: Cambridge UP, 2004. Print. Landmarks of World Literature.

Simpson, Anne B. *Territories of the Psyche: The Fiction of Jean Rhys.* New York: Palgrave Macmillan, 2005. Print.

Sitney, P. Adams. *Modernist Montage: The Obscurity of Vision in Cinema and Literature.* New York: Columbia UP, 1990. Print.

Sitwell, Edith. "Some Notes on My Own Poetry." *The Canticle of the Rose Poems: 1917–1949.* New York: Vanguard, 1940. xi–xxxviii. Print.

Smith, Mark M. *Listening to Nineteenth-Century America.* Chapel Hill: U of North Carolina P, 2001. Print.

Sousa, John Philip. "The Menace of Mechanical Music." 1906. Taylor, Katz, and Grajeda 113–22.

Spear, Jeffrey. "The Other Arts: Victorian Visual Culture." *A Companion to the Victorian Novel*. Ed. Patrick Brantlinger and William B. Thesing. Malden: Blackwell, 2005. 189–205. Print.

Stamm, David. *A Pathway to Reality: Visual and Aural Concepts in Dorothy Richardson's "Pilgrimage."* Tübingen: Verlag, 2000. Print.

Stamp, Shelley. *Movie-Struck Girls*. Princeton: Princeton UP, 2000. Print.

Stankievech, Charles. "From Stethoscope to Headphones: An Acoustic Spatialization of Subjectivity." *Leonardo Music Journal* 17 (2007): 55–59. Print.

Steinberg, Erwin R. "The Stream-of-Consciousness Technique Defined." Steinberg, *Stream-of-Conscious* 152–63.

———, ed. *The Stream-of-Conscious Technique in the Modern Novel*. Port Washington: Kennikat, 1979. Print.

Sterne, Jonathan. *The Audible Past: Cultural Origins of Sound Reproduction*. Durham: Duke UP, 2003. Print.

———. "Sonic Imaginations." Sterne, *Sound Studies* 1–17.

———, ed. *The Sound Studies Reader*. London: Routledge, 2012. Print.

Stewart, Garrett. *Reading Voices: Literature and the Phonotext*. Berkeley: U of California P, 1990. Print.

Sutton, Emma. *Virginia Woolf and Classical Music: Politics, Aesthetics, Form*. Edinburgh: Edinburgh UP, 2013. Print.

Swing High, Swing Low. Dir. Mitchell Leisen. Paramount, 1937. Film.

Szendy, Peter. *Listen: A History of the Ear*. New York: Fordham UP, 2008. Print.

Taylor, Timothy D., Mark Katz, and Tony Grajeda, eds. *Music, Sound, and Technology in America*. Durham: Duke UP, 2012. Print.

Thompson, Derek. "How Headphones Changed the World." *Atlantic*, 30 May 2012: n. pag. Web. 17 Jan. 2014.

Thompson, Emily. "Machines, Music, and the Quest for Fidelity: Marketing the Edison Phonograph in America, 1877–1925." *Musical Quarterly* 79.1 (1995): 131–71. Print.

———. *The Soundscape of Modernity: Architectural Acoustics and the Culture of Listening in America, 1900–1933*. Cambridge: MIT P, 2002. Print.

Tiessen, Paul. "A Comparative Approach to the Form and Function of Novel and Film: Dorothy Richardson's Theory of Art." *Literature/Film Quarterly* 3.1 (1975): 83–90. Print.

Trilling, Lionel. *Beyond Culture: Essays on Literature and Learning*. New York: Harcourt, 1978. Print.

Trotter, David. *Cinema and Modernism*. London: Wiley-Blackwell, 2007. Print.

Truax, Barry. *Acoustic Communication*. Norwood: Ablex, 1984. Print.

Varèse, Edgard. "Music and the Times." 1936. Albright, *Modernism and Music* 185–87.

Vertovec, Steven, and Robin Cohen, eds. *Conceiving Cosmopolitanism: Theory, Context, and Practice*. Oxford: Oxford UP, 2008. Print.

———. "Introduction: Conceiving Cosmopolitanism." Vertovec and Cohen, *Conceiving Cosmopolitanism* 1–22.

Rev. of *Voyage in the Dark*, by Jean Rhys. *Times Literary Supplement*, 1 Nov. 1934: 752. *TLS Historical Archive 1902–2006*. Cengage Learning. Web. 21 Feb. 2012.

Walkowitz, Rebecca. *Cosmopolitan Style: Modernism beyond the Nation*. New York: Columbia UP, 2006. Print.

Watts, Carol. *Dorothy Richardson.* Plymouth: Northcote, 1995. Print. Writers and Their Work.

"The Waves: Words and Frequencies." *Virginia Woolf Web,* 14 Mar. 2000. Web. 22 Oct. 2001.

Weaver, Jack W. *Joyce's Music and Noise: Theme and Variation in His Writings.* Gainesville: UP of Florida, 1998. Print.

White, J. Andrew, ed. *Wireless Age: An Illustrated Monthly Magazine of Radio Communication* 10.3–6 (1922–23). *Google Books.* Web. 6 June 2014.

Whiting, Steven Moore. *Satie the Bohemian: From Cabaret to Concert Hall.* Oxford: Oxford UP, 2002. Print.

Wilson, Elizabeth. *Bohemians: The Glamorous Outcasts.* London: Tauris, 2003. Print.

Wilson, Sarah. "Gertrude Stein and the Radio." *Modernism/modernity* 11 (2004): 261–78. Print.

Woolf, Virginia. "'Anon' and 'The Reader': Virginia Woolf's Last Essays." Ed. Brenda R. Silver. *Twentieth Century Literature* 25 (1979): 356–435. Print.

——. *Between the Acts.* 1941. New York: Harcourt, 1969. Print.

——. *The Diary of Virginia Woolf.* Ed. Anne Oliver Bell. 5 vols. London: Hogarth, 1984. Print.

——. *The Essays of Virginia Woolf.* Ed. Andrew McNeillie. 6 vols. San Diego: Harcourt, 1986–2011. Print.

——. *Jacob's Room.* 1922. New York: Harcourt, 1950. Print.

——. "The Leaning Tower." *The Moment and Other Essays.* New York: Harcourt, 1948. 128–54. Print.

——. *The Letters of Virginia Woolf.* Ed. Nigel Nicolson and Joanne Trautmann. Vol. 6. New York: Harcourt, 1980. Print.

——. "Modern Fiction." *The Common Reader: First Series.* Ed. Andrew McNeillie. New York: First Harvest, 1984. 146–54. Print.

——. "Mr. Bennett and Mrs. Brown." *Collected Essays.* Ed. Leonard Woolf. Vol. 1. London: Hogarth, 1966. 319–37.

——. *Mrs. Dalloway.* 1925. New York: Harcourt, 1953. Print.

——. "The Narrow Bridge of Art." Woolf, *Essays* 2: 218–29.

——. "Oxford Street Tide." *The London Scene: Six Essays on London Life.* New York: Harper-Collins, 1975. 19–27. Print.

——. "Street Music." Woolf, *Essays* 1: 27–32.

——. "Thoughts on Peace in an Air Raid." Woolf, *Essays* 4: 173–77.

——. Rev. of *The Tunnel,* by Dorothy Richardson. *Times Literary Supplement,* 13 Feb. 1919. Rpt. in *The Feminist Critique of Language: A Reader.* Ed. Deborah Cameron. London: Routledge, 1990. 70–72. Print.

——. *To the Lighthouse.* 1927. New York: Harcourt, 1955. Print.

——. *The Waves.* 1931. New York: Harcourt, 1959. Print.

——. *A Writer's Diary.* Ed. Leonard Woolf. New York: Harcourt, 1954. Print.

——. *The Years.* 1937. London: Grafton, 1977. Print.

Wyndham, Francis. Introduction. *Jean Rhys Letters 1931–1966.* Ed. Francis Wyndham and Diana Melly. London: Deutsch, 1984. 9–12. Print.

Zimring, Rishona. "Suggestions of Other Worlds: The Art of Sound in *The Years.*" *Woolf Studies Annual* 8 (2001): 127–56. Print.

Zwerdling, Alex. *Virginia Woolf and the Real World.* Berkeley: U of California P, 1986. Print.

Index

ANGELA FRATTAROLA is senior lecturer at Nanyang Technological University in Singapore. Her interests include modernism, the novel, sound studies, and writing studies.